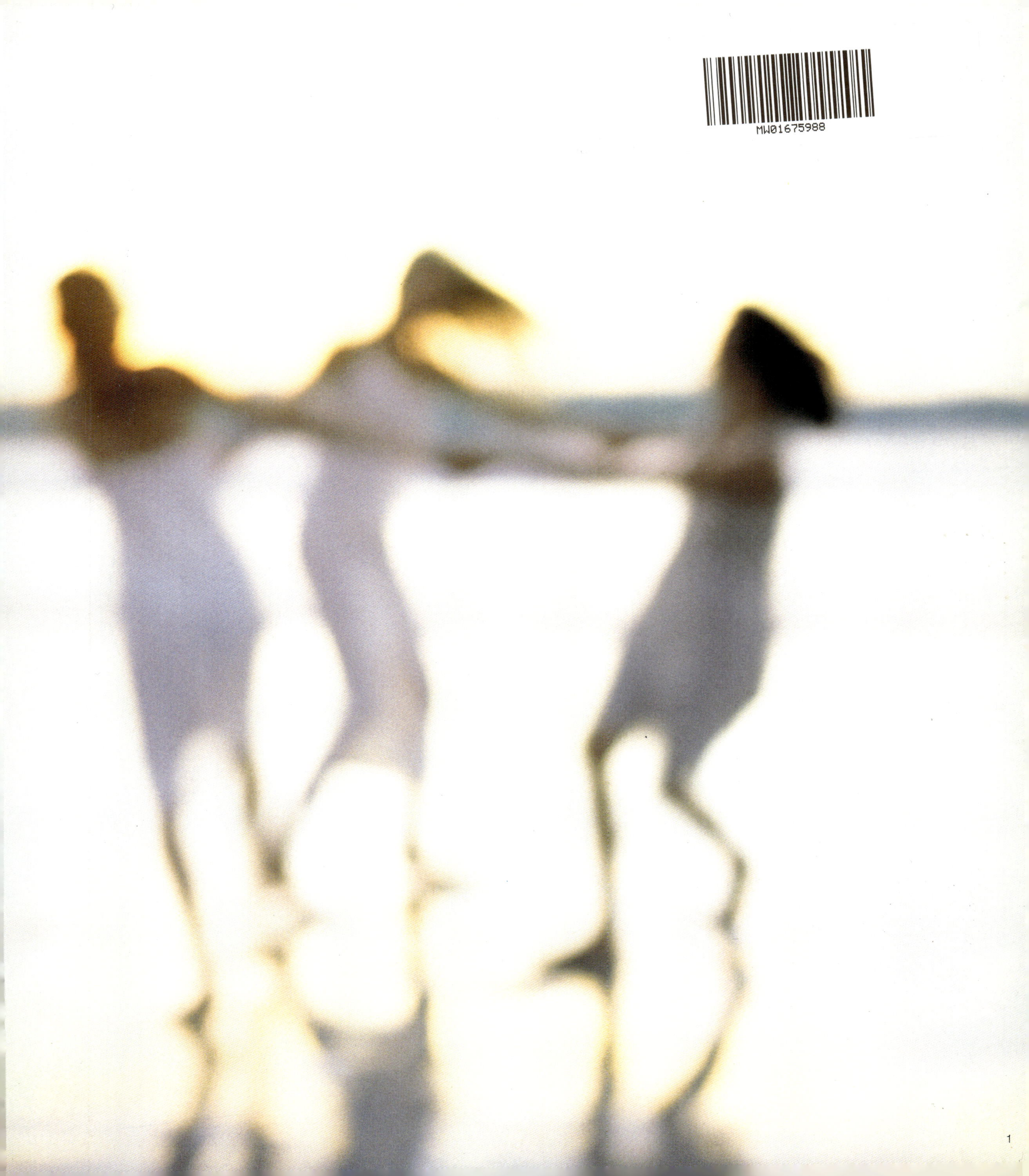

A RotoVision Book
Published and distributed by
RotoVision SA
Rue du Bugnon 7
CH-1299 Crans-Près-Céligny
Switzerland

RotoVision SA
Sales & Production Office
Sheridan House
112/116A Western Road
Hove
East Sussex BN3 1DD
UK

Tel
+44 (0)1273 72 72 68
Fax
+44 (0)1273 72 72 69
E-mail
sales@rotovision.com
www.rotovision.com

10 9 8 7 6 5 4 3 2 1

ISBN 2-88046-609-1

Design
SEA

Production and separations
in Singapore by
ProVision Pte. Ltd.

Tel
+65 334 7720
Fax
+65 334 7721

RotoVision

People Shots That Sell – How To Succeed in Stock Photography

Tracey Tannenbaum
Kate Stevens

Contents

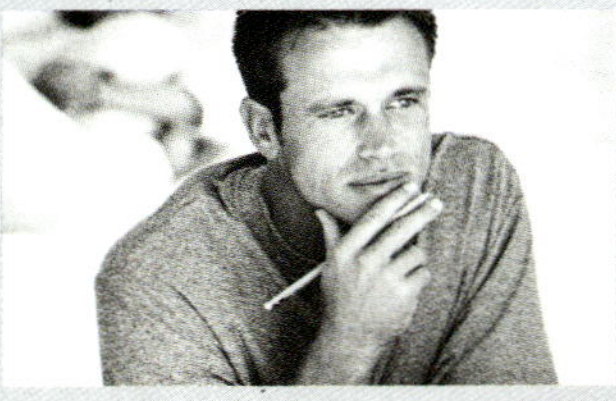

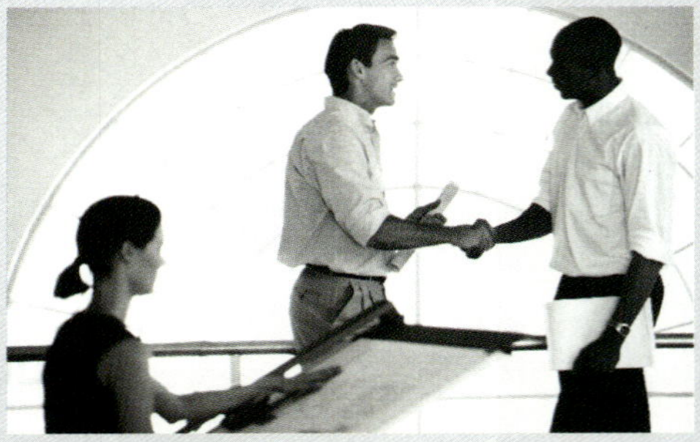

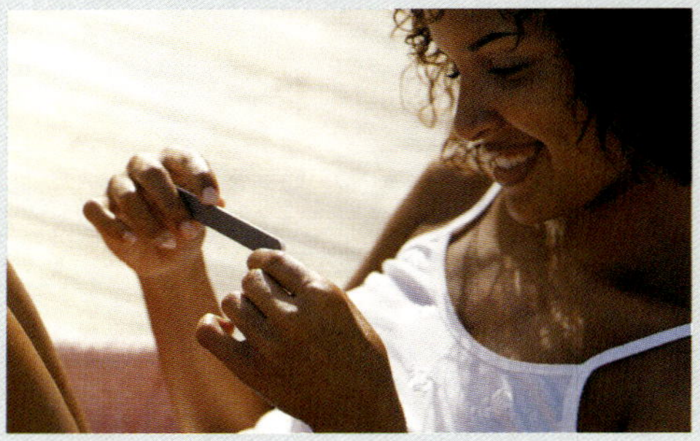

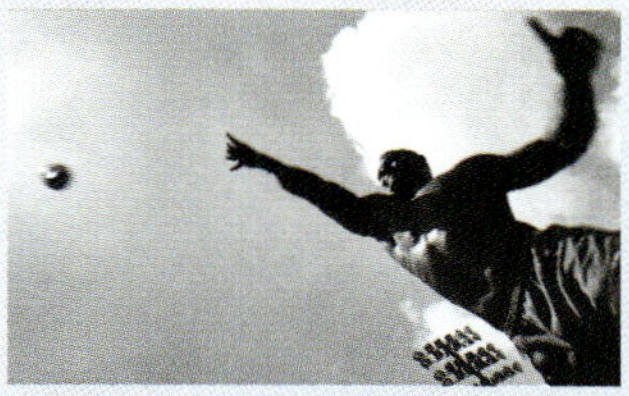
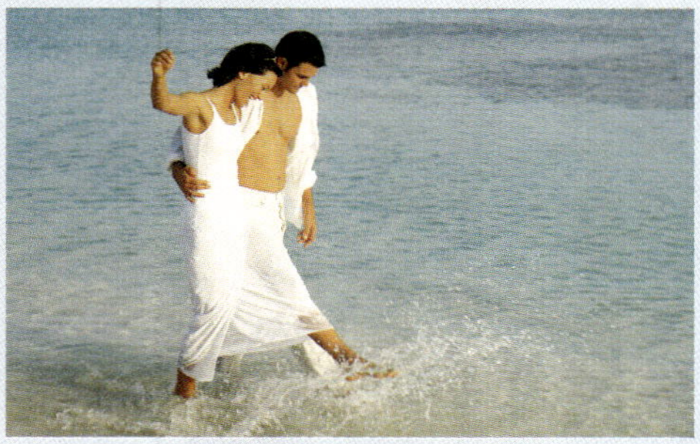
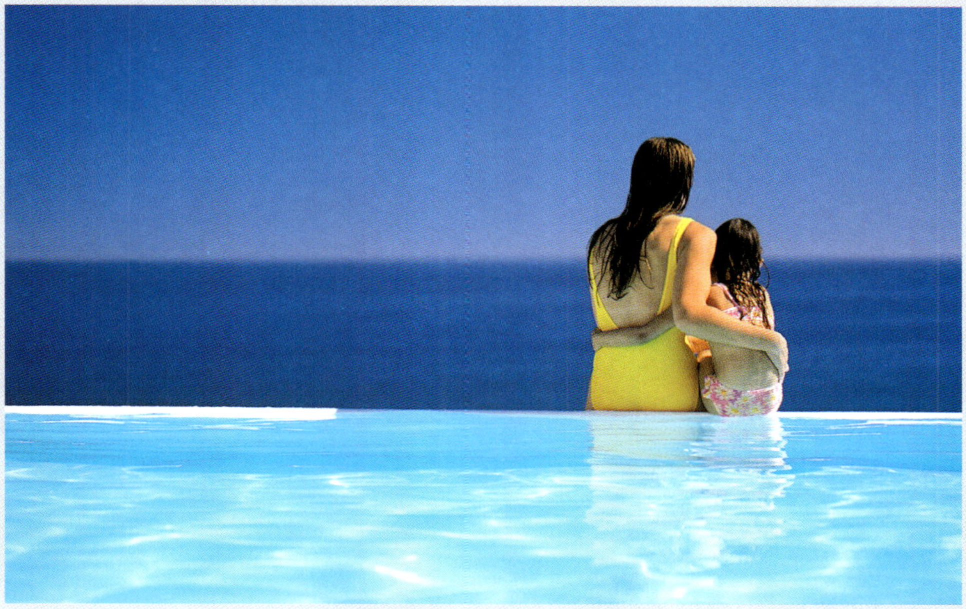
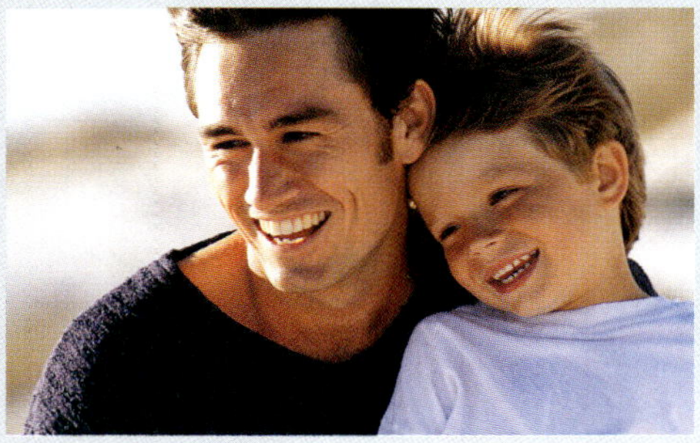
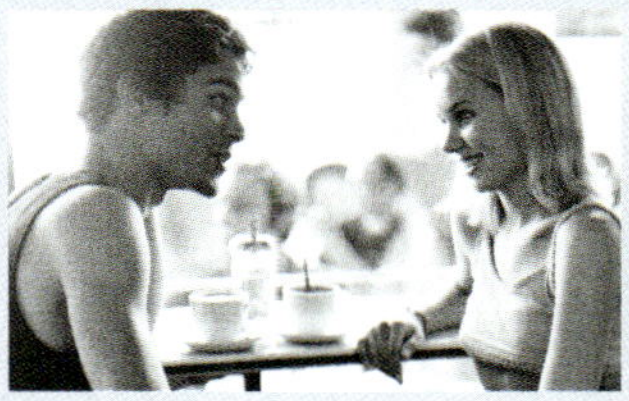
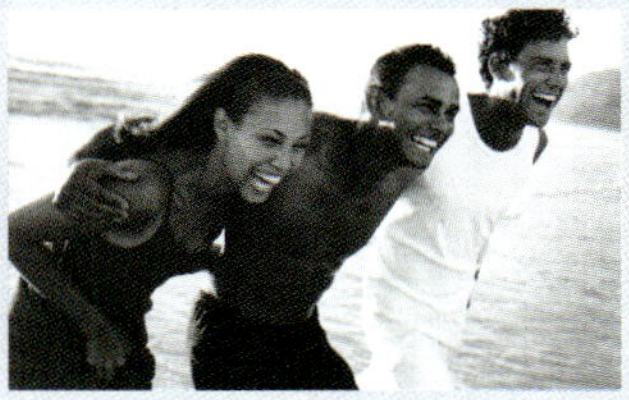
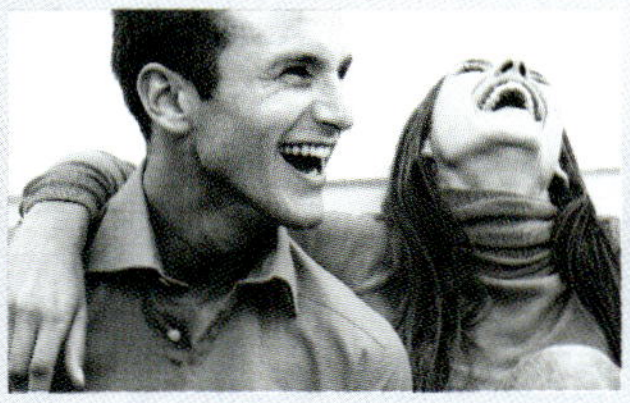
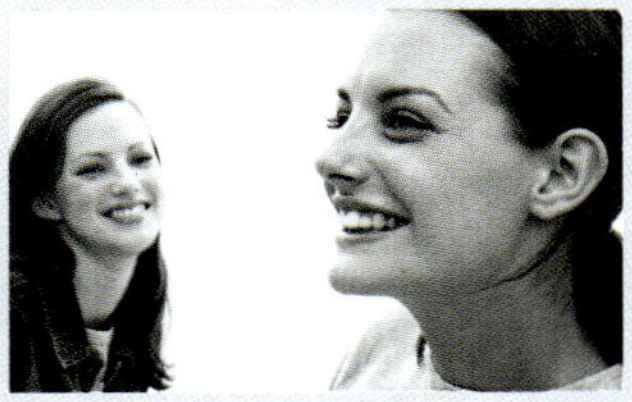

Introduction

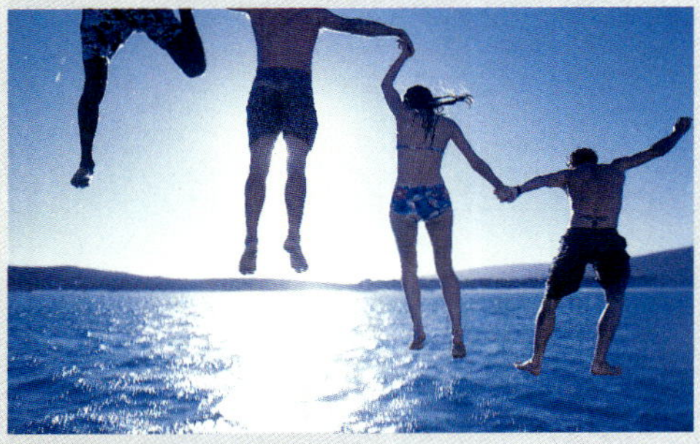

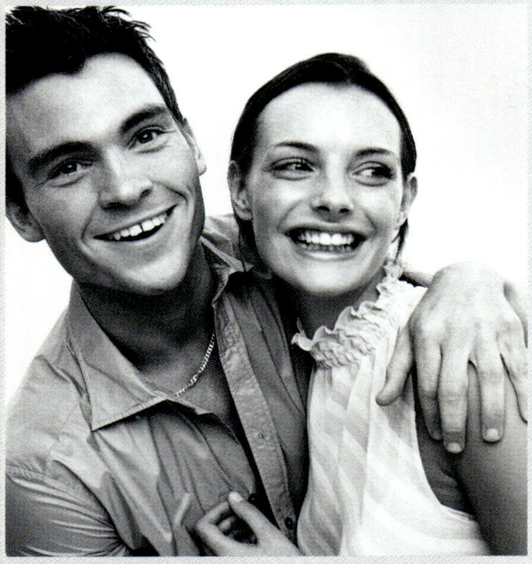

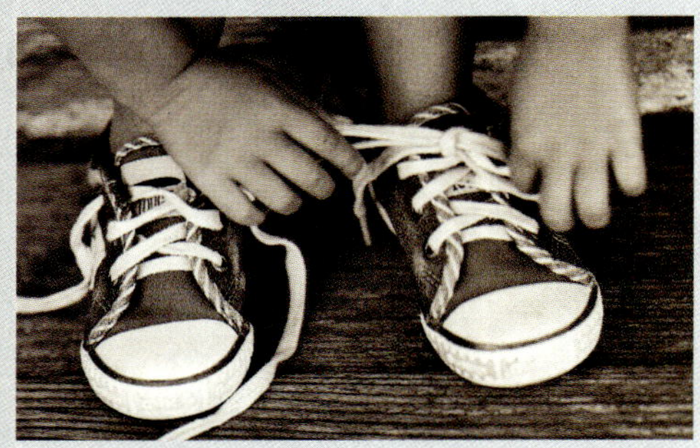

For some people, photography is more than a passion, it is work.

This group of people has been able to turn what for some is an enjoyable hobby, into a job which provides a livelihood, and for an even smaller number, a highly lucrative career. The question remains – how did they do it?

Surprisingly, many photographers will tell you that being a good businessperson is as important as being a good shot. And, while this may shatter some people's preconceptions of the craft, photographers who have an understanding of the business they are operating in have more of a chance of success. Knowing your worth in the marketplace and how to approach and market yourself is as important in the photography business as it is in any other.

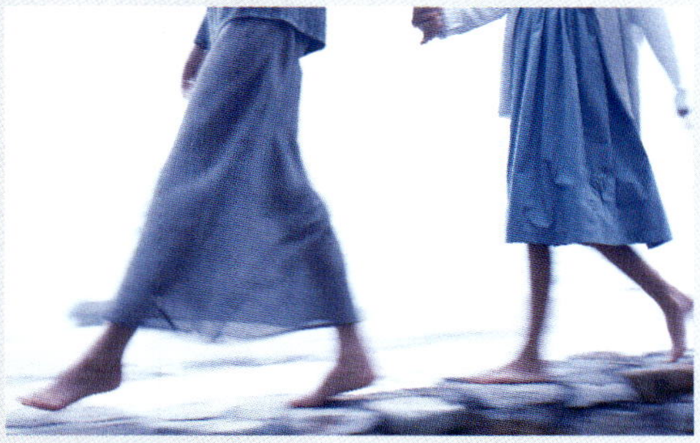

Stock photography is an exciting, although difficult, route to entering the picture business.

If you've picked up this book, more than likely you are a gifted amateur photographer or a professional who wants to explore how to enter the stock industry. You've heard about the way quarterly royalty payments can help ensure that you still have a cash flow when commissioned work is quiet. And you probably think – or have been told by friends – that your pictures are as good, or even better, than the ones you see on billboards, magazine advertisements and on the web. But, there's a small issue. You haven't approached the stock industry with your portfolio. You haven't negotiated a contract and you don't even know where to start.

Well, with this book, we will show you how to do all those things and more.

People Shots That Sell gives you in-depth insight into promoting your portfolio of pictures, marketing yourself to the best audience, and negotiating your contract to ensure that you are getting the most lucrative arrangement for your work.

To give you this insight, we've approached stock library professionals at all levels – from the influential creative buyers to the all-important stylists and art directors. You'll receive advice and insider tips from successful photographers who make their living from shooting for stock. They'll tell you what works for them, what mistakes to avoid and how to foster relationships within the stock industry to guarantee that you'll be on the 'A' list whenever the next project is conceived.

Starting at the beginning, we'll explore how the stock industry developed from those dusty cutting-room rejects offered through simply designed leaflets to today's sophisticated, global on-line channels of distribution. Whose idea was it in the first place to take once or never used photographs and rent them to customers? And for that matter, did the model always have to be… nude?

Exploration of the industry will bring us to the new battle of 'traditional stock photography' versus 'royalty free photography'. We'll define these terms for you and explain why the licensing of stock photography imagery is causing so many clashes within the industry. And how does the web change the rules of stock? We'll explain how you can benefit from quick, global delivery of your images.

We'll give you useful hints to initially getting a foot in the stock company's door. As you can imagine, there are thousands of photographers who want their work reviewed. We'll help you fast-track your way to the decision makers within the organisation – finding out what the stock company requires; how to most effectively do your 'homework'; the best way to prepare your portfolio to show what the decision makers really want to see; and lastly, how to choose a stock library. If your work is as good as you think, you'll want to find out all the nitty-gritty – with, of course, the most important question being "Will I be paid promptly – or at all?"

To visually complement these topics, we've included a wide range of quotes, case studies and on-set interviews. And, as a unique tool for both photographers and their customers, i.e. art directors, magazine editors etc., we've included a chapter entitled 'Understanding Your Creative Options'. This section will show how different photographic treatments can be used to illustrate the same single concept – such as 'Literacy' or 'The Winning Spirit'. The results are fascinating and give a better insight into the direction of contemporary stock photography and the various creative options available. The rules for stock photography might be tight – but those artists who are willing to challenge convention are often well-rewarded.

And what are the latest trends in stock photography? Will black and white be the next 'colour' and what about digital images? To answer these questions and more, we will conclude this first book in the series by discussing the future of stock photography – where is it going and what tips to follow to guarantee that you will be riding the next photographic wave.

So go on. Get out your best pictures and lay them out on your lightbox or dining room table. Now turn the page. Let's see if you have the skill, confidence and persistence you need to shoot for the stock industry.

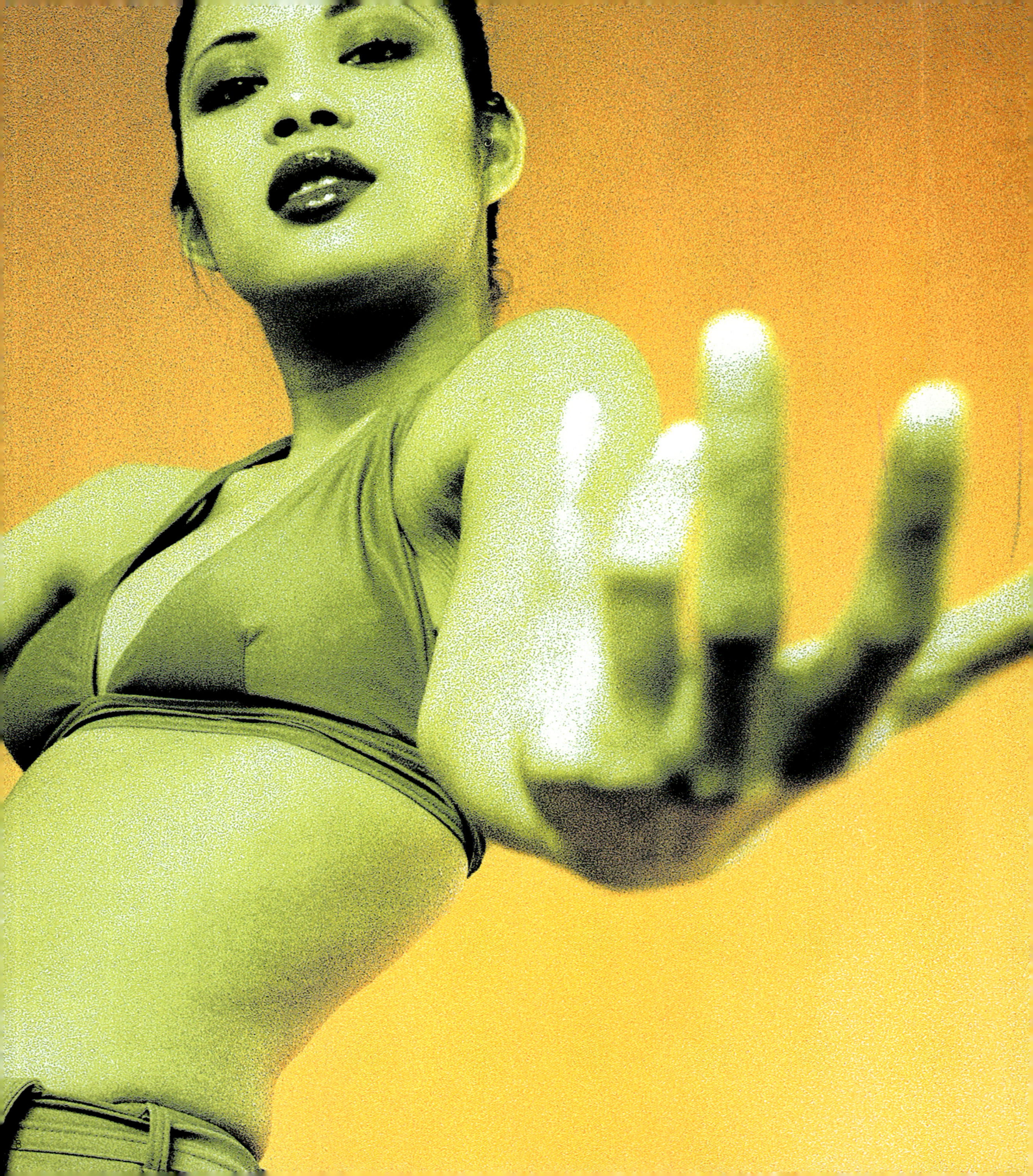

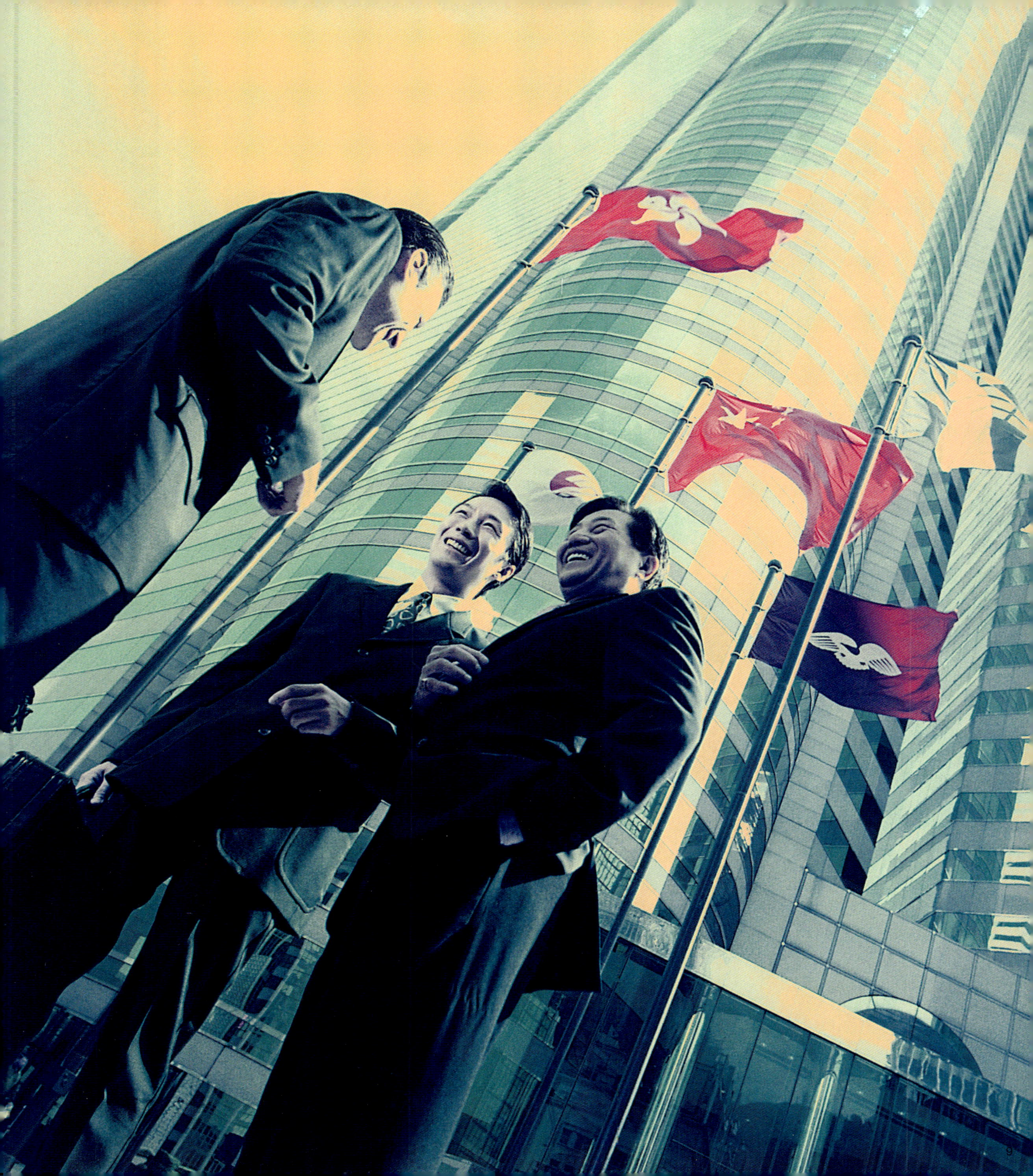

Chapter 1

The History of Stock Photography 10 – 17

At the Beginning

The actual business of selling stock photography has been around since the American Civil War, when Matthew Brandy sold images he and other photographers had made of the war for use in stereoviewers.

In France, the famous 'postcard' market had taken off when erotic images of models were duplicated and distributed for sale. However, it was the printed piece that sold – and not the actual images that were distributed.

Later, hoards of beautiful hopefuls landed in Hollywood and they all took the required screen test. These images were then quietly sold through the newly growing stock industry for use in the new field of advertising. Until then, illustrations – often photo-realistic in nature – were used for this growing media. In general, at this point, advertisers still preferred to arrange their own commissioned shoots.

Stock photography libraries continued to conduct business for most of the 20th century, but it wasn't really until the 1980s that the business of stock gained ground in popularity. Prior to that it was never regarded very seriously by advertising, editorial and design companies. They still continued to commission shoots as a way of controlling results and getting larger project margins.

Part of the problem was that stock library collections before this time were often built on outtakes from commissioned shoots.
In the 1980s, libraries realised that if they wanted people within the creative industry to purchase their images, they had to commission shoots specifically around the needs of the market. As with all businesses there was no blueprint for coming to the industry. Some libraries built their businesses on being photographers themselves, as in the example of Tony Stone (UK). Others have founded businesses following an evolution of events, for example The Telegraph Colour Library (UK).

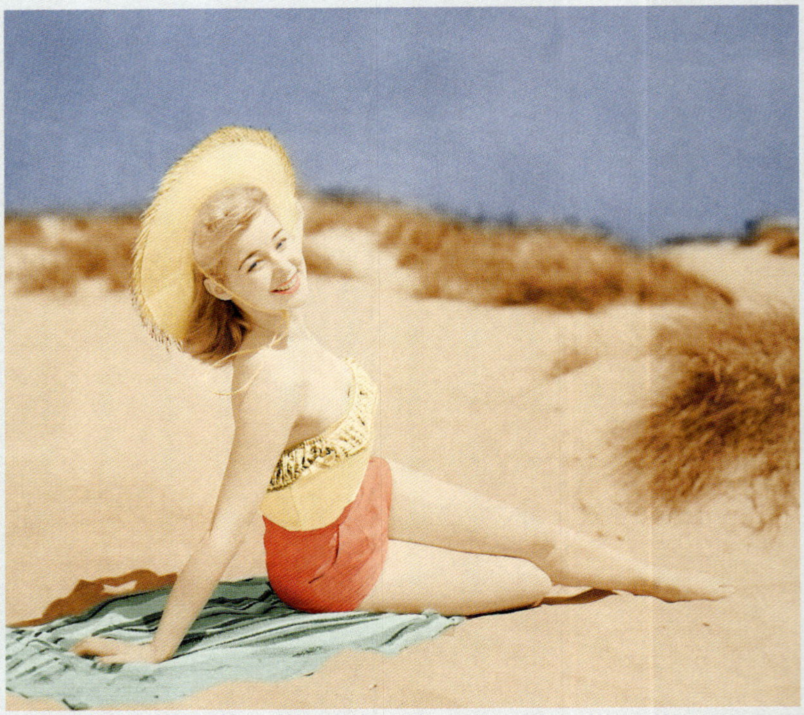

An Early Mover and Shaker

When The Telegraph newspaper (UK) launched its own magazine, it commissioned images for it and then syndicated pictures and stories. The demand for these quality pictures soon became apparent. Through various economic situations, commissioned work dried up and the newspaper started to represent various stock agencies to syndicate images. As the company made an increasing success of selling the rights to images, it became easier for people to buy images and the business of stock really took off.

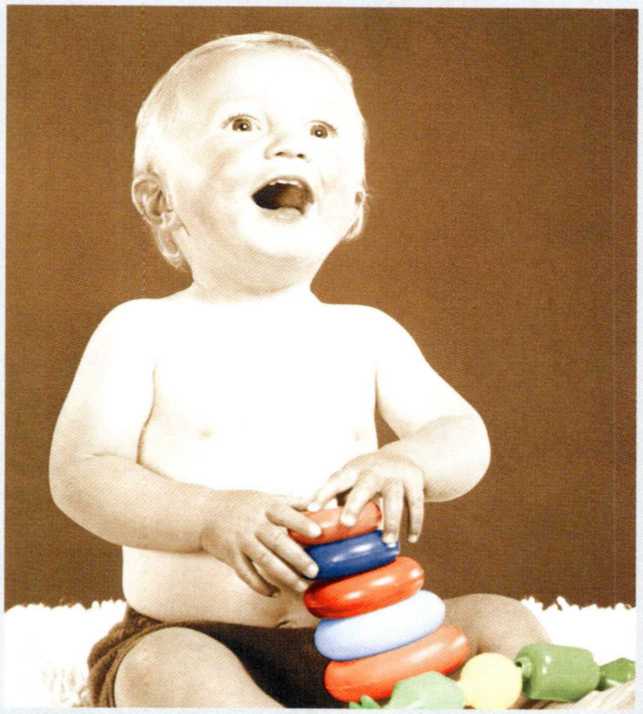

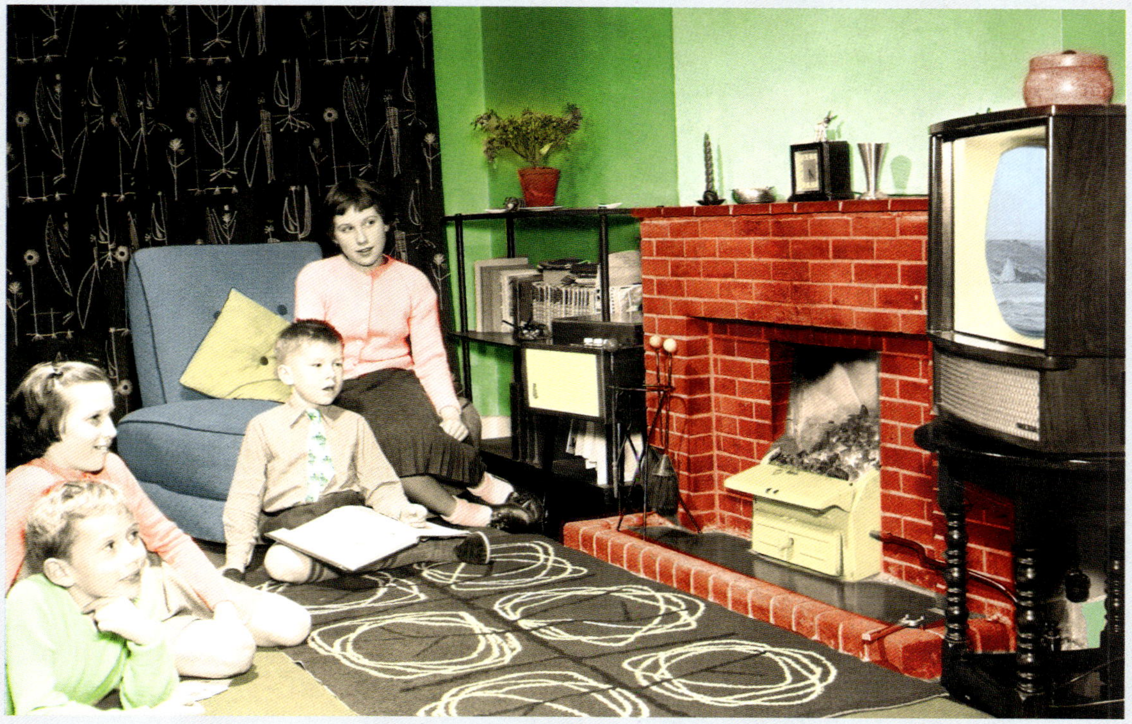

The Royalty Free Revolution

As the stock industry evolved, another player entered the market – PhotoDisc (UK). They took the original and ground-breaking step of grouping images by subject matter and putting them on a single CD. While this step was in itself original, their pricing model went even further – they charged a fixed price for an image. No negotiation, no repeat fees.

This was the beginning of the royalty free business model and it caused an uproar within the photographic community, which prior to this was dependent on repeat usage fees or negotiated rights per image. Now, over ten years later, many associations still shun photographers and illustrators that enter the royalty free market. There is still anger against the economics of the royalty free sector – although, oddly enough, it has followed the same pattern as traditional stock – from original less-than-ideal imagery to that which is of a high-quality standard.

Initially though, these 'royalty free' images were considered by the creative community to be a last resort. Usually the pictures were outtakes from commissioned shoots and did not include models who, like the photographers, demanded repeat fees. Therefore, these pictures were primarily of items – such as business equipment like phones or computers. Or, if the pictures did include models, they would be the same model throughout the whole collection with no variation!

Today, royalty free carries less of a stigma since this sector is setting the same quality standards as traditional stock. It is in fact a badly kept secret that the more successful stock photographers shoot for both markets. And, as a photographer, you may want to consider weighing the financial benefits of each before deciding not to pursue the libraries involved in royalty free distribution. See 'Expectations' in Chapter 2 to calculate your options.

Technology Enters the Scene

Another reason for PhotoDisc's success in the creative marketplace was that it marketed its images digitised and ready to drop into digital artwork files. Remember that at this point Apple Mac computers were beginning to remove the traditional need to do work by hand. When the artwork was needed, it was scanned from a transparency and produced as a digital file. Once the image was scanned, however, it still required the usual colour correction, resizing and retouching to be done by the designer. This was very time-consuming.

So, even if the original royalty free images and subject matter were not ideal, the benefit of having them in a format that saved the designer time was considered extremely advantageous. Interestingly, it took a long time before traditional stock libraries embraced this new digital technology. As you can imagine, the amount of images – as in the case of Corbis (UK) – was in the millions. The sheer operation of digitising the images was formidable, but the e-commerce revolution changed all that.

Creatives, being under constant time pressure, were still seeking ways of getting to images as quickly as possible. Ordering a CD wasn't fast enough – they wanted immediate gratification. Enter the downloadable image, put your credit card or account number in, and immediately download your picture. This change in working habits was the major reason why all libraries, whether rights controlled or royalty free, eventually digitised and now feature images to purchase on-line. The customer demands it.

Now, traditional stock libraries ask the customer to self-select usage descriptions which carry a pricing structure. This saves negotiating and customer service time for the library – and may even mean higher commission rates for the photographer who is dependent on a percentage of sales cost.

With the introduction of broadband technology, more and more customers will be working on-line. And, if you have any doubts as to where the industry views the future of stock purchasing to be, take a look on-line. Some new stock companies don't even publish a catalogue!

Your Move

This introduction should have given you an understanding of what the stock industry does and how it has evolved. From this point, the focus will turn back to you and to how you can ensure that you can be successful within the industry. We will discuss everything from your all-important portfolio to helping you with essential interviewing techniques. We will also give you in-depth information as to what the industry pays for your images – and on how to maximise your royalty cheques. The next move is yours.

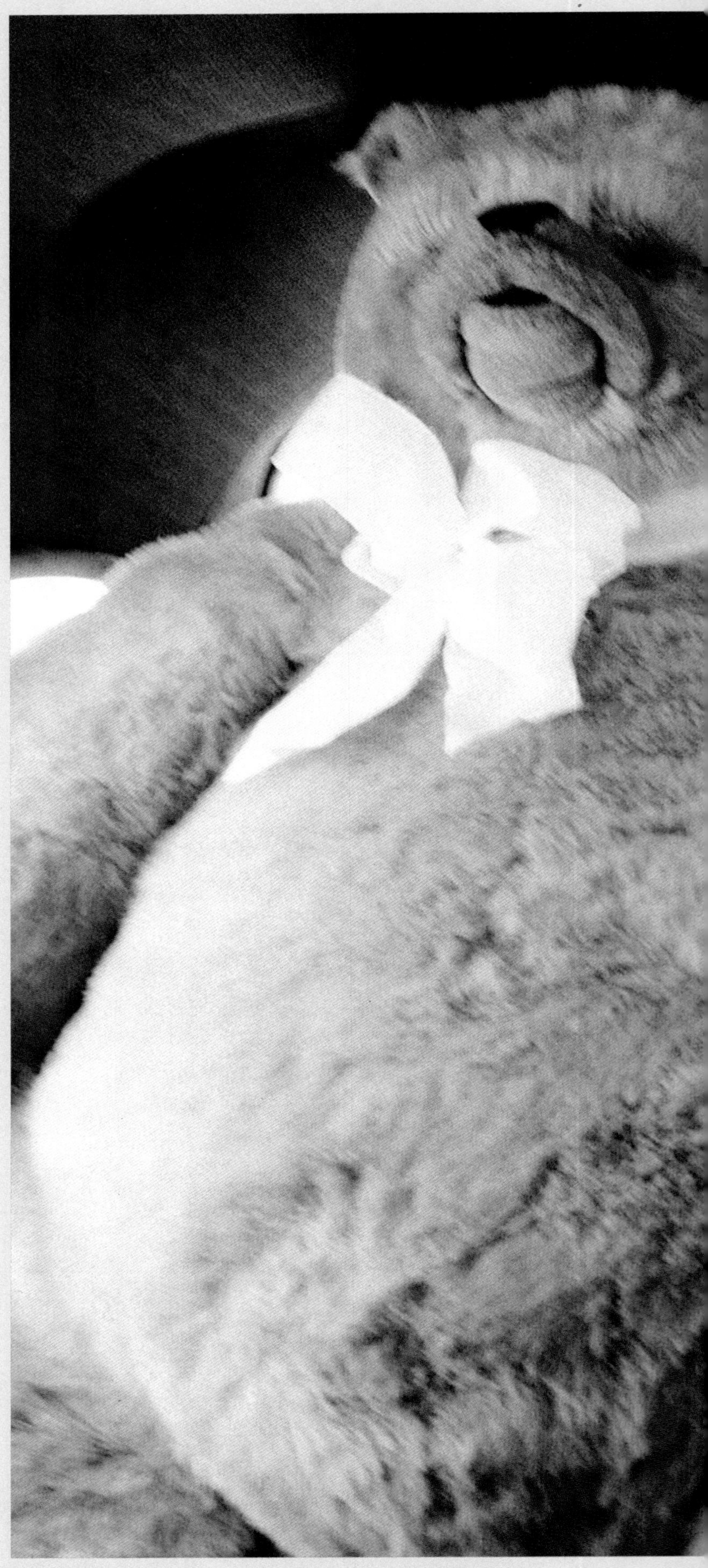

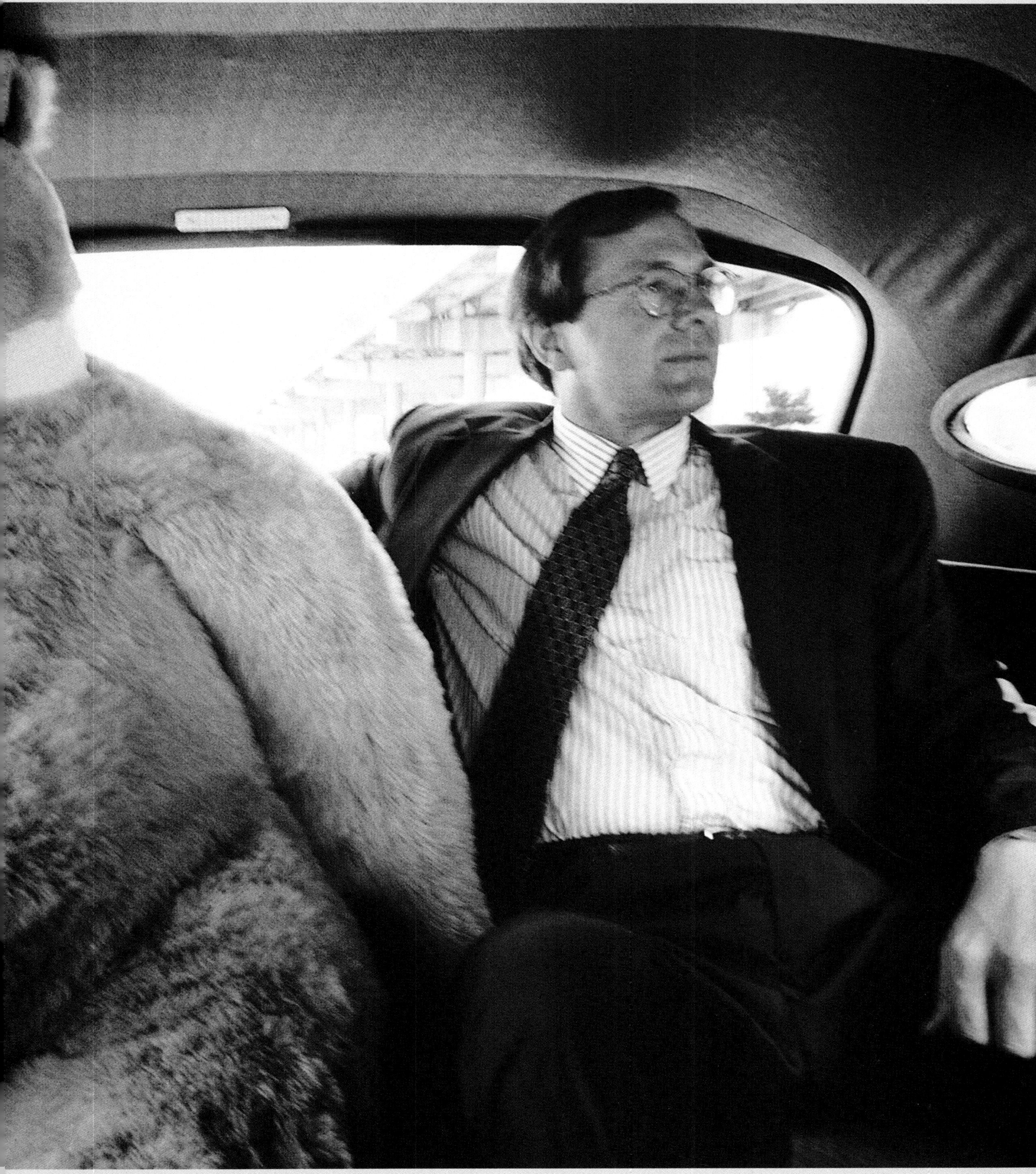

Chapter 2
How to Break into the Stock Industry

Where to Start

You've probably been thinking of entering the stock industry for a while. For some photographers it is a 'can't beat them join them' opportunity. They have seen their commercial business decrease as more and more decision-makers choose stock rather than commissioned shoots.

Other photographers might be contemplating the idea of entering the stock industry as a way of using royalties to fund their personal, less commercial work. Whatever your motive is, here are recommendations to ensure that you can get in the door, present your work in the best possible way – and get the maximum benefit from your stock images.

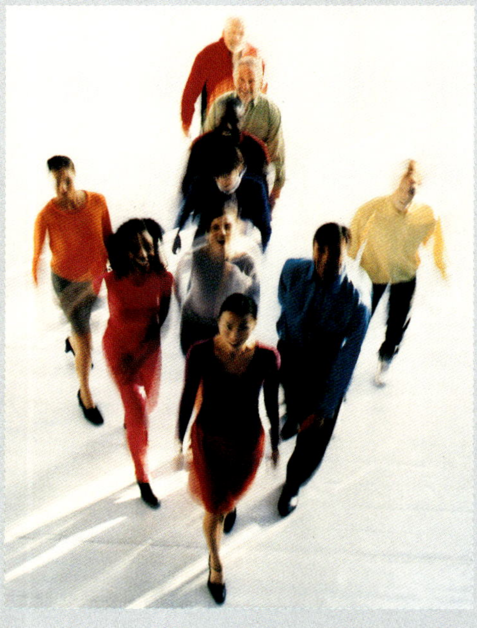

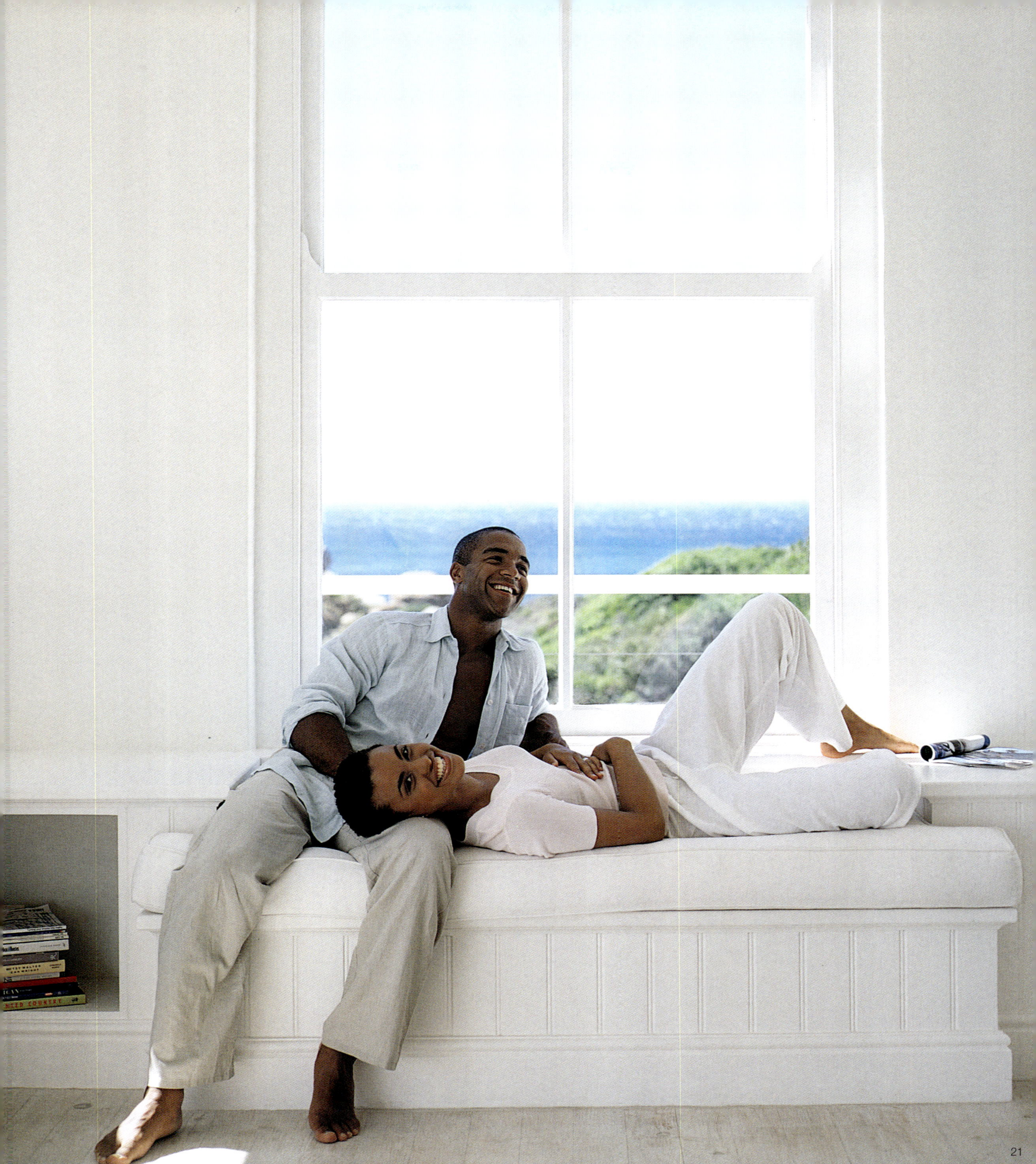

Preparing Your Portfolio

Have you ever noticed that everyone has a different opinion on this topic? Some say show as many images as possible with the maximum amount of variety. Others will recommend just presenting your most commercial work. While all of these suggestions may be valid, the most important thing to remember is that your portfolio is your most valuable marketing tool.

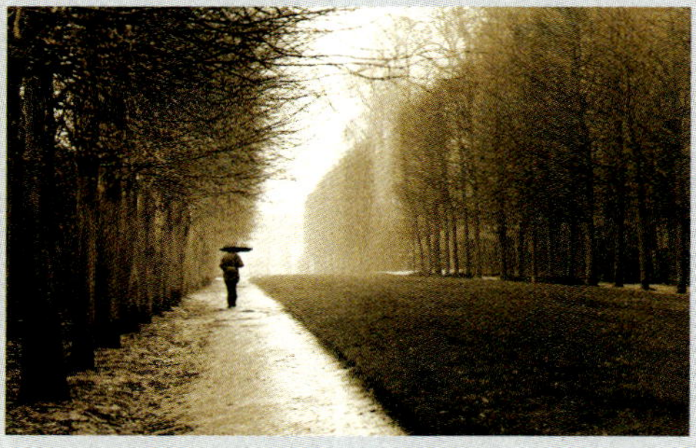

Think of it as an advertising campaign. You may only have seconds to 'sell' the decision-maker, normally an art director, your work. One thing to keep in mind is that many art directors are photographers themselves. They want to be motivated by what they see and to be able to envisage how your work would fit into a project they know is on the books. What they are looking for is originality, competence, confidence and the ability to capture people naturally.

As hinted in this book's introduction, the classic irony in stock photography is that photographers are chosen for their personal work but are commissioned to do commercial shoots. Art directors want to see what you are capable of doing without the restraint of a brief or another's direction. How creative can you be and how far 'out of the box' can you push your work? A capture of a child's elusive smile or an interesting composition of people and their everyday surroundings will certainly be of interest. Take chances by putting your personal work in your portfolio, but you may want to limit these images to the absolute best in your collection.

To balance your personal work, include what you view as your house style. Do you have a special look such as reportage family scenes or close-cropped portraits? In truth, your style is what will spark the art director's attention. But again, try to balance these types of images so that you show off all your skills and your capability to capture a large range of styles.

Limiting the number of images is also key. One top tip is to put your portfolio together and have a friend or trusted photographic colleague review it. Anything which doesn't register a 'wow', simply remove from your book. One less-than-ideal image can undermine the rest of your work.

You've now chosen your images and placed them on the recommended black board if they are prints, or transparency sleeves if they are in slide format – but there are other more useful marketing tricks to putting your portfolio together.

Envisage this – instead of just placing your images in a book, why not add 'value' to the individual pages? This can be done with the addition of captions telling the art director what the work was commissioned for, which advertising agency (if appropriate), and most importantly the response. If the client came back for additional work, put that in. This establishes a linear success trail – exactly what the stock industry wants. If you have access to the printed advertisement or the web page where your image was used, mount it beside the image. This also encourages the art director to further interact with both your work and you. In the end, this will enable you to ask the question: "Can I really see myself working with this art director?" If not, keep looking. There are other agencies which might be a better fit.

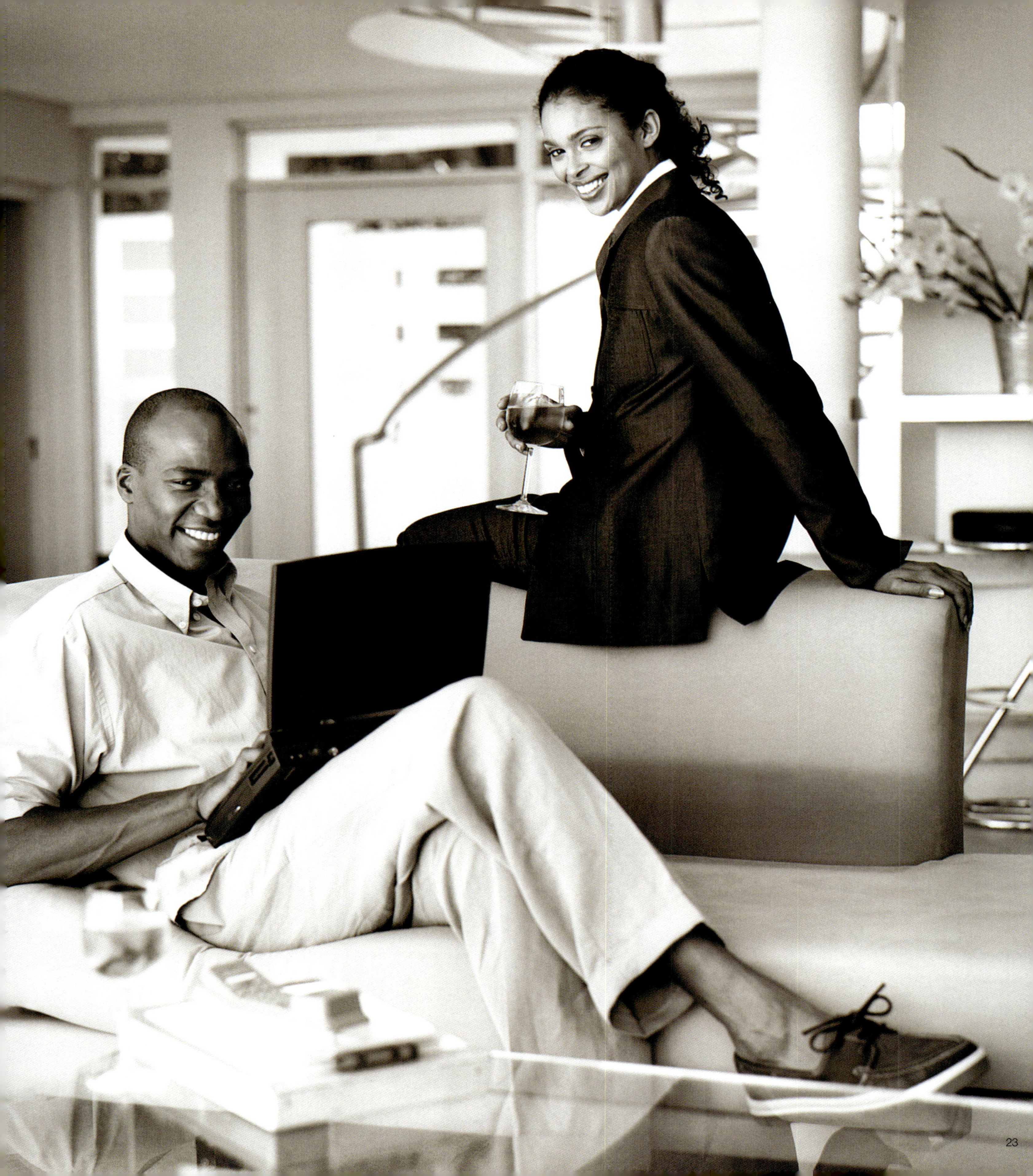

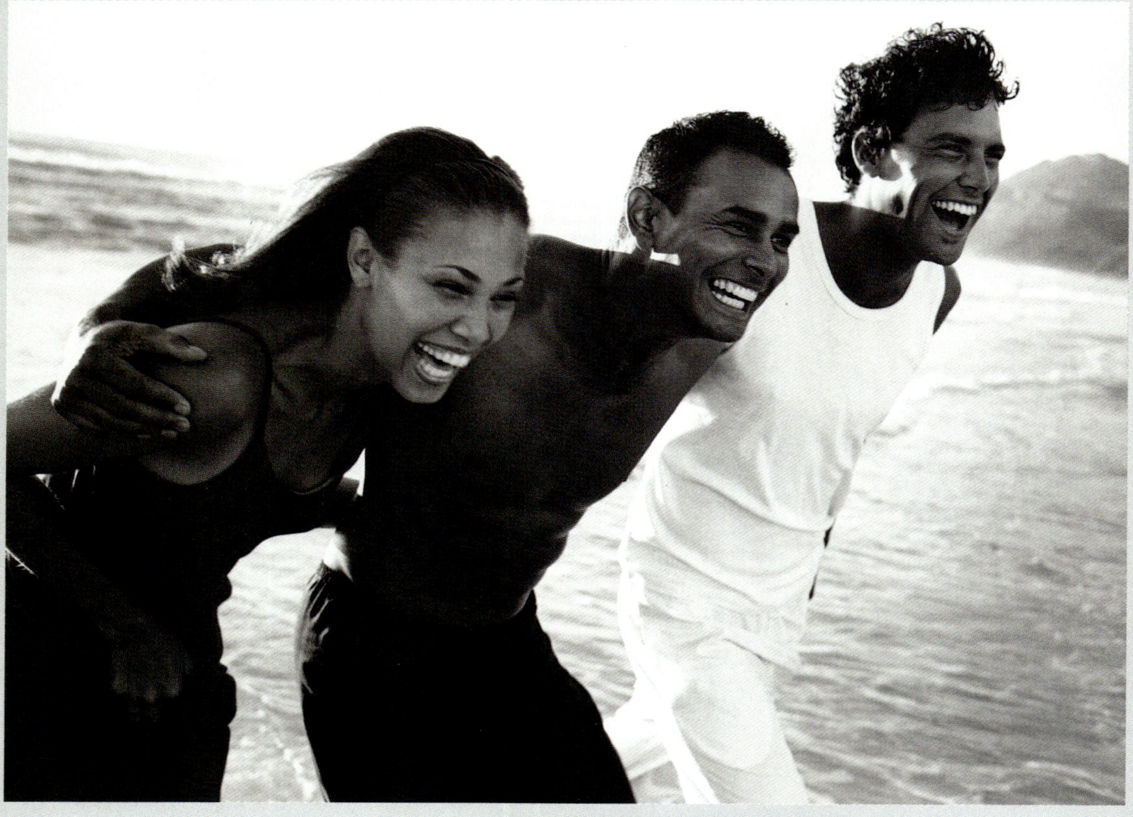

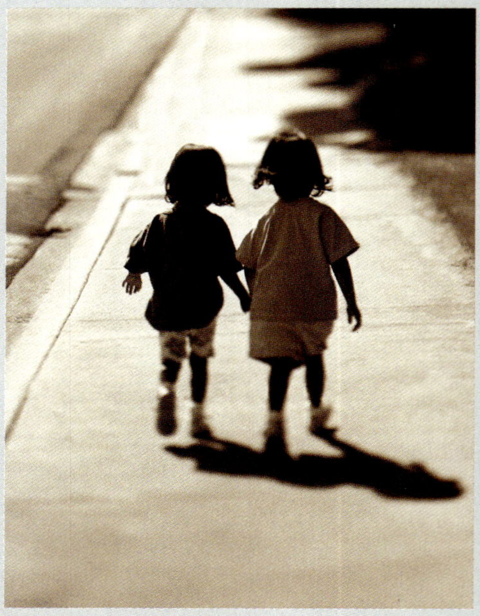

Professionals in the stock trade recommend showcasing both personal work, like the black-and-white pictures shown on this page, and commercial stock images in your portfolio.

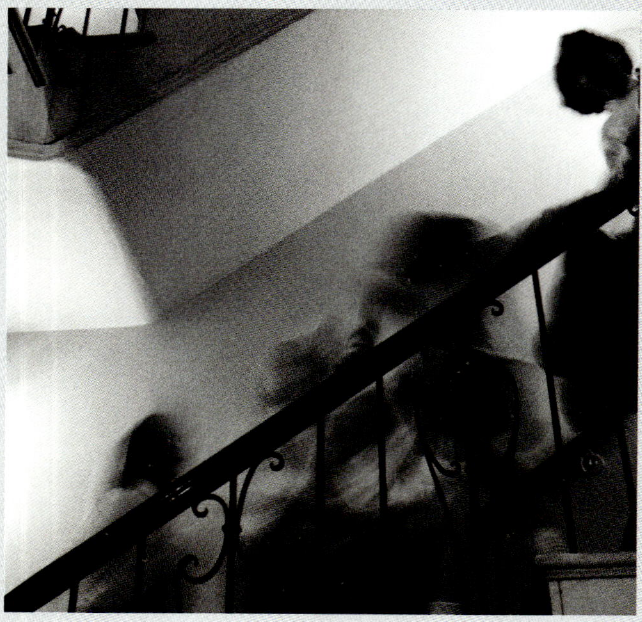

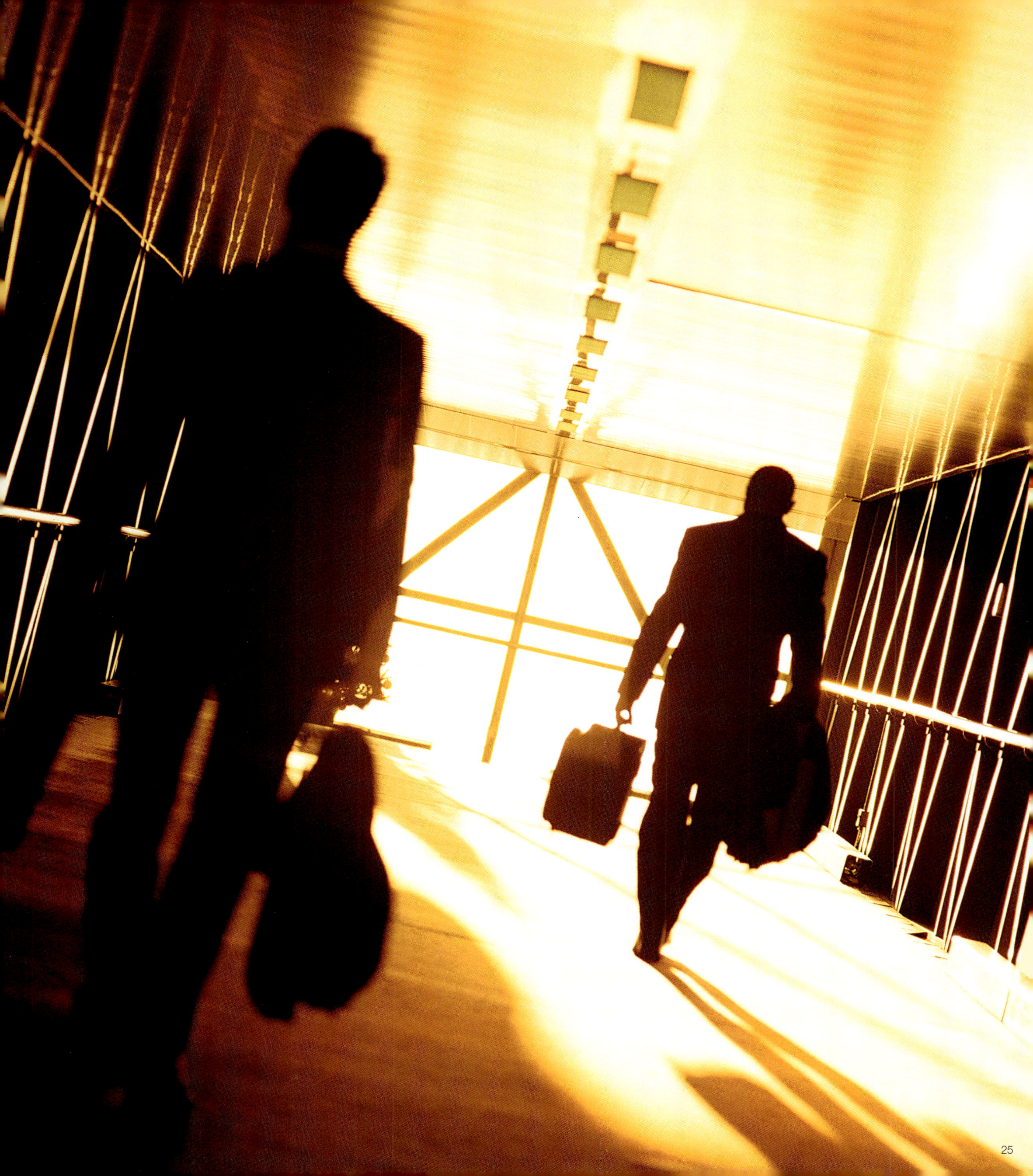

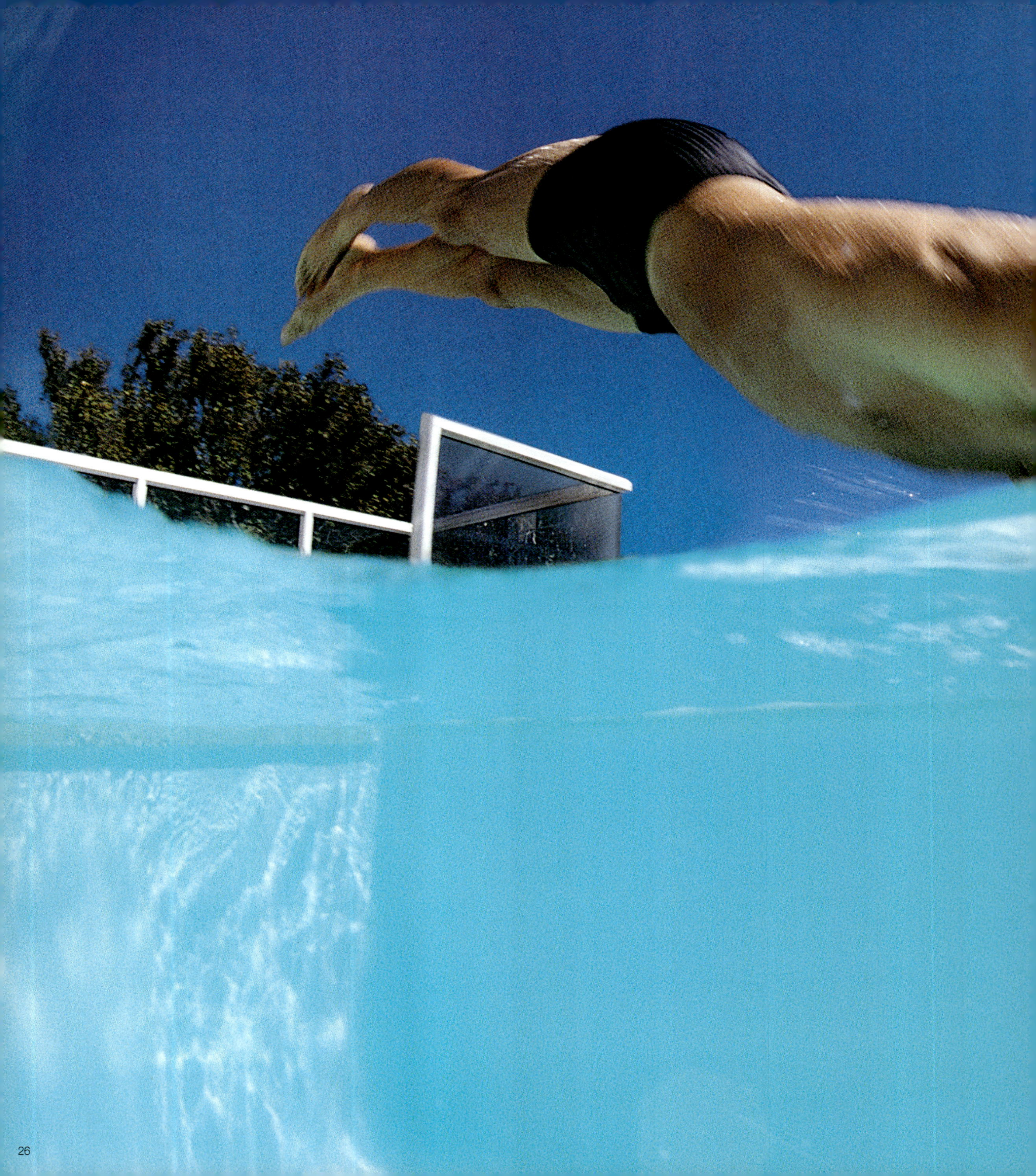

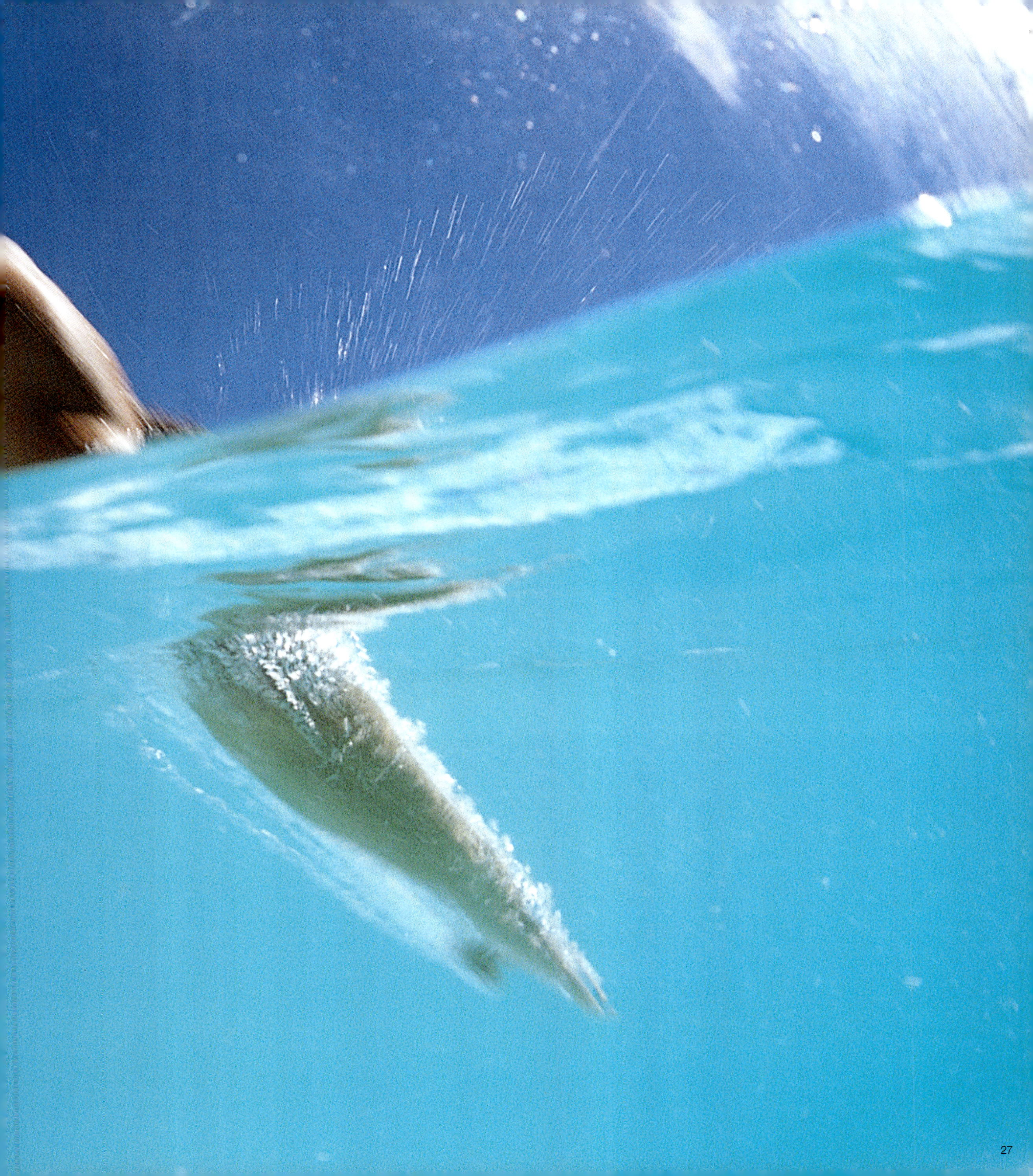

Doing Your Homework

In many ways, presenting your portfolio is the equivalent of interviewing for a new job. Knowing a bit about the company before you enter the door is invaluable. To do this most effectively, you may want to visit the company's website, ask other photographers their opinions on the company and lastly, and most importantly, call your national photography professional association.

Websites

The stock industry is relying more and more on the electronic channel of distribution. Given this fact, companies are putting more information on-line for their potential and existing photographers. This is a good source for finding out about fee structures, how royalties are calculated, and the company policy on 'buy-outs'.

Also on-line, you can view 'want lists'. These may be everything from research and technology images to modern lifestyle pictures that may be a hole in the stock company's collection. Consider these lists carefully as you may want to structure your portfolio around these stock requirements. If all the lists call for a variety of styles and compositions you have more freedom – if they are looking for black-and-white or sepia-toned prints then be sure to include them in your portfolio.

Your Colleagues

Another way of finding out about a company is to ask other stock professionals their opinion. Ask them if they have personally worked for the company you are presenting to and what their experiences were like. If artistic freedom is important to you, you might find out that the art direction is strictly provided by the company. This may not fit the way you work and it is better to find out now rather than after you've committed to doing a shoot.

Photographic Associations

Photographic associations are ideal for finding out the 'nitty-gritty', including whether or not the company has a history of paying its photographers' royalties on time, and if there are many complaints filed by fellow members. Doing this type of research is highly recommended, especially before you are impressed with plush offices or a very likeable art director!

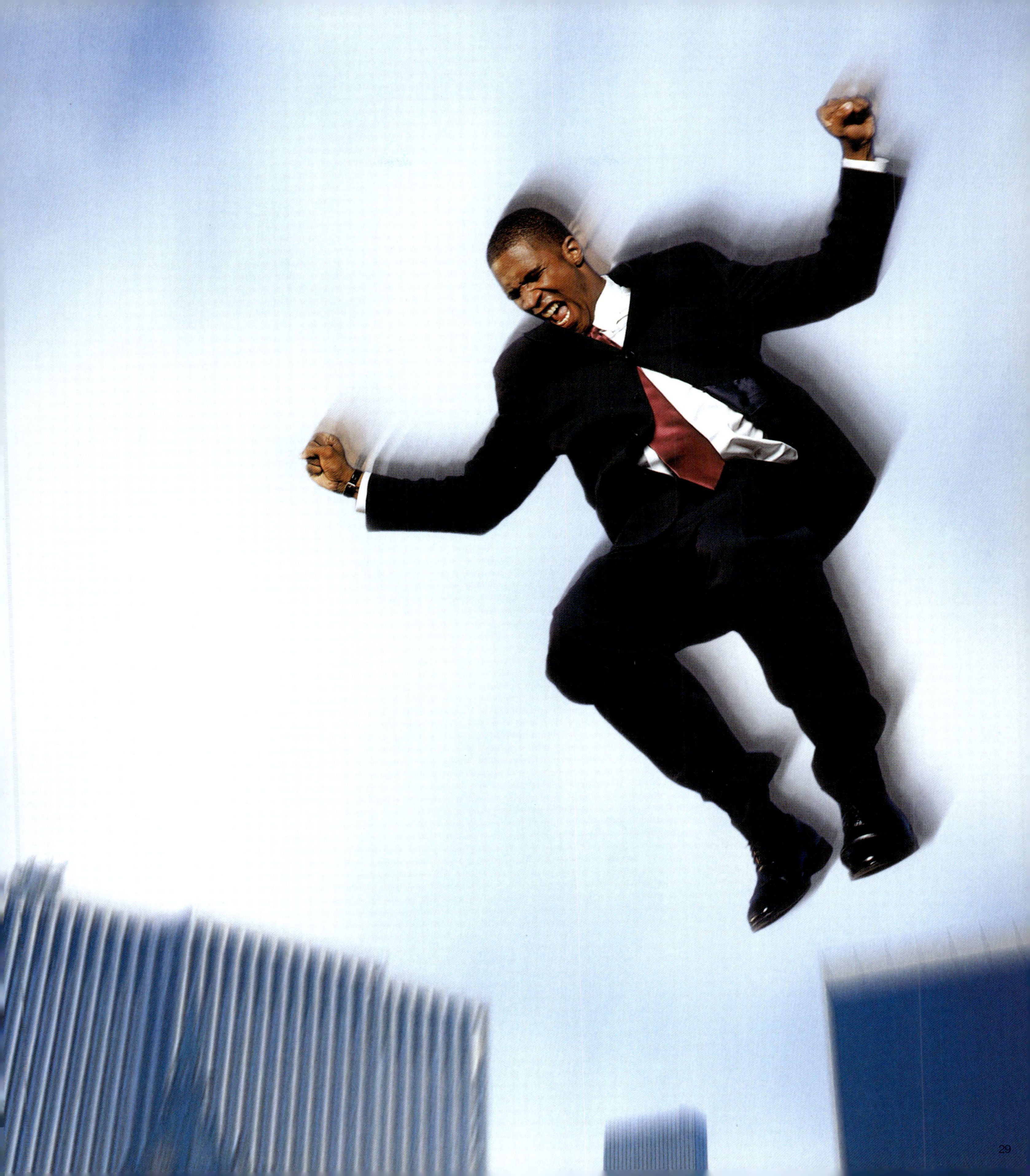

Choosing a Stock Library

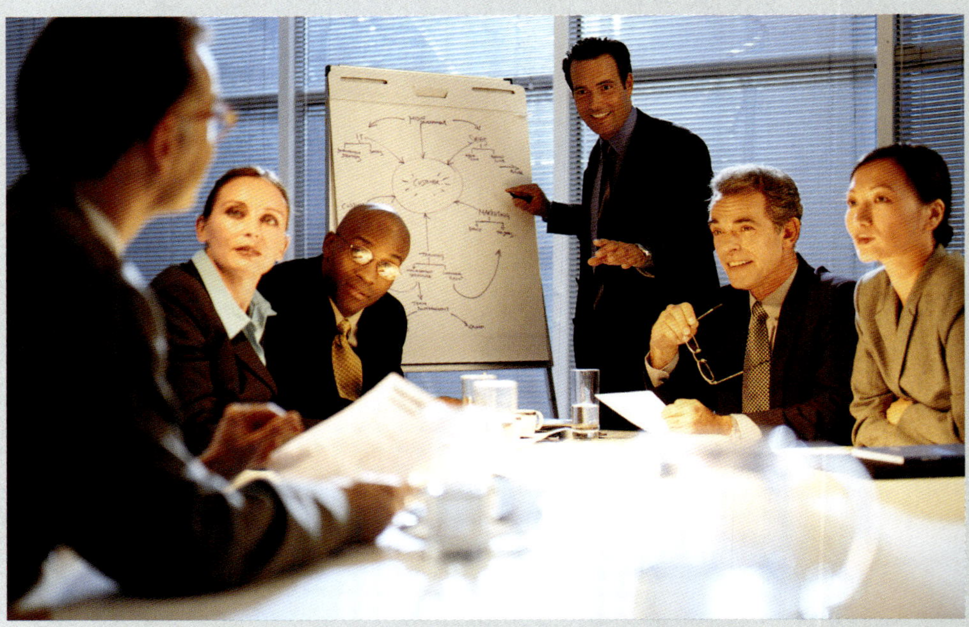

After you've done your homework, you will probably feel more comfortable about approaching the different companies. However, there are additional issues you should address before making your final choice of company. As with any type of employment, it is in your best interests to find out your worth in the marketplace – so be sure to see more than one stock company. If you are fortunate enough to have piqued the interest of more than one company, you may want to consider the following:

1 – Time to market
Ask yourself how long from image acceptance to promotion of this image, whether on the company's website or in a stock catalogue. This time frame can be up to a year for inclusion in stock catalogues or as little as a month or two for web-based sales. Realistically, even if your images are successful, you won't see substantial royalty figures for at least six months after they are initially brought to market.

2 – Distribution network
What follows is an issue commonly overlooked by photographers, but it can mean the difference between a good royalty cheque and a great one. In simple terms, the more agreements the stock company has with international stock distributors, the more chances you will have that your images will be sold. You want to ensure that the stock company you choose has a strong network in the US, Japan, France, Germany and the Netherlands, which are traditionally the most active markets.

3 – Space allotment
With stock photography, even if you have an established name, creative professionals buy on sight. They need to see your images and be inspired to buy. A good question to ask the stock company is "How often will my images appear in stock catalogues/the home page of the website/direct mail etc.?". Even if you have no marketing training and you shy away from anything to do with sales, you need to ensure that you get the coverage if you want to get your royalties. There is a proven relationship between placement and sales – think of the wars fought in supermarkets for the shelf space at eye level. When your images are with the stock library, they may be part of an image collection of more than a million other pictures. Photographers who are smart will push for the maximum amount of space. Remember, once your pictures begin to sell well, your battle for the mindshare of the marketing department will be much easier!

4 – Traditional or royalty free
One of your big decisions will be whether to promote your work through a stock photography company that is 'traditional' or 'royalty free'. While the differences between the two were broadly explained in Chapter 1, for you this might be more of an emotional decision since the differences in royalty cheques can be nominal. The royalty free industry has long been considered the 'poor relation' to traditional stock, but there is a movement to change that perception. These companies are no longer the dumping ground for 'seconds' and they have the same quality standards as traditional stock. They are, however, hungrier than traditional stock companies, and if they view your work as star quality, you may be able to negotiate a better deal.

There is a caveat here. Within your profession, you may encounter some backlash against royalty free because it goes against the business model of commissioned work. In the past, if a client commissioned a photo shoot they would have to pay repeat fees. In royalty free, the client pays for an image once and can use the image over and over again. This is the main reason why there is some resentment against royalty free. But, times are changing and royalty free has been an option for almost a decade. If you do choose royalty free, you still have the ability to become the 'big fish in a little pond' and for some photographers, this is as important as status.

Some photographers, however, still enjoy the prestige associated with Tony Stone and Photonica (US), the perceived quality suppliers within the traditional stock industry. Stone was actually started by a leading photographer, Tony Stone, and this has historically given credibility to the company. Photonica's inclusion of 'non-commercial' photographic work within its collections has also assisted with its positioning within the marketplace.

5 — Buy-out or royalty based

When you approach a stock company, you may be offered two choices: a straight buy-out or ongoing royalty basis. This means that you have the option of selling your images for a fixed price or taking the risk that in the long run, you will receive more from your images as a percentage of sales. Most photographers make this decision on their personal cash flow situation. If they need the money, for example to fund the purchase of new equipment or make up for a shortfall in their ongoing commissioned work, they will choose the straight buy-out. Others will take the gamble and hope to achieve ongoing royalty payments. If a photographer does take the royalties option, it is even more important to negotiate percentages of sales and placement before committing to a contract. Being a hard negotiator is not seen as a negative by the stock industry – as long as you are well informed and have realistic expectations.

Whatever you decide, the important thing is to ensure that you are comfortable with your choice, you have chemistry with the stock company itself, and have negotiated the best possible deal for your images.

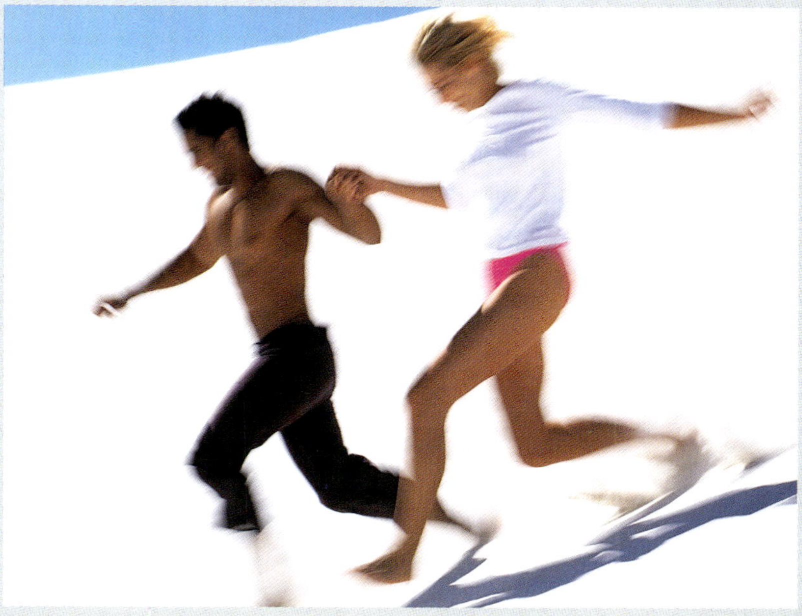

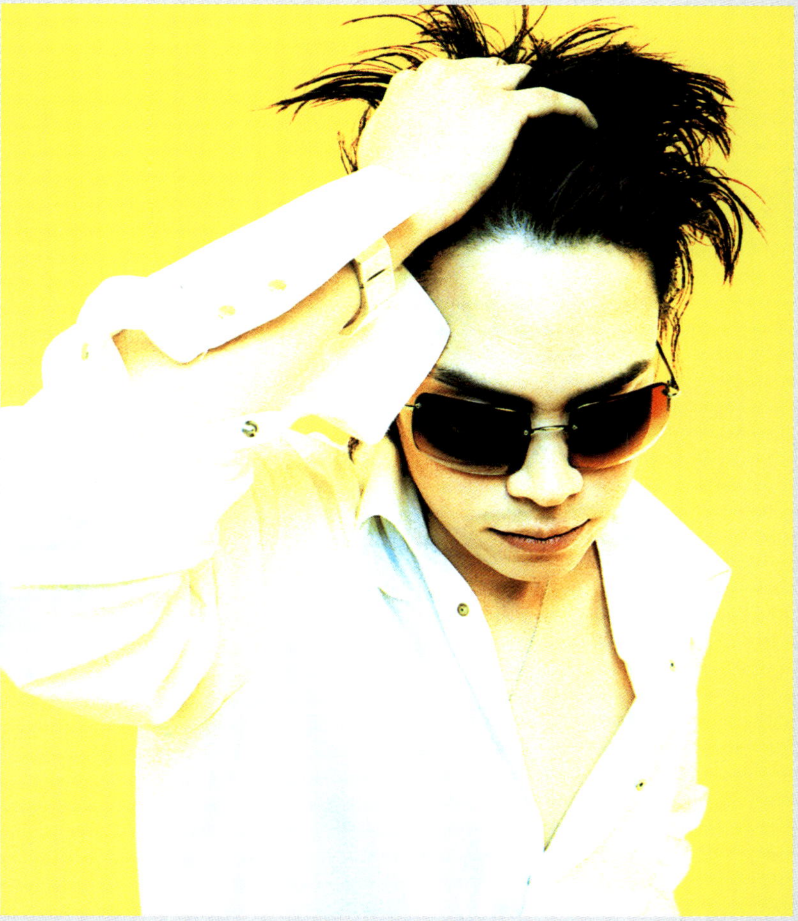

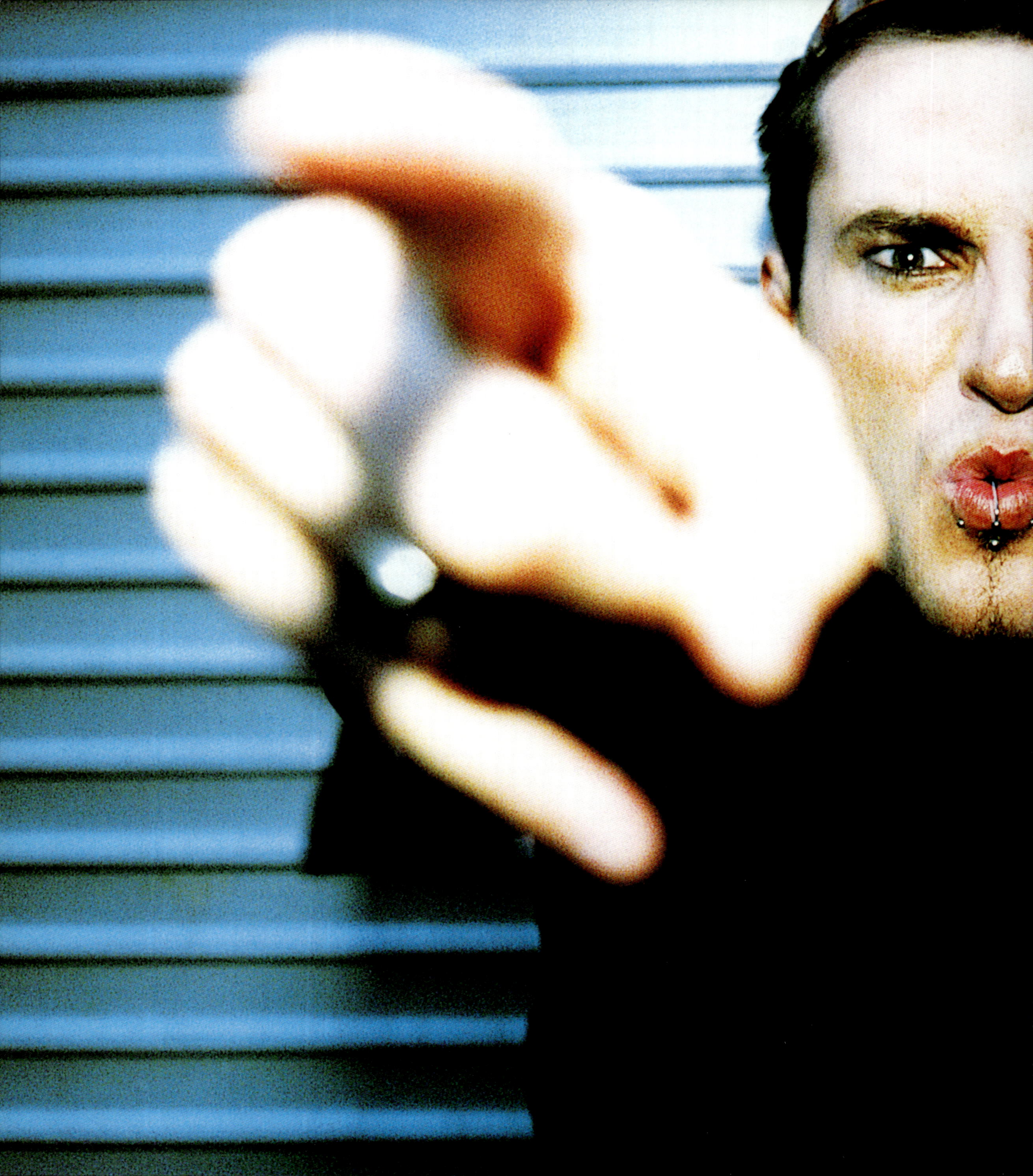

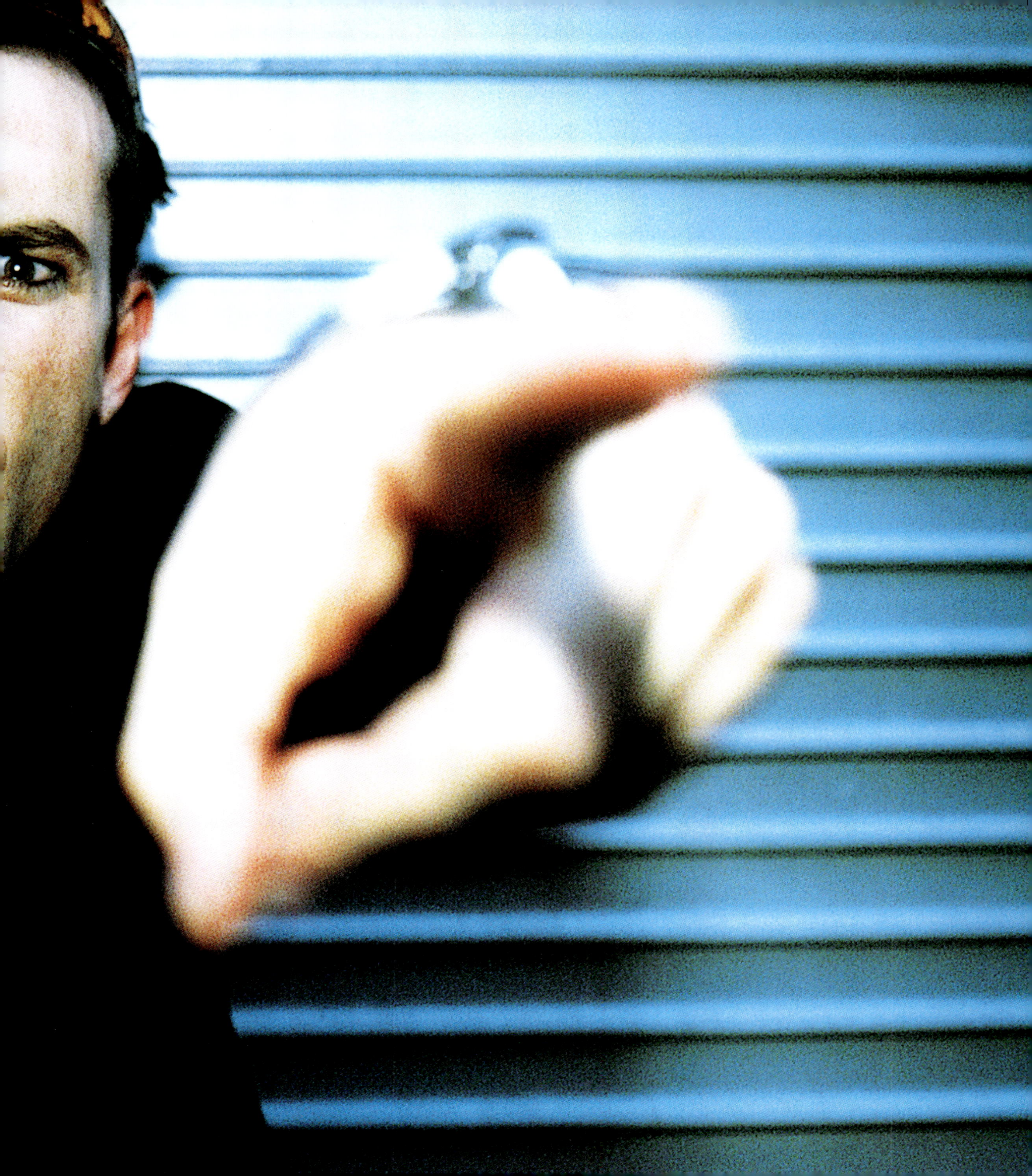

How the Libraries Price Images and Pay You Royalties*

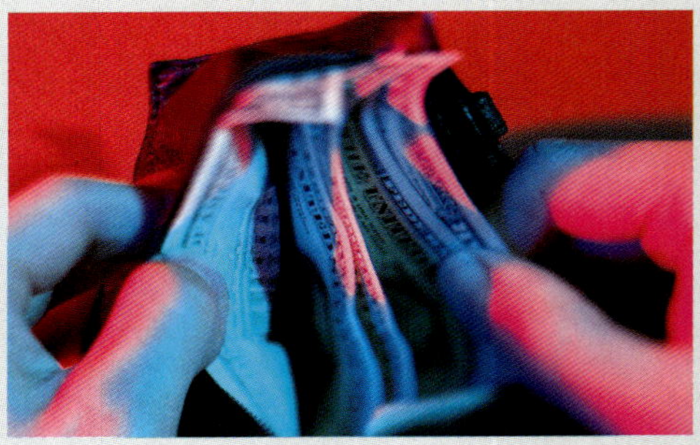

*Note that while the information is current, pricing is in a state of constant change. Photographers should use the information as a guideline for negotiations when approaching the industry, but they should not anticipate that the pricing structures will be the same as stated.

Rights Controlled Libraries

What a creative professional will pay for an image will depend on where he or she buys an image and for what type of project. Rights controlled libraries work to a different pricing model than do royalty free companies. They determine the price a customer will pay by asking the customer: where the image will be seen – single territory or global; the print run (if used in printed material); for what usage – whether it is for advertising or editorial; and the size the image will be used at.

In general, the cost for single usage will vary from £35 to £450, but as with any other business, high volume customers are in a position to negotiate better discounts.

Stock images sold for advertising offer more pricing permutations than editorial ones. As well as the criteria applied above, the number of insertions the advertisement will have and the length of time they wish it to run, i.e. six months, a year etc. will be considered in the customer quote. Importantly in the field of advertising, there is greater demand for rights protected images, or exclusivity in the business area in which the client operates. This equipment is becoming less and less critical to those agency customers who don't want to pay for the large exclusivity tariff.

Prices quoted will depend on the library pricing structure and to a degree this is dependent on their position in the market. All-media, rights protected buy-outs (these don't include TV) are some of the most lucrative deals. A library which charges out at the higher end of the scale would, for example, offer a rights protected buy-out in all media in the UK for only one year at approximately £12,000. If the agency wished to include one other country, France for example, another 10% would be added to the cost. If the whole of Europe were added it would be approximately a further 50% and worldwide a further 100%, bringing the total to £24,000. If they wished to waiver the rights protection the costs would drop by about 15%. Conversely, editorial deals are far less lucrative. Exclusivity is normally only requested for images used for front and back covers of publications.

Rights controlled libraries will usually take a 50% commission for all 'home' or 'domestic' sales. On overseas sales, the commissions can increase to 70–90% depending on the distribution model of the company and how many overseas agents/sub-agents will represent the photographer's images.

Over the past 18 months, some libraries are moving away from the 50/50 model to embrace renumerating the photographer through part commission/part royalty. For example, the library will pay for the shoot costs and give the photographer a flat fee – this will be costed according to the photographer and how successful their work has been with the library – and then pay out a 10% royalty on all subsequent sales. The advantages to the library are that they make money in the long-term on successful multiple-selling images. Some libraries will charge the photographer for showing their work in the catalogue, often up to £400+ per image. For a photographer who has had 30+ images chosen, this can mount considerably. To make this more palatable, most agencies will offset the catalogue entry against sales.

Royalty Free Libraries

Royalty free companies have a different business model and pricing structure which is product rather than rights determined. Image prices in royalty free are generally fixed with standard costs for images. Pricing is determined on image resolution or file size – not usage. A general ball-park scale for image pricing is approximately £20–£50 for low resolution images (at 72 dpi); £50–£200 for medium resolution; £80–£250 for high resolution to £300+ for super high resolution. Although fixed, image pricing from company to company can vary considerably.

Image CD prices are also at a fixed rate (in other words non-negotiable by the client, unless buying in multiples when a discount may be offered). Within a collection of image CDs there is likely to be a variety of price points. Once again prices vary from company to company but as a general guide, image CDs sell for anywhere between £150–£350 for 50 to 100 images per CD. Most companies will include all file sizes of the images on the CDs. The general trend in the industry is for CD prices to increase while the number of images per CD is decreasing.

Royalty free companies work with photographers and artists in a variety of ways: commission, image buy-out, and royalty percentage.

1—Commission based
As with straightforward work-for-hire, commission jobs are negotiated on a daily rate or project rate. The amount a photographer can expect to receive varies from library to library and, as with any other commission work, the library would expect costs quoted to reflect the volume of work they may be asking the photographer to undertake. Daily rates can vary from approximately £500–£1,000, or more, but it would be fairly unlikely for royalty free companies to front advertising day rates of £1,800 or more. Shoot costs are often advanced by the company if the photographer is billing, otherwise they will be invoiced directly to the company. Most royalty free companies would expect the photographer to assign all copyrights on commission jobs over to them.

2—Image buy-outs
Image buy-outs usually favour the specialist photographer who may have existing large image collections in certain areas such as travel or nature. A per image cost is offered, normally between £10–£250, often on a non-exclusive basis. This will enable the photographer to still sell the image if, for example, a client rings them directly and wishes to purchase it. They would not however be able to sell that image to the client exclusively.

For this type of arrangement, libraries will usually be seeking generic images which can be used widely. This is advantageous to the specialist photographer since there is usually very little conflict with the photographer's own client base, who are more often than not editorially based and require specific images.

3—Royalty percentage
A royalty percentage on image CDs and single image web sales is the third pricing model. Once again there are different permutations of this pricing model across the industry and different percentages are offered. In general, the royalty percentage is calculated on the sale of the CD or single image rather than the sale of the image rights (usage).

In many respects, the model is more akin to the music industry than traditional stock. Percentages vary from around 15% to approximately 25% usually of the net cost (once distributor costs are deducted). The amount a photographer can expect to receive per image disk depends on the cost of the CD and whatever percentage has been negotiated with the distributor.

The amount a photographer can earn is therefore also dependent on volume and the expected lifespan of the CD title. This could be from two to four years and more. Sales volume of a title is obviously dependent on the strength of imagery and crucially, the company's marketing strength and distribution network. For a photographer to do well from a royalty deal, it is important that their CD title be represented in the company's catalogue and marketing materials.

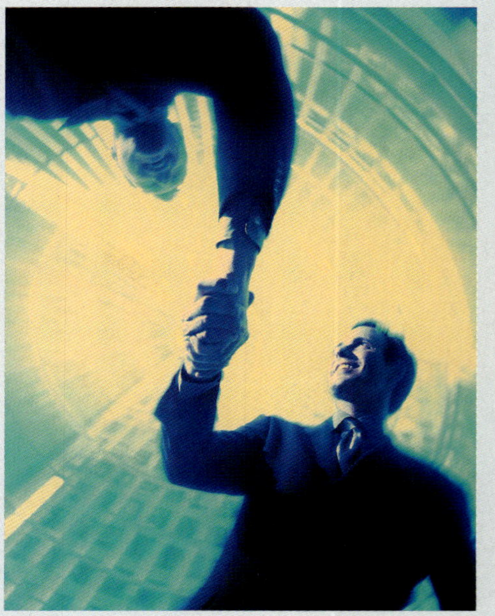

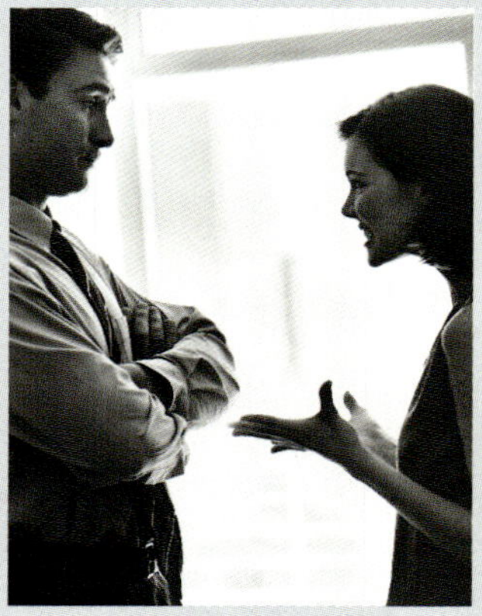

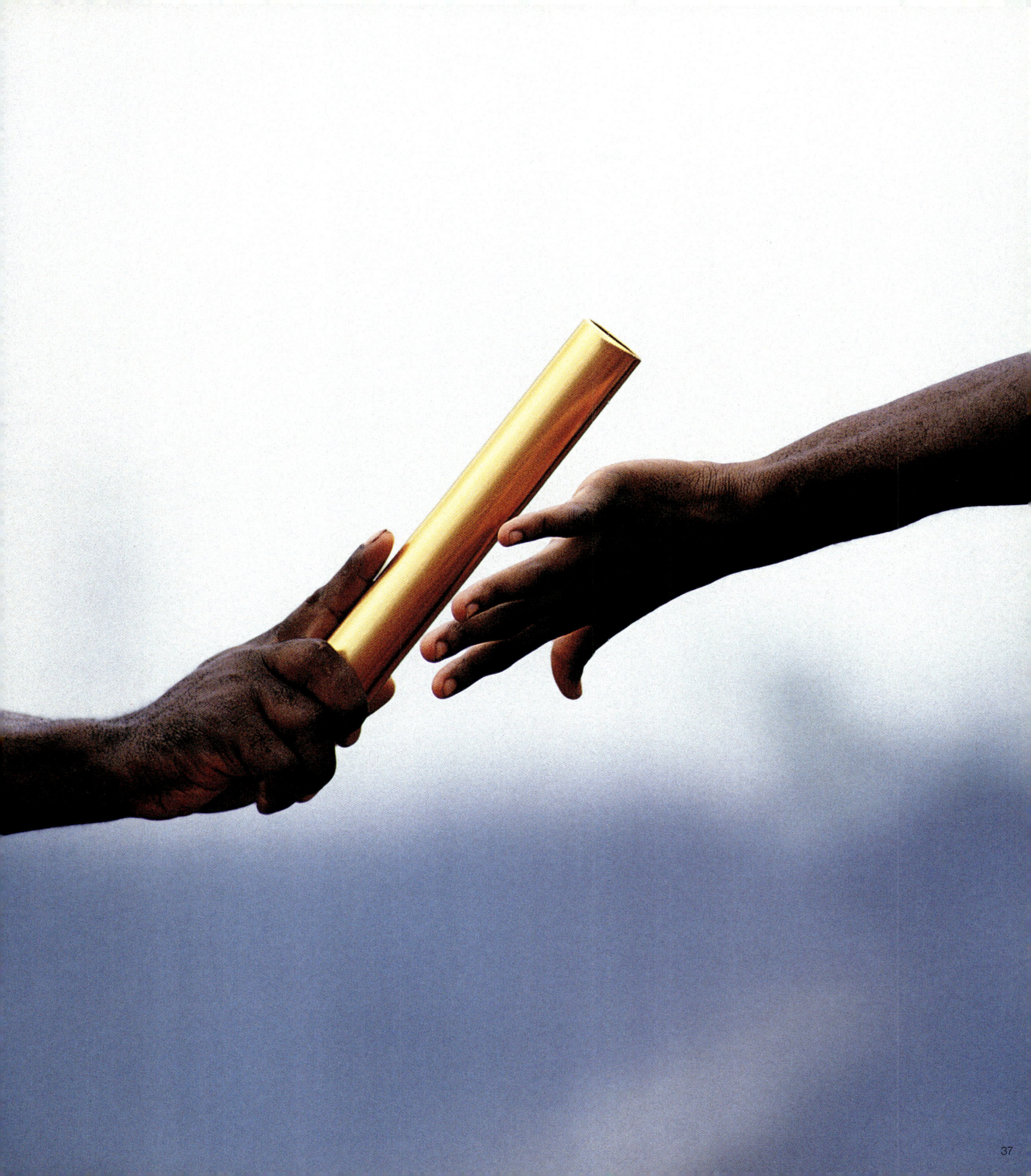

Top Ten
Creative Directors' Tips

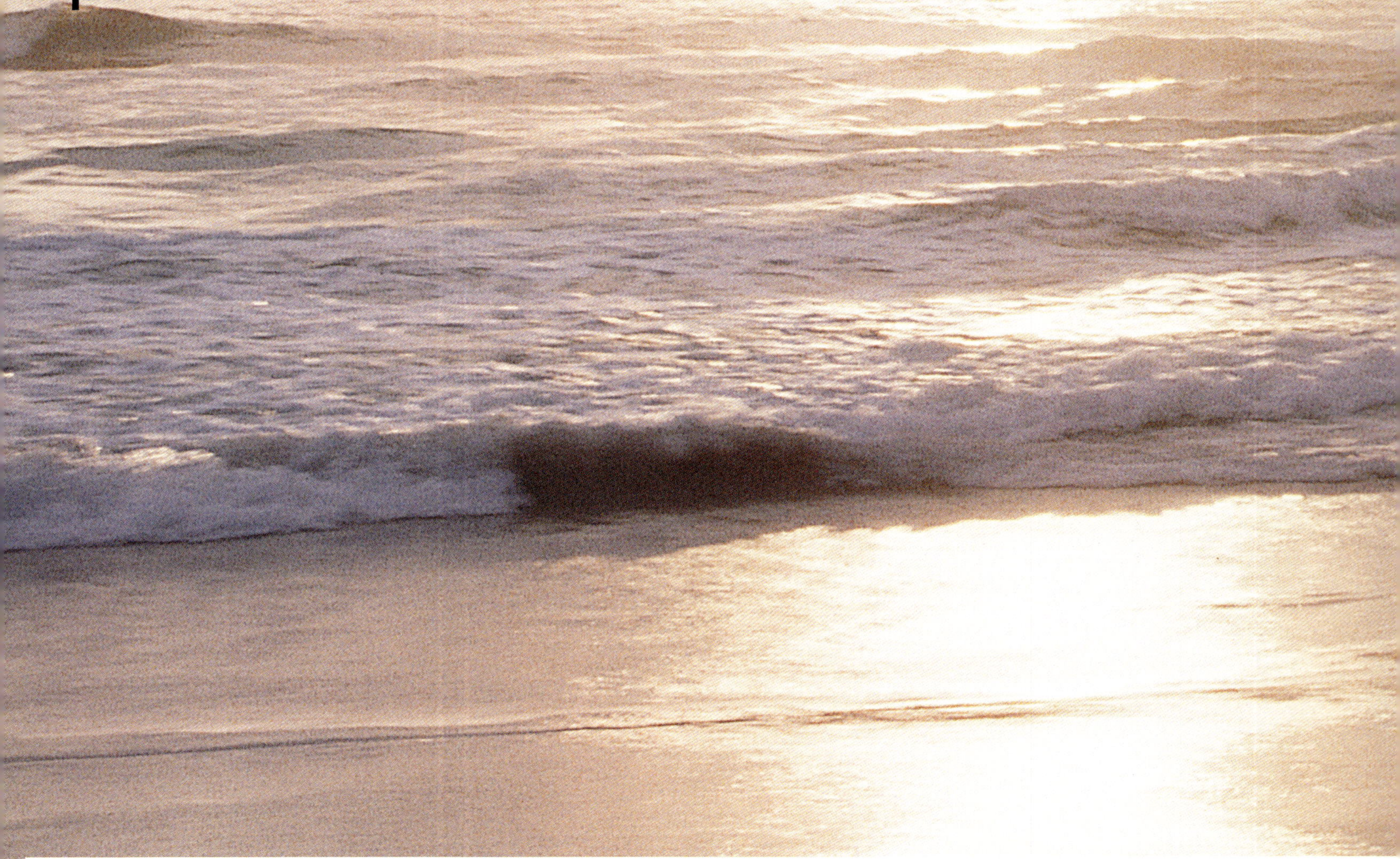

1
Find out who you should see – and find a way of getting to them directly. If your focus is on baby shots for example, find out which creative acquisitions person deals with this area. Persistence pays. If you get a 'not interested' over the phone, don't give up right away.

2
Talk to other photographers who the stock company admire. Find out why they value that photographer – is it his/her style or way of working?

3
Don't be insecure about money matters. This is an absolute turn-off. If you are worried about being paid, do your research with due diligence before you present your portfolio.

4
Be knowledgeable about how the stock industry works. While creative acquisitions staff will spend time explaining how they like to do business, your lack of knowledge about the industry and the creative market is another turn-off.

5
Send digital files – not transparencies. When you send transparencies, they need to be logged and kept in a safe for security reasons. This creates work at the stock company's end, plus they are now slower to review images provided in this format. The best way to send your images is by a link to your own website that features your pictures.

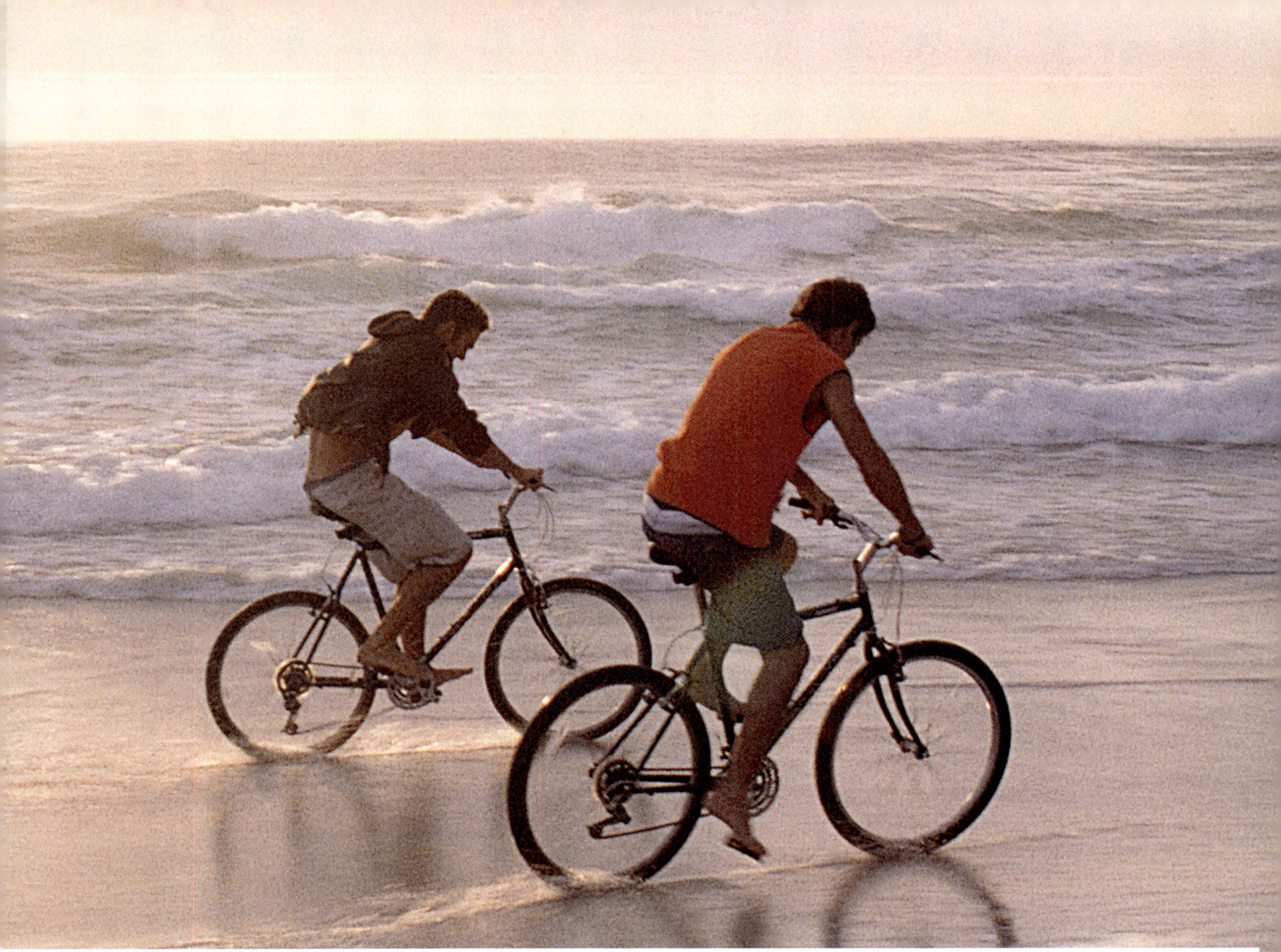

6
If you are a professional photographer, don't complain about your lack of assignment/ commission work. Stock professionals are wary of photographers who once had lots of work, but now don't. They start to think that the photographer views stock as 'second choice' and doesn't respect the industry. An absolute no-no.

7
Be aware of your own style – and how it works in the commercial world. If you can prove that your imagery is wanted by the creative community, you will have more credibility. This may be as simple as bringing in cut-outs from magazines showing similar styling/ lighting/composition.

8
Don't oversell your portfolio and picture collection. Let the stock industry professional make comments and address weaknesses.

9
Ask how the company likes to work. Be interested in the partnership aspects of working within the industry by asking if they provide stylists and art direction. In turn, make it clear that you have a network of professionals to call upon.

10
Be a trendspotter. Look at what the music and fashion scenes are producing. If you have the talent and the courage, try to capture the zeitgeist so that that stock photography agency will have the most current imagery in the marketplace. In business terms, this means you will have 'first-mover' advantage – filling a gap before the rush flows in.

Chapter 3
Marketing Yourself and Your Work
40 – 49

Where Will it Be Seen?

In the last ten years, there has been a trend in the stock photography industry to provide the most exciting platform to launch new images. This image showcase, usually the annual or biannual stock catalogue, has undergone a transformation from the traditional standard book sizes to catalogues which include pull-out bound pages, tabs, and even covers with pink acrylic fur! Attention has even been given to the external packaging with one company sending out stock catalogues in suitcase-style styrofoam boxes or luminous silver bubble-wrap envelopes!

All this expense is logical – the customer who is searching for stock images is visually driven. They may be a graphic designer, an art buyer or a marketing professional, but they are all excited by well-designed catalogues which use contemporary materials or concepts. The stock industry recognises this customer response and spends a large portion of their marketing budgets on these catalogues. In fact, this fascination with 'design meeting photography' has led to many of the stock companies seeking the help of graphic design firms who specialise in music industry materials such as CD covers and posters. The cooler, quirkier and more cutting-edge the better.

But beware that paying for this new, high-production value material is not only in the hands of the stock company, but is often billed to you. Libraries that offer traditional priced stock require photographers to pay for the 'space' that the images take up in the catalogues. The justification for these costs is that these books are a method of 'advertising' – like paying for space in photographers' contact books. In general, royalty free companies do not charge for image placement. This is another area which separates the two types of companies.

The catalogue only plays one part in a growing photographic arsenal of marketing messaging. Quarterly magazines are a mainstay of royalty free companies with the quality of these publications increasing rapidly. The on-line presence of stock photography libraries is the newest and most lucrative area of business.

When making your decision about the company you choose, take a look at the materials it produces. If you can visualise your work in that company's catalogue or on their website, then it will probably be a good fit for you. If not, keep looking.

On this page are some examples of what is currently seen in the stock photography marketplace.

Websites

Stock photography websites are becoming the primary way that the creative market searches and purchases imagery. The reasons for this popularity are threefold:
1. Speed – the images can be downloaded and placed directly into designs;
2. Choice – all the stock library's images are placed in one location thereby taking away the need to search through a pile of stock books;
3. Usability and Payment – accounts can be set up on-line which eliminates the need for the designer to raise a company cheque.

Another reason why searching for images on the web has become more popular is the development of better on-line search engines. Search engines look through 'key words' which are linked to all the images on a library's site. When a designer needs an image, they will type in a descriptor such as 'businesswoman + office' and a variety of images featuring this topic will appear. Technology has now evolved and natural language search engines are becoming increasingly popular. You can simply type in 'contemporary businesswoman in her office talking on the phone'. This further narrows down the choices for the designer, therefore increasing the efficiency.

From your perspective, you want to ensure that your images appear as frequently as possible during on-line searches. An insider tip is to request the total list of words attached to your images. Read them, and if you think any key 'conceptual' themes are missing, then request to add these keywords to your images.

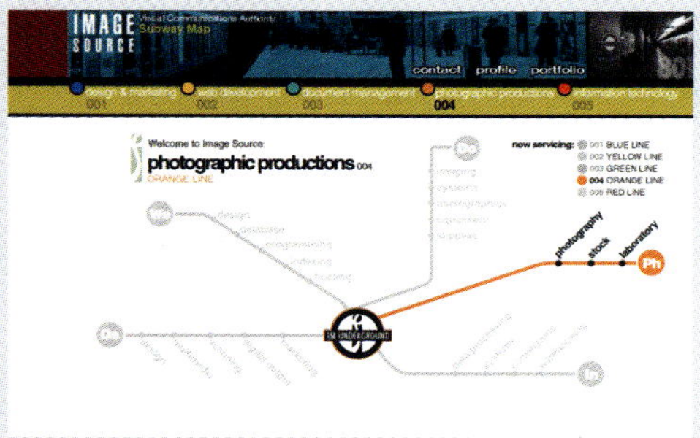

Imagesource
www.imagesource.com

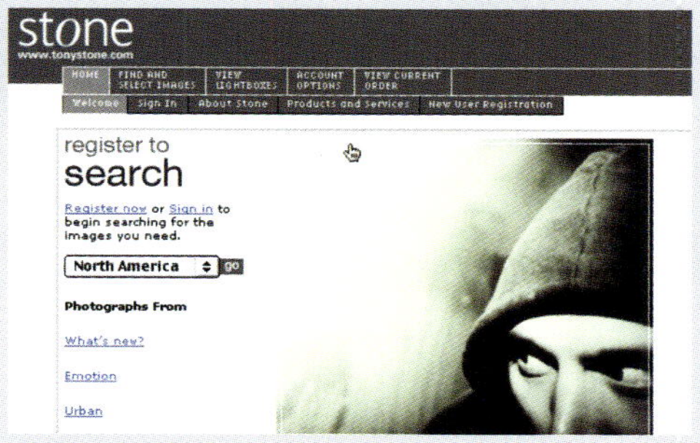

Tony Stone
www.tonystone.com

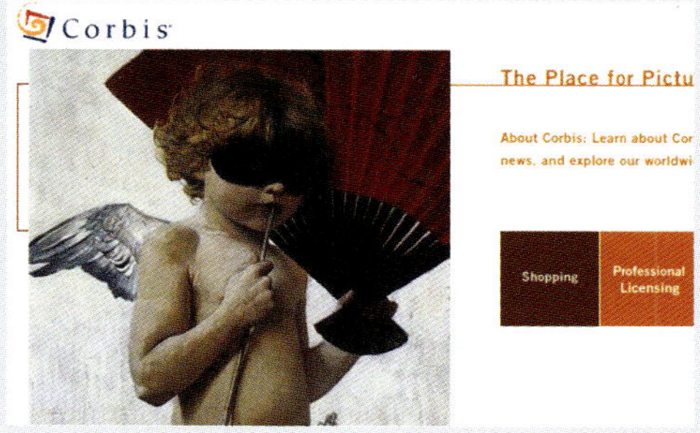

Corbis
www.corbis.com

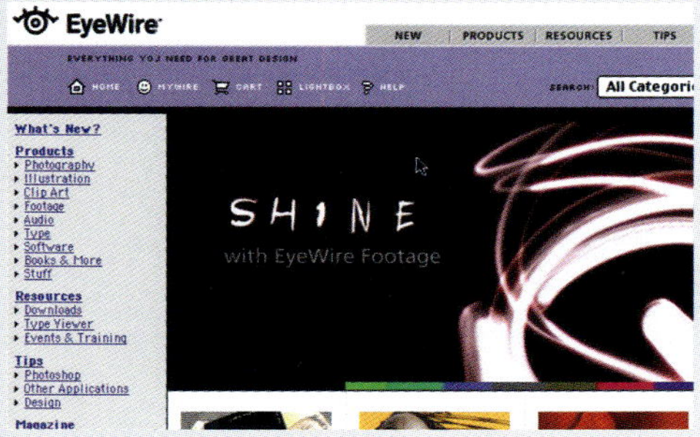

EyeWire
www.eyewire.com

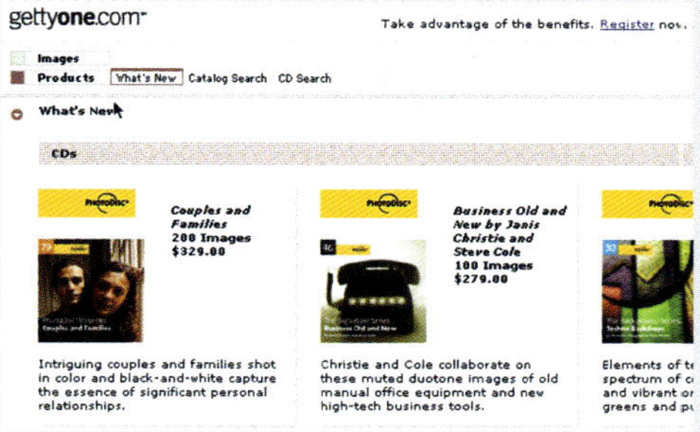

Getty One
www.gettyone.com

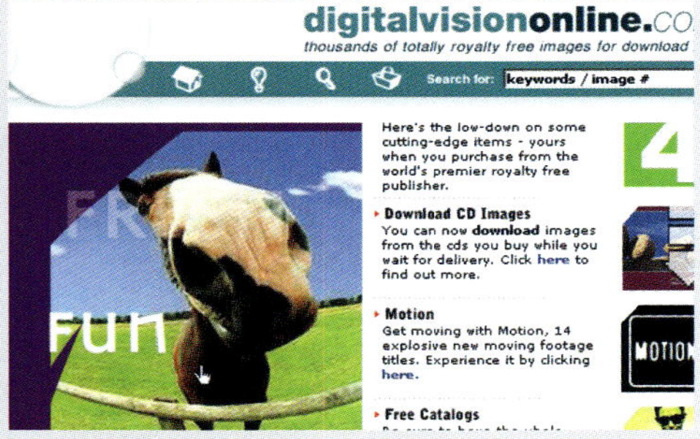

Digital Vision
www.digitalvisiononline.com

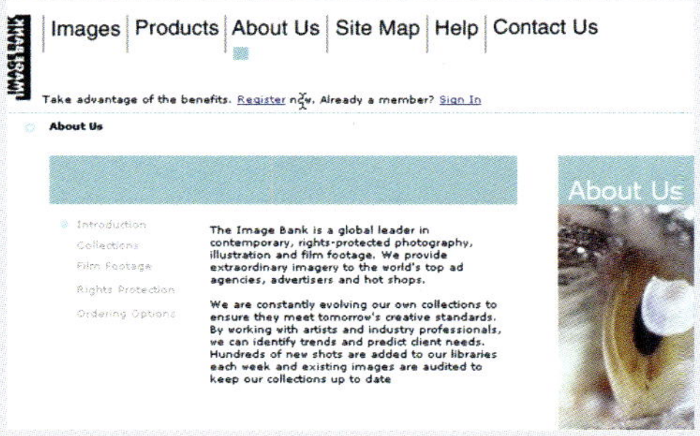

Image Bank
www.imagebank.com

Catalogues are still a key part of the marketing mix. They still represent the completion of a photographic collection and represent the market positioning of a company. Stone, for instance, has continually bucked the convention of the oversized A4 catalogue. They have experimented with a metal binder, a hard-bound book, and a half-sized catalogue with the pages bound on the short edge. This creative experimentation has helped Stone keep its marketshare as designers look not only to Stone for high-end photography – but for design inspiration, too.

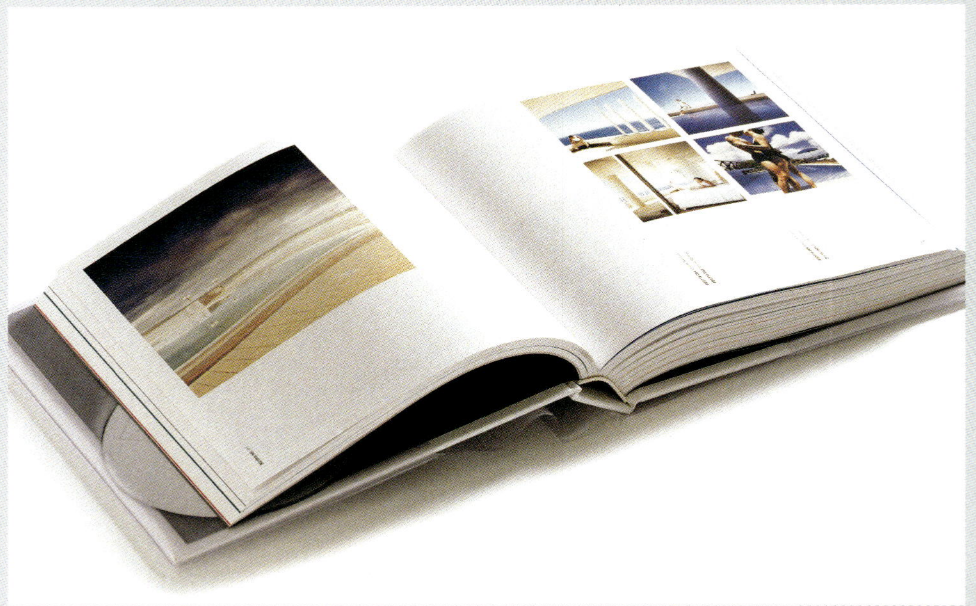

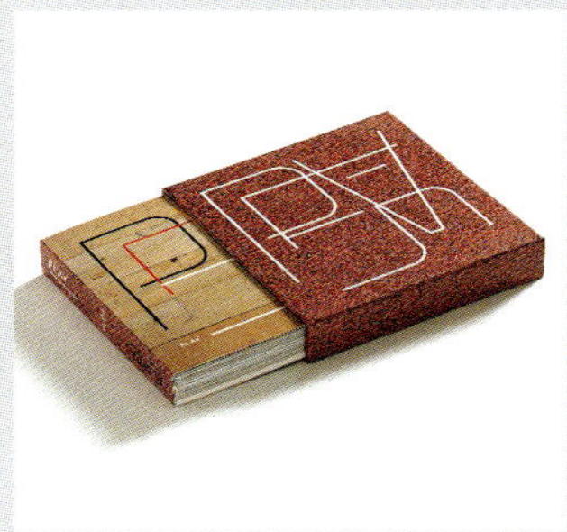

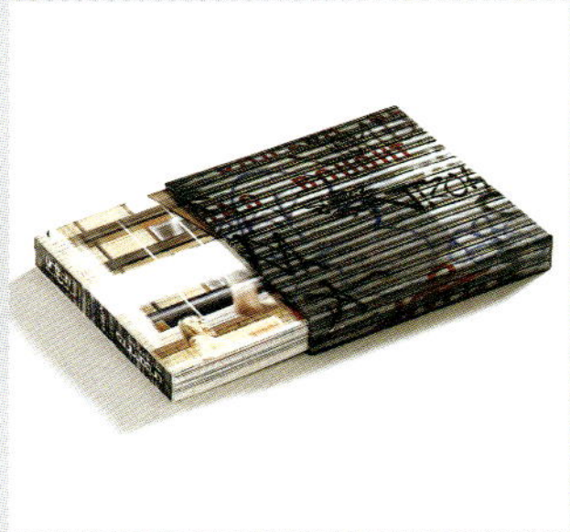

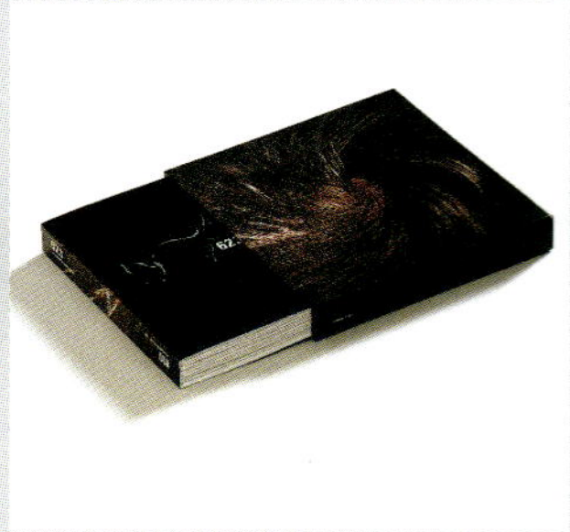

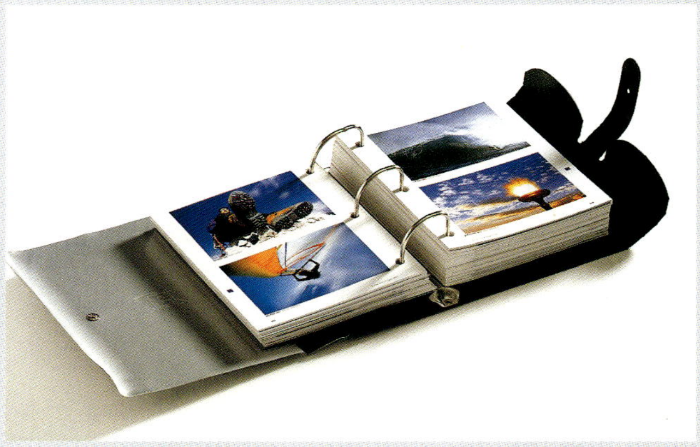

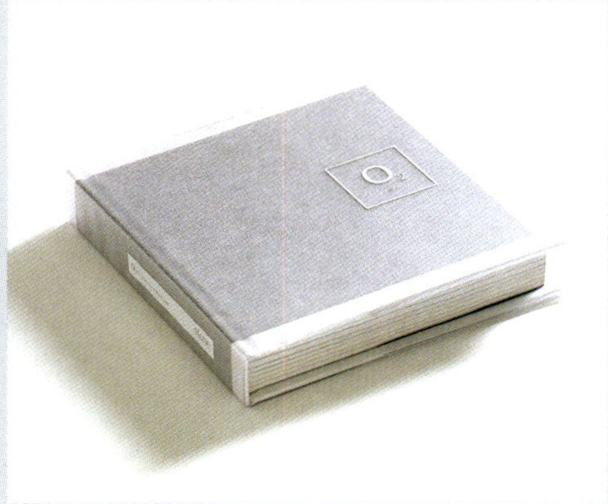

The Image Bank, another stock library, has also recognised this 'design = positioning' trend, and has hired a well-known British design company to rebrand and redesign their materials. In their case, they chose to use a strong typographic treatment instead of photography to transmit their message.

In the past, royalty free stock photographic catalogues were, in general, not of the same creative quality as traditional stock. Their focus was on illustrating 'value' over 'quality' by showing every single image from a collection. More recently, however, the line is being blurred with royalty free companies' catalogues starting to focus on the quality within their collections. Some royalty free companies are even taking the brave step of not promoting every single image within a collection. Instead, like the traditional stock business model, they are showing the best images much larger and to better advantage.

Interactive CDs

Interestingly, the use of interactive CDs is the most controversial item within the marketing mix. These CDs are normally included within a stock catalogue and feature 'low-res' versions of all the images printed within the book. The *raison d'être* of interactive CDs is so that the designer can place these images into designs 'for placement only', enabling their clients to buy into concepts. In the past, creative agencies would scan the images from the stock catalogue, place the images and then, if their client approved a project, negotiate the rights to use those images. It is simply a matter of changes in technology.

However, the web can provide exactly the same type of low-resolution 'for placement only' images – so why do stock companies still provide CDs? The answer is simple – all designers work differently and the stock library wants to ensure that it satisfies everyone.

From a business standpoint, CDs are easy to produce and are light and therefore inexpensive to mail. Marketing professionals will often spend time adding more information to this interactive medium so that their customers will feel more affiliated with their company. Some have even added computer games to the interactive CDs to give them more value and fun.

Looking forward, however, it will be interesting to see if these interactive CDs will be dropped in favour of low-resolution images on the web.

Direct Mail and Company Magazines

Just as technology has moved forward, so has the philosophy of how stock photography marketing professionals view campaign management. When they know a new themed collection is going to be published, they plan what is called an 'integrated campaign' which takes into account the catalogue, the web, the interactive CD and direct mail.

Direct mail can take the form of a periodical magazine, or mailings which ask the recipient to return a business reply card. Magazines are becoming a more important part of the marketing schedule because they fill the gap between catalogue launches. Currently, they are used more frequently by the royalty free sector.

These magazines, like the catalogues produced by the royalty free companies, have improved in quality over the last few years. Once seen as the 'sales brochure', many have evolved to include features, design tips and non-picture products such as fonts, software, and even CD shelving! EyeWire's magazine is considered, by many, as one of the best examples of the customer magazine. It sets a tone within the copy and it has a good balance between the editorial, product and sales promotion.

Other direct mail can also link into large campaigns such as the one recently launched by The Telegraph Colour Library in London. Wanting to position the company as a stock company with English roots and bias, the company put together a promotion which allowed any new customer to enter a draw for the ultimate British design icon, the Mini automobile. The campaign culminated in the draw being held in a West End theatre followed by a screening of the movie **The Italian Job**. An enjoyable, quirky way to sell images.

Marketing Your Work

In Chapter 2 we discussed how to market your work to the stock photography company by using some commercial acumen and some presentation tips. Once your work has been accepted and printed in a catalogue, you may want to consider how to draw attention to your imagery. Even if you don't have exceptional selling skills, there are some effective ways to get your work seen by your target audience.

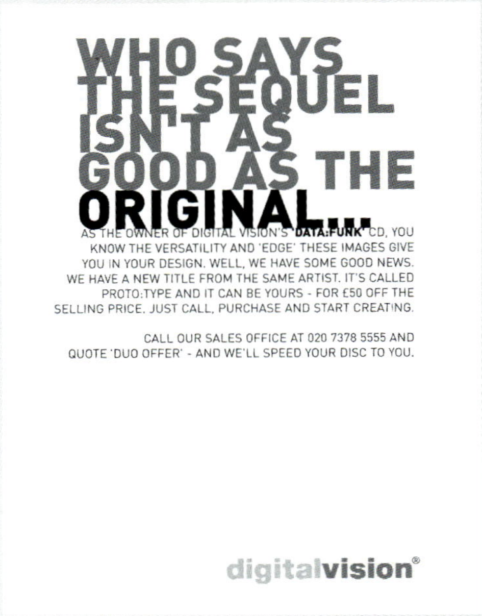

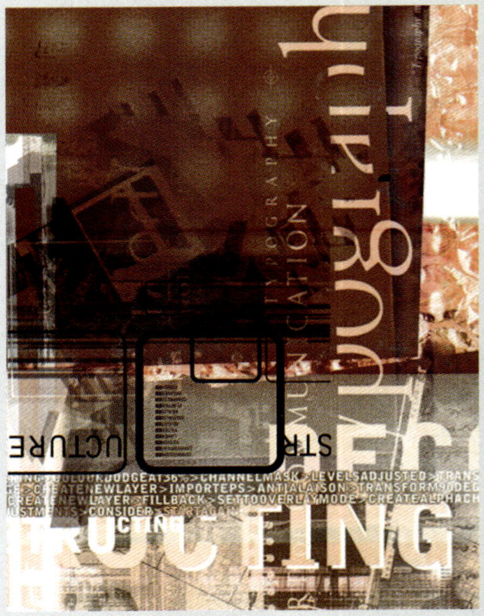

Digital illustrator, Paul Price, designed his own direct mail to promote his second royalty free title (above).

Illustrator and digital artist Daniel Mackie, is an example of someone who markets his work extremely well. Through his unusual Francis Bacon-esque style of editorial illustrations, he has developed a large database of freelance journalists, art editors and publishers. When he produces new work for a stock agency or completes an exciting project, he e-mails his contacts with a short note telling them to view this work on his website – which he has also designed. This interaction with his existing and potential customer base keeps him top-of-mind for future work, or it might spark a journalist to write an article about his art and technique.

Paul Price, another digital artist who uses his own images to complement his high-tech designs, also markets his images well. As a former magazine art director, he approached a stock company for freelance design work, and ended up designing the company's main publications. Guess whose images appear frequently? The company doesn't mind, however, since Paul's images are top sellers.

Many photographers have their images printed on postcards to send out to their friends. Others consider hiring gallery space and have framed versions seen by invited guests. In the end, the trick is to use your natural creativity and consider ways to get your images seen by the right people.

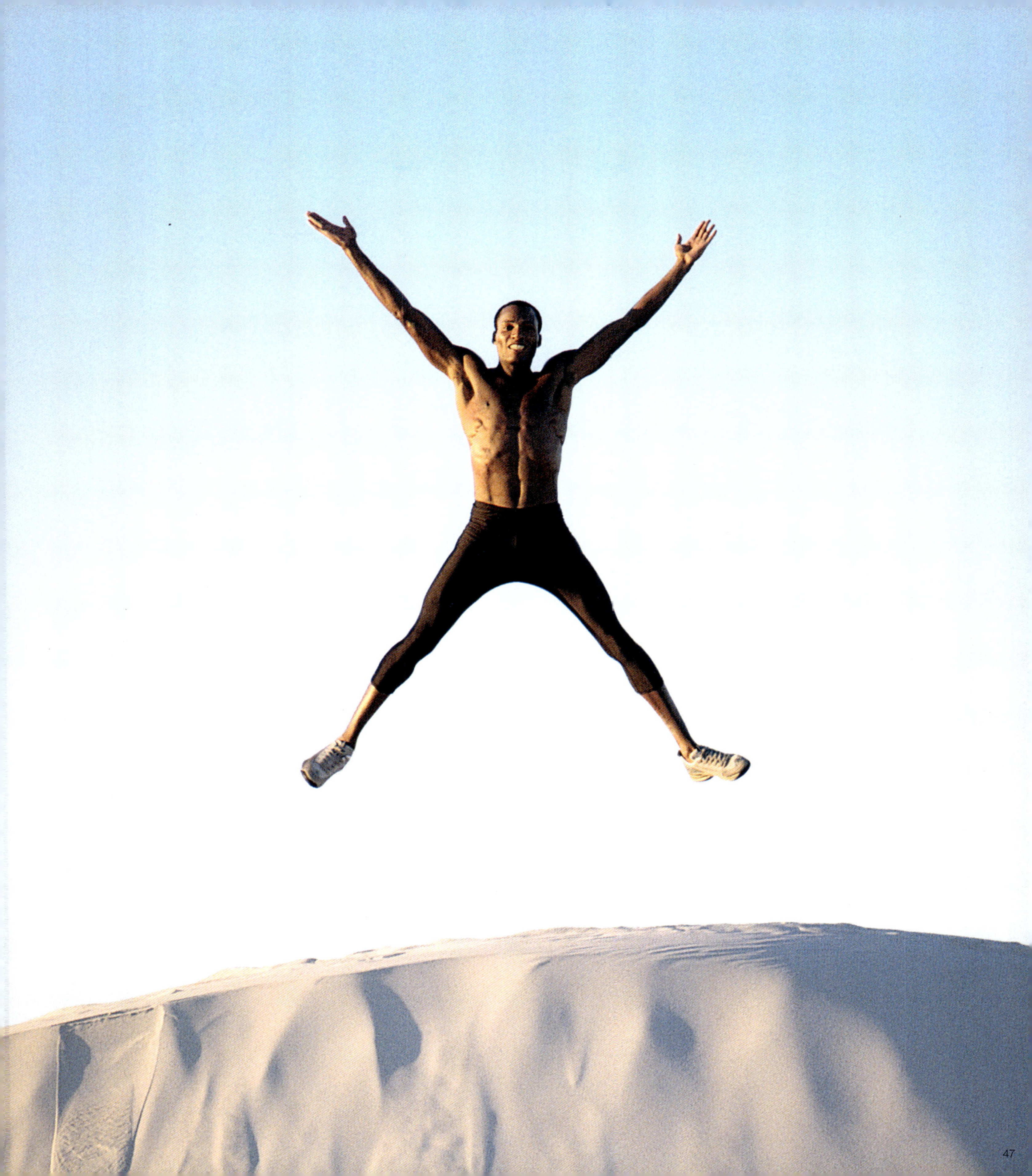

Approaching the Marketing Department

Stock agencies are always looking to keep in touch with their customers – if you offer something they can send out, then more than likely they will.

Depending on the company, the marketing department may or may not be receptive to your assistance. The trick is getting the mindshare of the marketing director by offering some value to their current campaigns. If, for example, the coming month's focus is on 'Sports' and you are a sports photographer, you may offer to co-fund some of the printing of a sales brochure if your images are used and credited.

Or, you may want to design (or have a graphic designer create) a postcard advertising the best pictures you have on offer.

Another trick is to talk up your book. Put your camera down for the moment and consider how you can get the maximum publicity for your images. Do you have some writing skills? Put them to the test by writing a press release and sending to both the local newspaper press and the editors of creative publications. Be sure to include a reason why they should feature your work – such as new techniques or new styling or describe what you see as the value in these images. Read these publications in advance to see what they publish – then tailor your release to fit their tone of voice.

You may be asking "Isn't it the marketing department's job to ensure sales for my images?". Yes, is the answer, however, with hundreds of photographers on their books, you want to ensure that you get the exposure you need to maximise royalties.

Marketing Quotes

"If a photographer gives me print-ready or web-ready stories – I am happy to use them. Providing written content is part of my job – and if a photographer wants to promote his or her images, it is in their interest to be pro-active supplying both words and sample images to show."

"Public relations is a function of marketing – if a photographer approaches me (extremely rare by the way) with a story about how they produced their images, what lighting they used etc., I'd send it to my press contacts pretty quickly. The trick is finding mutually beneficial things to do – that frankly don't require a huge drain on my time, but that I can see have possible tangible results."

"I'd like to do more promotion – but sometimes the photographers become too temperamental about how we show their work. If a photographer becomes a prima donna, I'll just look for another one to showcase."

"Some photographers still have a hang-up about being affiliated with royalty free. I'll work harder for the photographer that is not only proud to be working with my company – but one who will put effort in on their part, too."

"One of the things I may do is print postcards or flyers – if the photographer gives me print-ready artwork that is well-designed. Especially if the work reflects how we promote our company and the associated 'brand'."

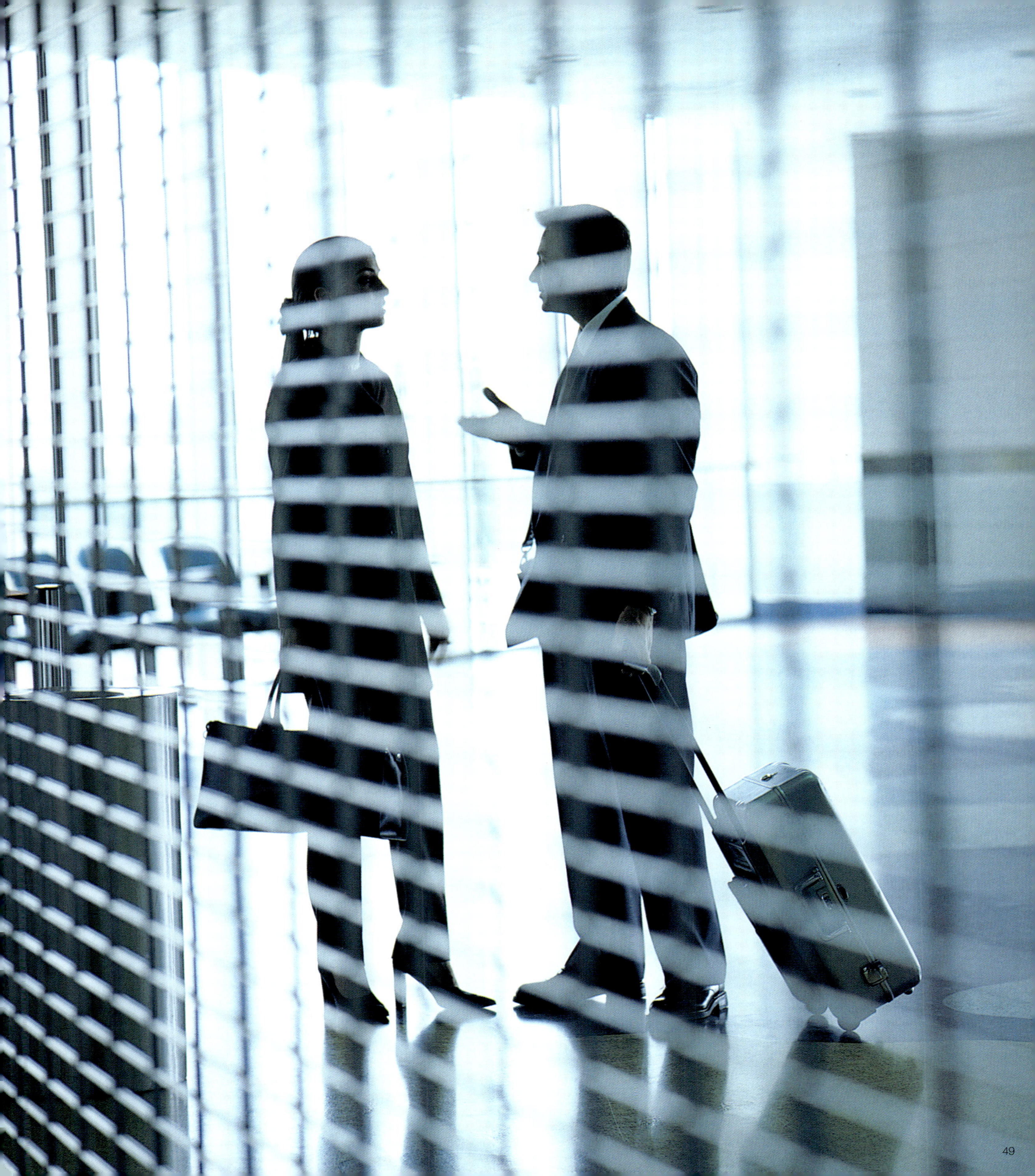

Chapter 4
How to Take Pictures for Stock
50 – 87

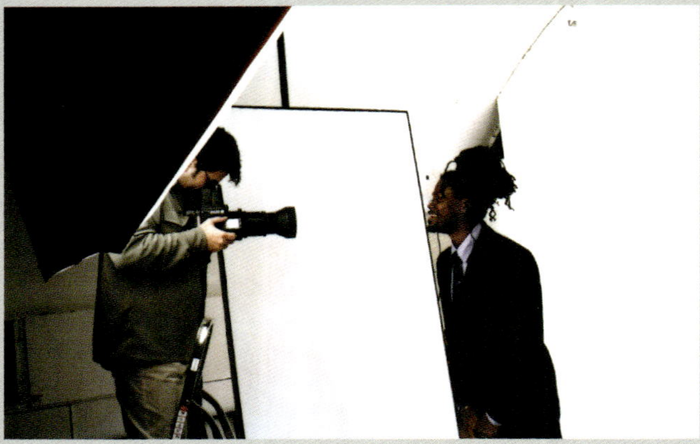

Shooting against a white background enabled the photographers to digitally manipulate the images post-shoot.

Case Study 1
Fashion Meets Stock

The Photographers

and-images

Nad and **Enamul** are **and-images**. They have been in partnership for four years and are known in the industry for their ability to capture up-to-the-minute fashion themes.

The Brief

To shoot a series of business-themed images in a strikingly contemporary and amusing way. The photographers were encouraged to use their fashion background to achieve quirky yet highly commercial images with the anticipation of their use in editorial and corporate brochures. They were instructed to use the same mood, types of models and lighting as they had in two previous shoots for the stock company.

The Location

The photographers' own studio in London.

The Models

A mix of professional and 'found' models were used on the shoot. Getting the right-looking 'character' models demands that both the photographer and art director scour the streets, clubs, bars and appropriate venues for that special look.

"Sometimes you have to hunt hard and on other occasions the right people seem to just fall into your lap," says Nad. "On this particular shoot, the found models included a trainee doctor, hairdresser, graphics student, a jeweller and an unemployed man!"

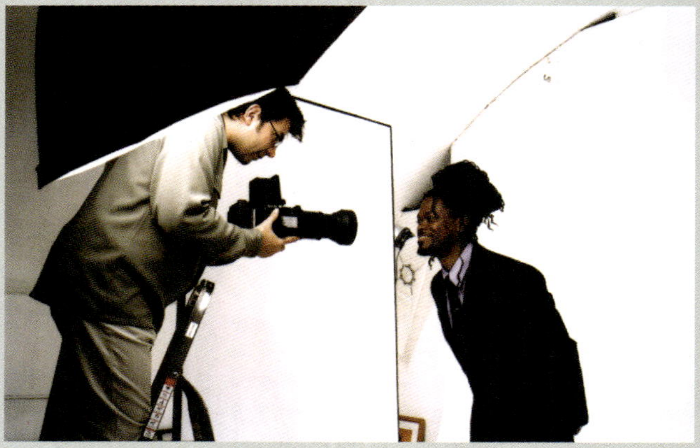

A close-up on the face allows strong detail.

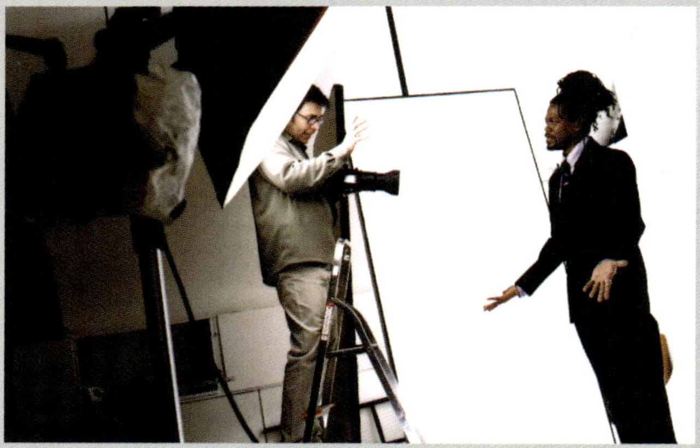

Using gestures brings out character.

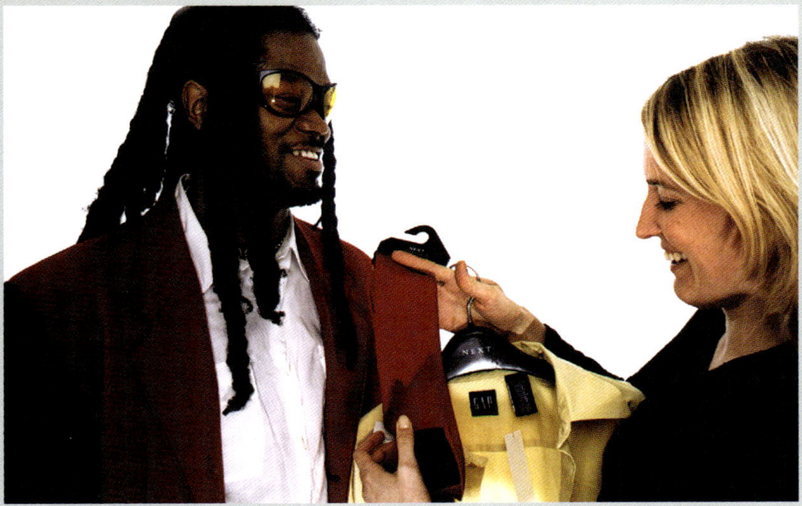

Experimenting with different styles.

The Art Direction
Art direction of an and-images shoot is, like their photography, a collaborative affair. Kate Stevens of Digital Vision provided the initial brief and storyboarded shots. These allowed for a high energy mood and utilised the photographers' signature dynamic, wide angle shots and varied lighting set-ups – from graphic high key events to filter-enhanced muted shades that emphasise shadow detail.

"One of the refreshing aspects about working with Nad and Enamul is their spontaneity… it allows them to get the best work out of the models, many of whom are often in front of the camera for the first time," says Kate. "This also gives them a high hit rate of winning shots. Rigid art direction doesn't apply here. When the guys are on a roll, it is far better to work alongside them and suggest composition, model gestures, and camera angles than demand the shots be exactly as storyboarded… they need the freedom to play!"

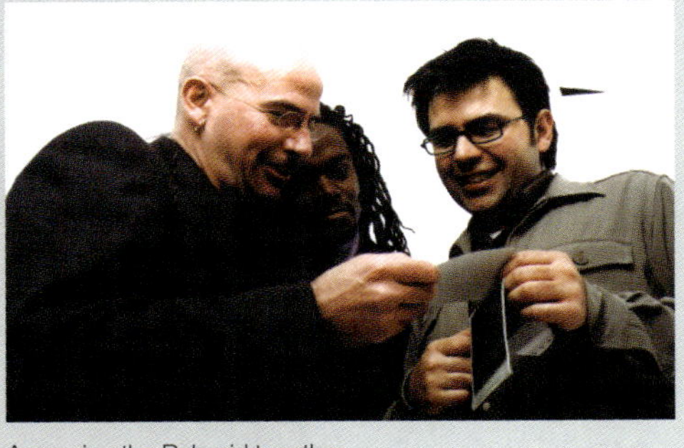

Assessing the Polaroid together.

The Styling
"Styling was both very important and a big investment on this shoot," comments Kate. "The location was minimalist studio space and props were kept to essentials so the clothes had to do the talking. Straight traditional business stock shoots demand considerable styling input and this was business, but also demanding a funky, fresh mood out-of-step with the mainstream. We wanted to embrace all from a casual entrepreneur to a geek; from a sharp corporate boss to the stylish and brash male executive. The female look varied from the power-suited corporate decision maker to smart-casual independent woman. When we did go down the stereotypical route, we did it stylishly!"

The Results
The photographers' thoughts on the final images: "Looking at the film post-shoot there were no surprises… the days you felt went really well yielded great film and those that didn't were a little more subdued – perhaps because the model wasn't as practised or the shots were not as dynamic.

"Trying to maintain the balance between commercial and 'cheese' wasn't always successful, in fact on a number of occasions, we asked the model to overtly ham it up with the intention of giving an ironic edge… or, as the stylist commented, 'ironic cheese'! And, the single model shots rather than variations of couples were stronger in the end."

Overall, the series offers an upbeat, strong range of shots with the possibility of a diverse range of uses.

On Location...
"An unsuspecting Italian neighbour popped by one day to speak to Nad who happened to be out buying film," recalls Enamul. "We all assumed she was one of the models so the hair and make-up girl gave her a makeover ready for the shoot. The girl couldn't speak English but was laughing and apparently enjoying it. When Nad finally arrived back, she revealed that she just assumed we felt she needed a change of image as she wasn't a model at all!"

How the Image Could be Used

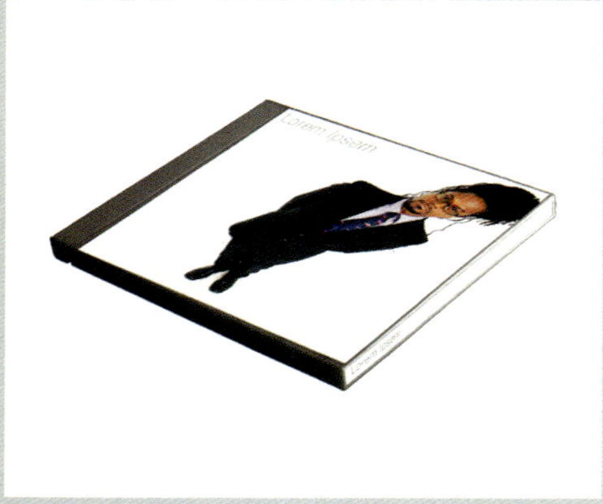

Use 1
The composition of this image makes it perfect for use as a CD cover for a music artist.

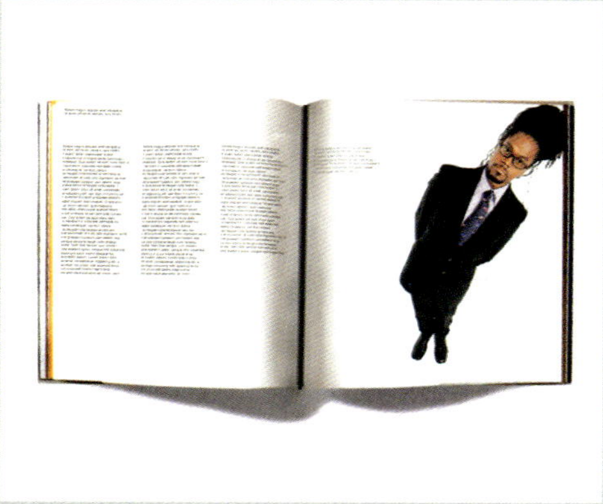

Use 2
The funky clothes used and the jaunty angle at which the model is standing create a very young and hip mood.

Up-and-coming businesses of any type could use the image in brochures, annual reports and prospectuses to indicate a forward-thinking company.

This image is so strong in every way that it has great potential for any customer's projected end-use.

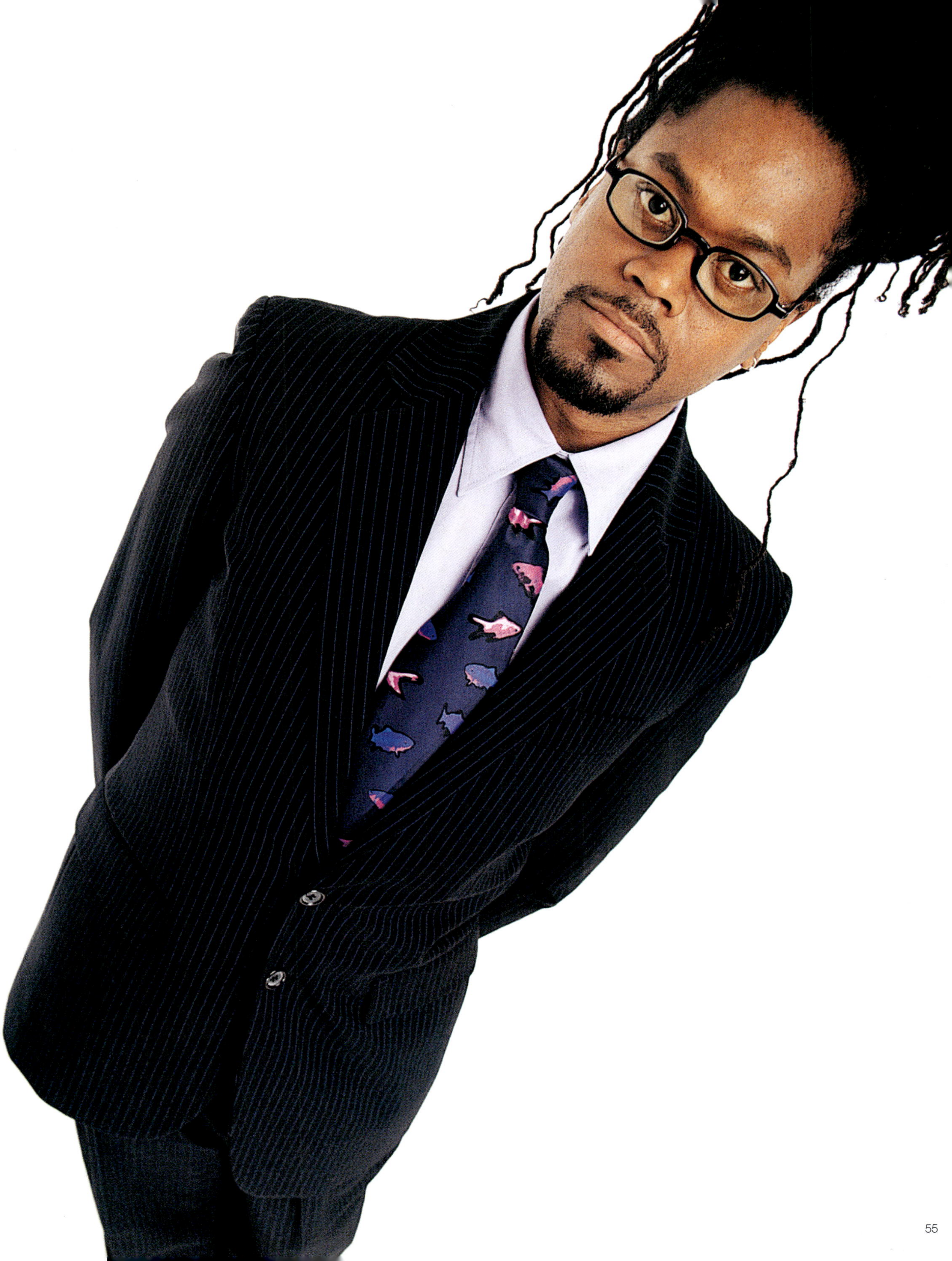

Case Study 2

'Non-Traditional Lifestyles'

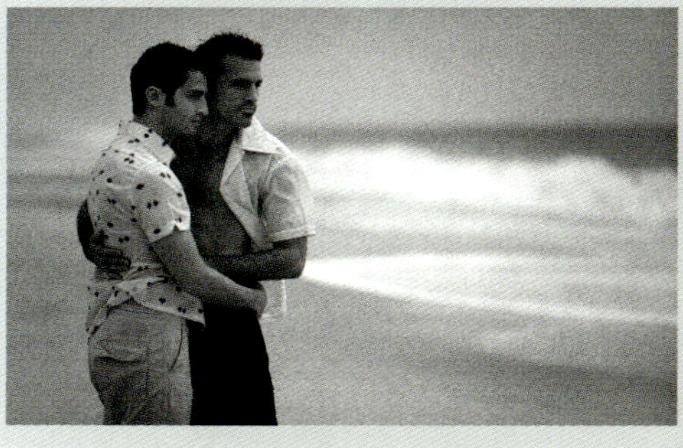

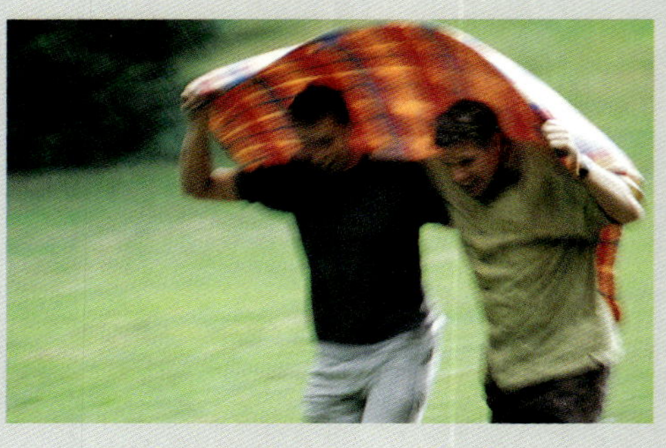

The Photographer

Jack Slomovits

Jack is a New York-based photographer who is known for his sensitive interpretations of homosexual life.

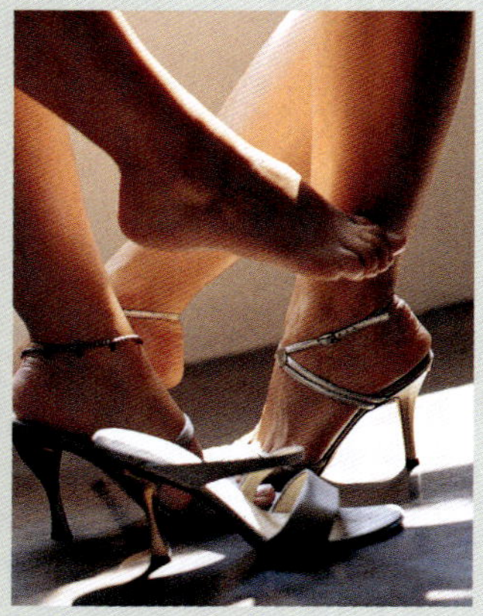

For the shot above, staff members stood in for models who failed to turn up on the day of the shoot.

The Brief

To shoot a series of gay lifestyles images which would show the subtleties of everyday homosexual life, rounded off with a few intimate portraits. To ensure that the images were as authentic as possible, the art director, Jo Kennils, insisted that both the photographer and the models were gay themselves. Her feeling was that a heterosexual photographer would not truly capture a lifestyle they themselves did not lead.

The Location

The shots were done primarily in New York apartments, streets and bars. The outdoor sequences were shot on Fire Island, New York.

The Models

Jack Slomovits' everyday work as an intimate portraiture artist brought him in touch with a number of available models. To fit the brief of 'authentic people in everyday situations', his choices were models of more average appearance than the stereotypically beautiful models used in the usual stock shots.

The Art Direction

The art direction was provided by Jo Kennils, who initially presented and sold in the concept to Digital Vision.

"Even though the stock industry is by nature conservative, I could see the growing need for lifestyle imagery with this subject matter – especially high quality, well-composed and well-lit shots. These are a rarity in stock and most importantly I wanted to find a photographer who understood my vision for this series.

"Jack understood immediately what I wanted from the shoot and pretty much got on with things from the beginning. We had a closed set for the intimate shots to ensure everyone was comfortable, but with the lifestyle images he really pushed the models. I remember a picnic scene in Central Park turning cloudy closely followed by a really heavy downpour, thunder and lightning. Jack shouted for the models to carry on acting natural while he continued to shoot film. The result was a giggling couple running for cover under the temporary shelter of the picnic blanket (above right). It was a priceless moment and a great shot."

The Styling

"We kept the styling as natural and 'everyday' as possible," recalls Jo. "Given the sensitivity of the subject matter, we tried to avoid the stereotypical gay uniform of tight jeans and t-shirts for the majority of the shots."

The Lighting and Film

"Wherever possible on the shoot, we used available natural light," notes Jack Slomovits. "Obviously some locations were better than others in this respect.

"The outdoor location days as always were very dependent on the weather. One of the days on the Fire Island shoot was fairly grim and it needed an injection of brightness, so we used tungsten light film in daylight to give a blue hue. Conversely, daylight film with tungsten light was used on some of the indoor locations, particularly in those instances where daylight was restricted and the location didn't allow for a lighting set-up.

"Fine grain, slow speed film was used for the black-and-white shots to bring out the highlight and shadow detail. The atmospheric, intimate shots were printed with soft greys to enhance mood while some of the nightlife images were given high contrast treatment to set the scene."

The Results

The final work was thought to achieve the right balance of very natural, relaxed, almost candid lifestyle imagery with some artsy and very beautiful portraits of same sex couples. There is still a debate, however, as to the commercial success of these 'non-traditional' images and the usage of black-and-white film for the majority of the series.

On Location...

Through no fault of the photographer, several female models couldn't make the shoot on the day. To keep the shoot going, the art director and a member of the stock photography staff were asked to strap on some stilettoes and play footsie under the office table (facing page, below left).

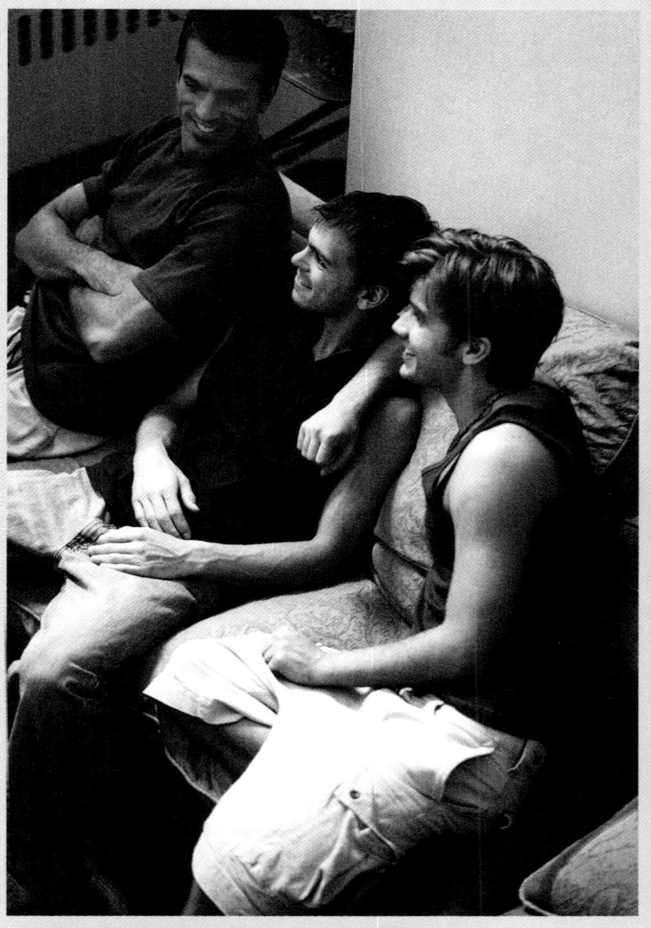

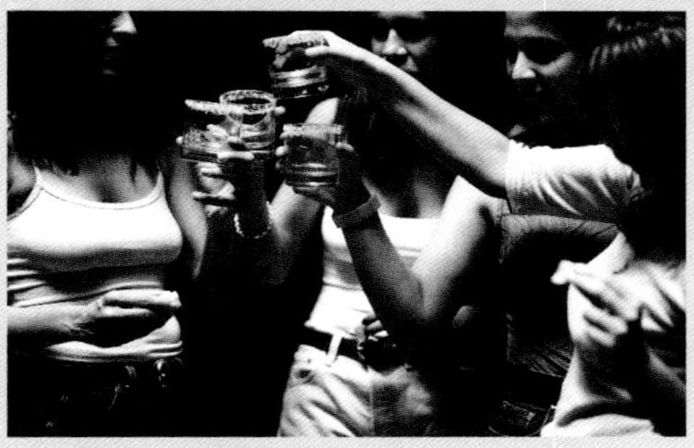

Mainstream lifestyle images like these featured (above and facing page), now extend to what were until recently considered 'alternative' living situations.

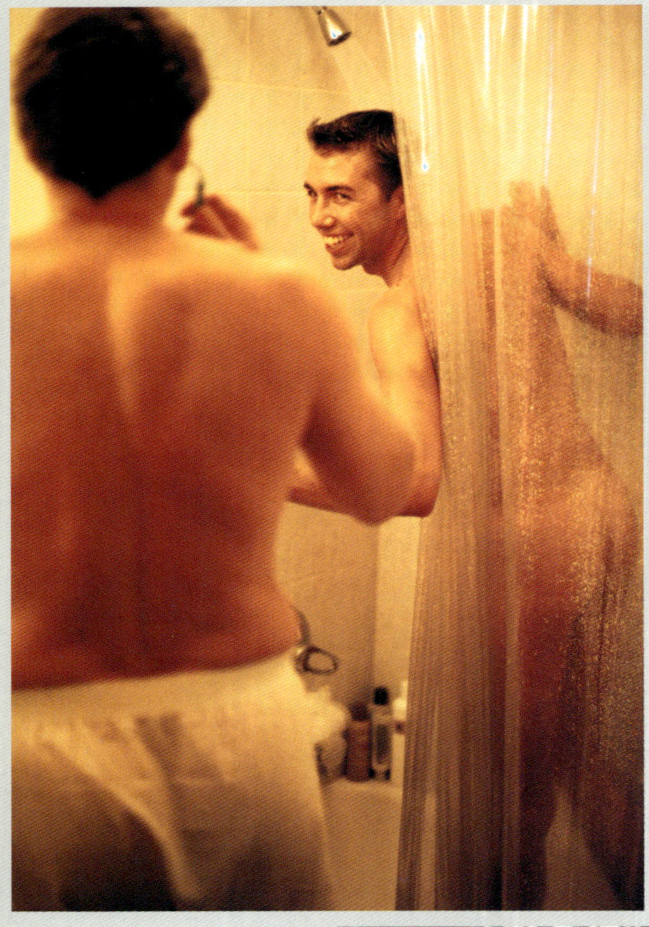

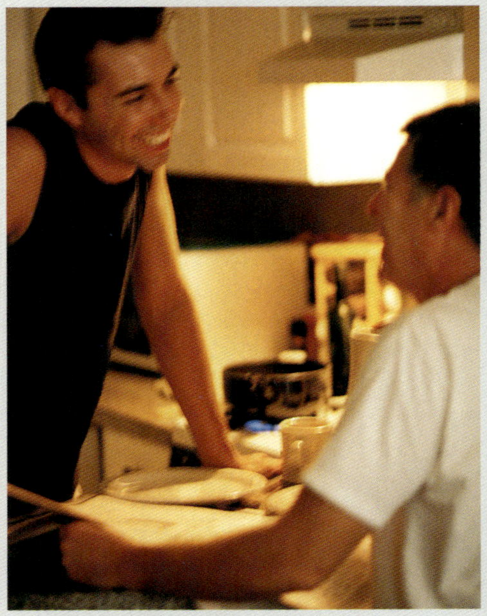

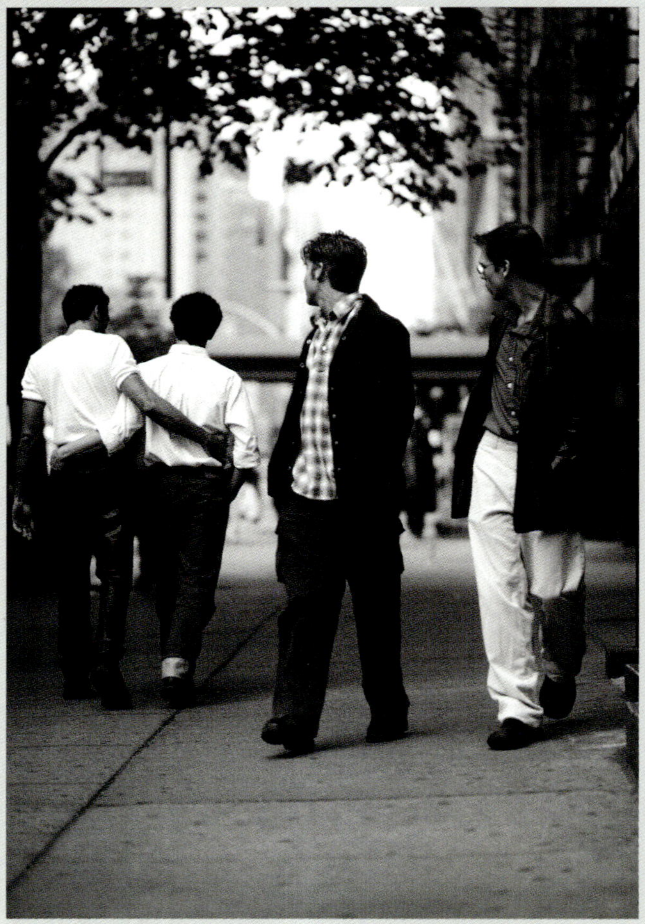

Images featured on this spread are modern interpretations of same-sex lifestyles. The subject matter is increasingly requested by insurance, financial and pharmaceutical companies.

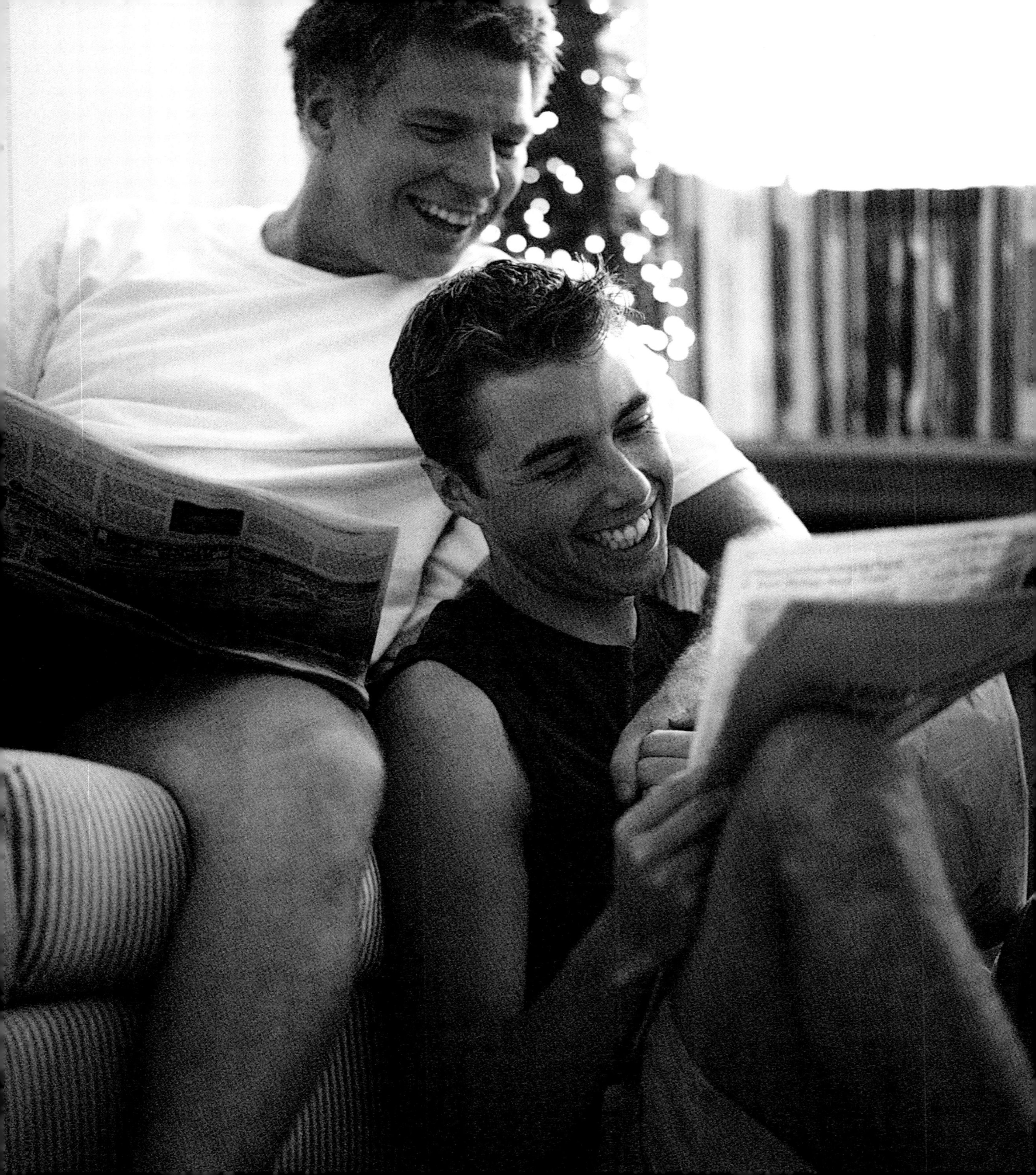

Case Study 3
Capturing the Human Body

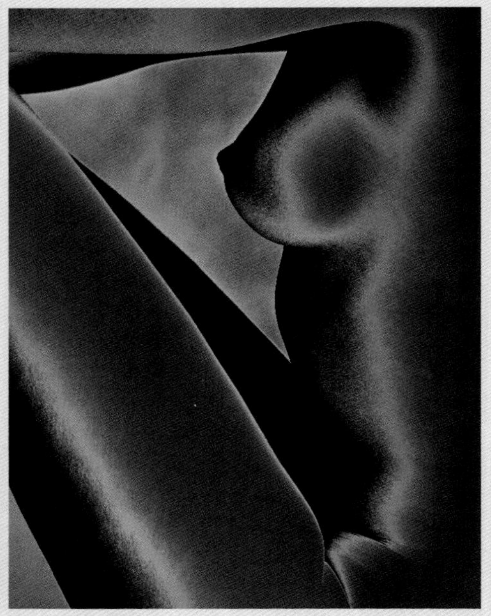

This image has been solarised and the result is both intriguing and unusual.

The Photographer
John Knill

John was selected for this assignment for two reasons: he had a stunning portfolio that included body shots, and he was well known for his expertise in photographic printing. For this project, he would be required to use different tones including selenium, sepia, blue and variations of these.

The Brief

To develop 100 'gallery' quality black-and-white images of the human body. These would be used to illustrate the themes required for the beauty, health, medical and/or finance industries etc. The series would also include some strong commercial icons such as eyes, indicative of visibility and insight, a muscled torso for strength and a man's arm representing power.

The Casting

John and an art director from the stock library handled the casting of models and as he says: "It was quite an economic shoot really because each model provided a lot of shots – we rarely focused on their faces therefore recognition wasn't particularly an issue… we only had seven or eight models in the end."

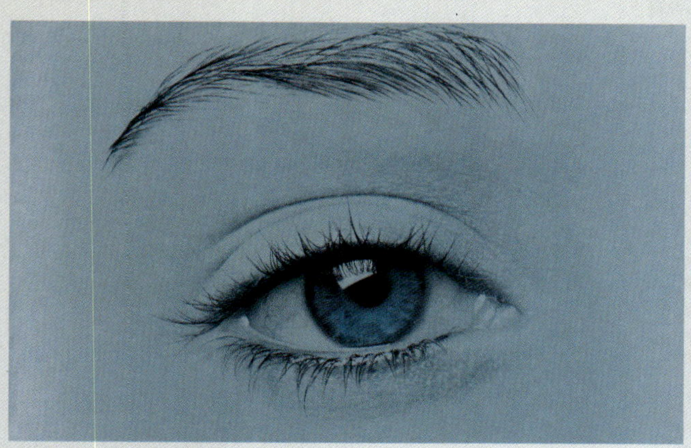

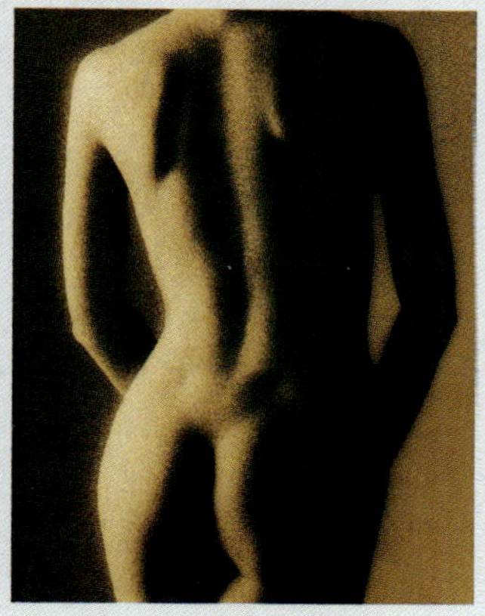

These images show a variety of toning and lighting effects.

The Shoot

The title was shot at John's London studio in stages, which allowed room for input from both client and photographer. "100 images is a lot so you need to be sure, dependent on your schedule of course, that you don't rush in head first and shoot like crazy with no room for evaluation," comments John.

"Every 'body' is different with its own strengths and weaknesses and each presents a different challenge.

"I would shoot one or two days at a time, then edit the work for print with Digital Vision and then edit again once we had the prints.

"I would produce two or three versions of the same shot or similar with different tonings… or perhaps solarised. With some shots it was obvious that they looked best in black and white, others with some sort of tone, but I had also to consider the overall look and balance of the title as a whole.

The Lighting, Film and Technique

A variety of lighting set-ups were used throughout the shoot – some shots were lit with strong, direct light to give a sharp, defined feel while others utilised reflected light to give a softer, more atmospheric mood. "I find that much photographic work is overlit, with several light sources, often creating a hard mood and ugly multiple shadows… I am a great believer in one source of light, you have so much more control over it… you can create and work with shadow and accentuate form. I treat bodies like pieces of sculpture, with the lighting enhancing their abstract nature."

The different film types used also gave variety; fast film for large grain and slow film for none, enabling John to achieve great differences in mood. John also used a specially adapted lens attached to his Nikon camera which gave a pleasing loss of definition, throwing the extremities of the subject out of focus but keeping its centre or focal point sharp. Using the lens also makes the highlights glow.

The shoot was carried out using both a 35mm camera and a medium format. "I like the flexibility of shooting with 35mm and the quality and feel of prints you get are very different to medium format."

The Results

This CD title's market appeal is global and spans the variety of market uses… from healthcare to finance… in fact John commented while contributing to this piece that another image used from the title had just landed on his desk: a two-hand shot, palms facing forward with ten splayed fingers… it was for an estate agent's brochure which was announcing the opening of their tenth outlet."

'The Body' was one of the first classic titles for Digital Vision. It set a precedent for quality, and is unhindered by the vagaries of time and fashion.

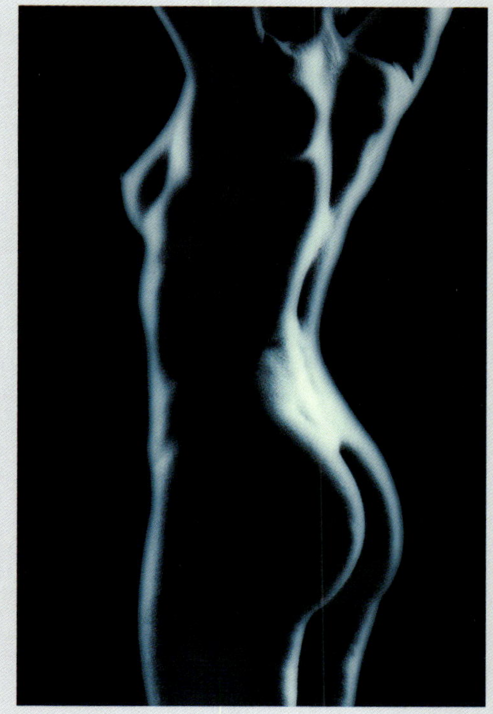

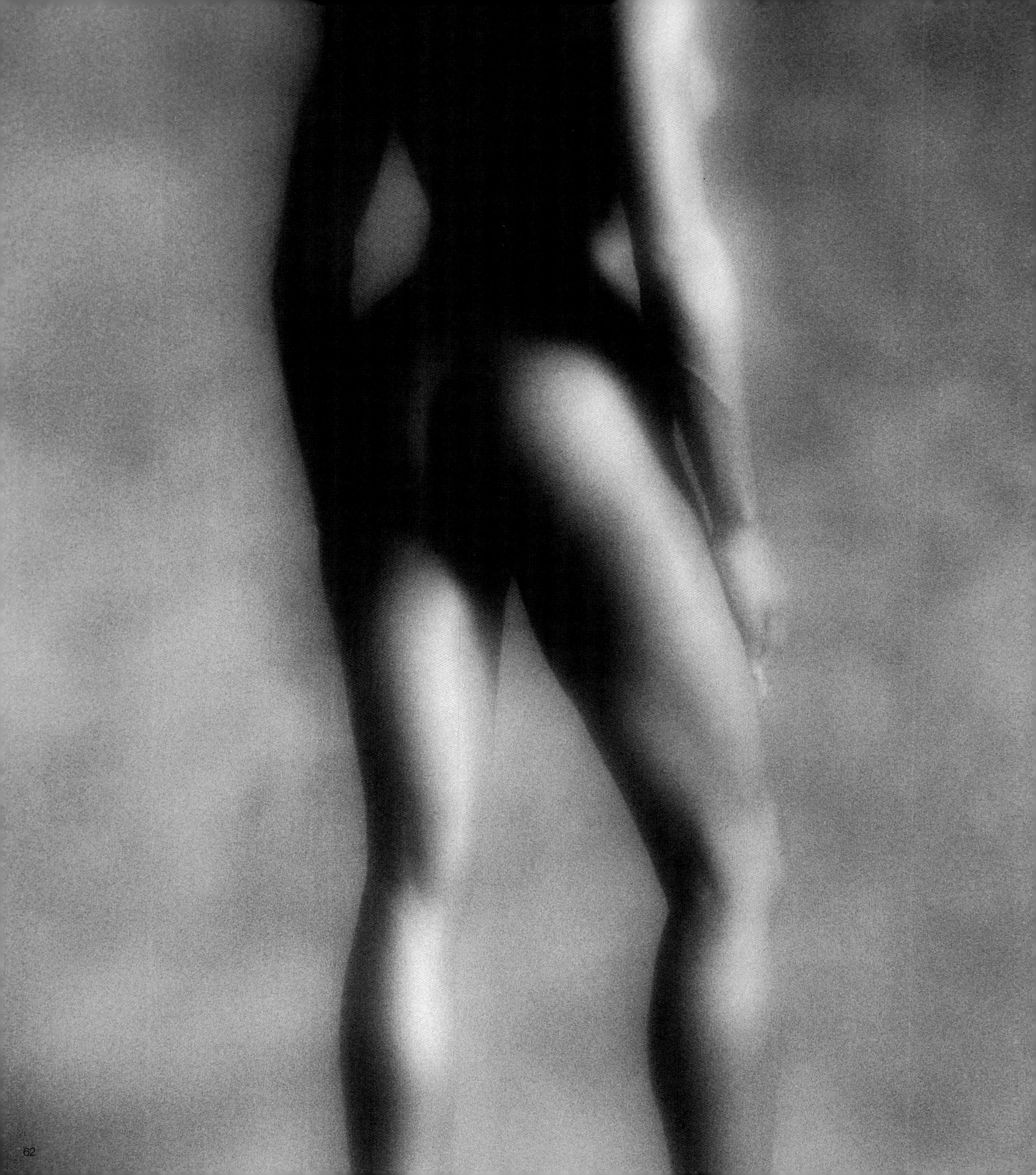

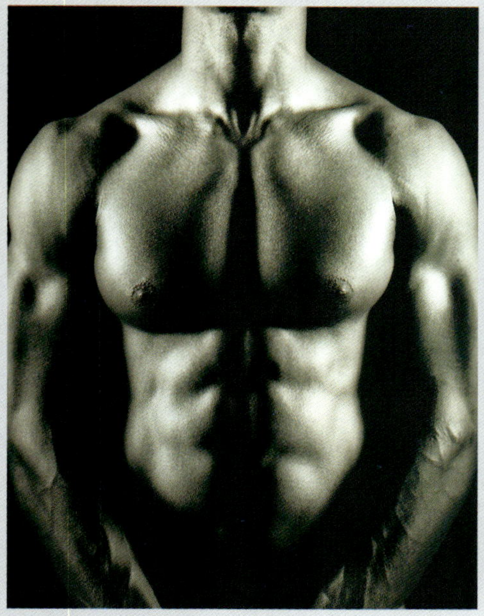

This image is pin sharp and has been shot on slow film which gives no grain.

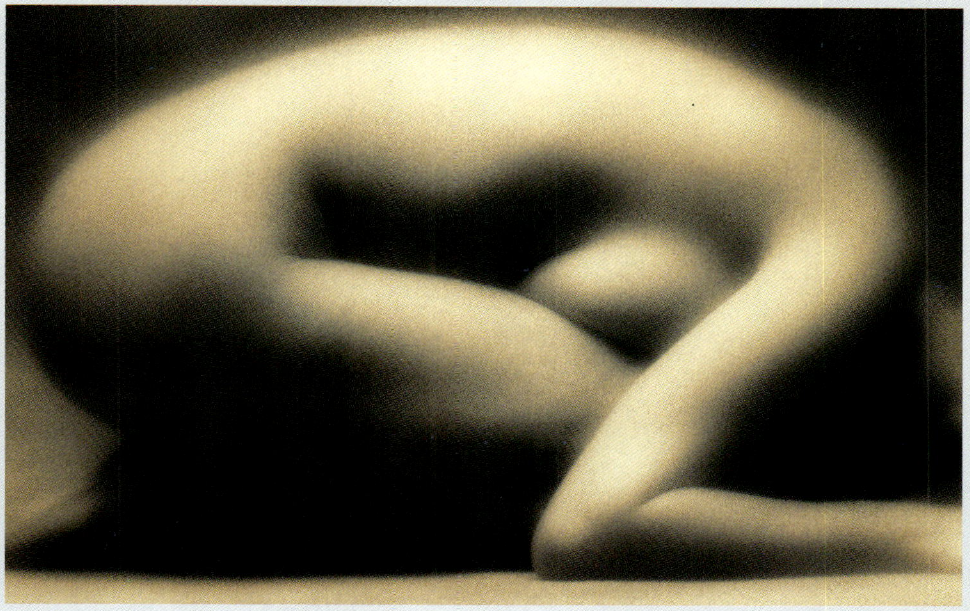

This image has been shot using a diffuser over the camera lens which gives the effect of softening the highlights and creating a semi-halo around the subject.

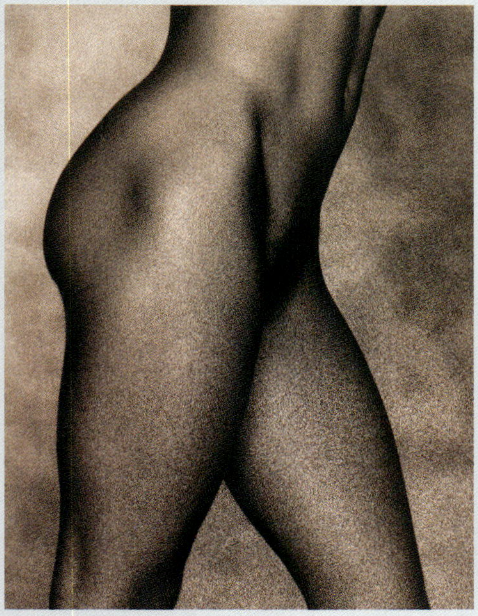

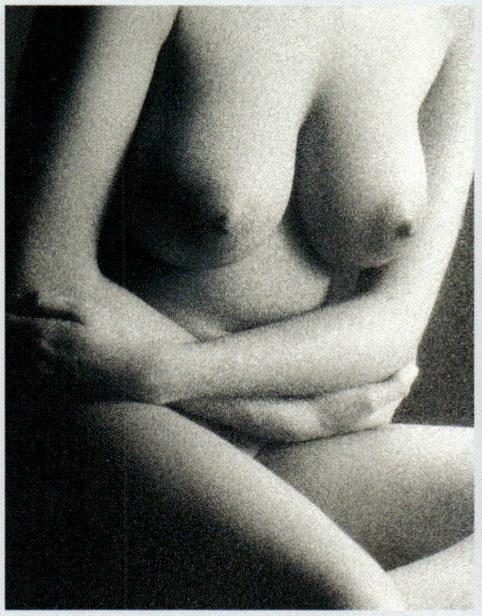

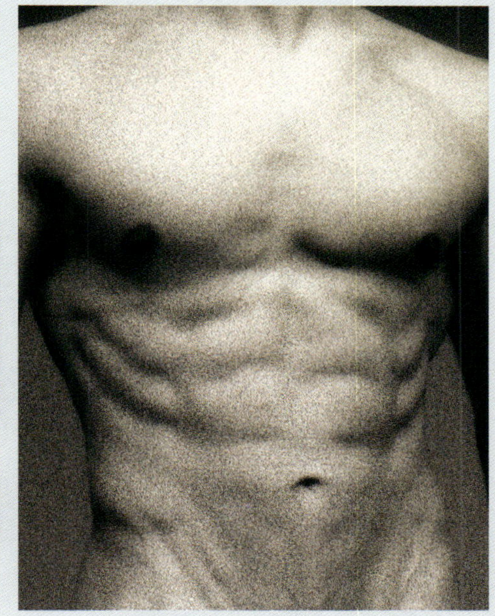

These images have been shot on fast film to provide large grain.

This image is a perfect example of a shot using John's adapted lens... You can see around the backside, but it is in focus, albeit soft, and the model is thrown out of focus as you move down towards her feet.

Case Study 4

Staging a Dinner Party

The Art Director
Carrie Beecroft

A London-based art director whose eye for styling makes her popular within the stock industry. She makes constant photographic trips to South Africa, New York and Miami.

The Photographer
Paul Viant

The Brief
To create a 100-image colour and black-and-white title of a dinner party scenario. This series of images would feature a strong spontaneous and aspirational mood to fit in with a catalogue of disks devoted to personal-based photographic work.

The Location
The entire shoot was shot in a mezzanine, loft-style studio with kitchen, bathroom and dining area.

The Art Direction
Carrie Beecroft, who is known in the industry for her up-to-the-minute casting style, was asked to art direct this innovative shoot. Her experience in handling groups of models, primarily for The Telegraph Colour Library and Digital Vision, was the basis for her selection. As an art director, she commissioned the photographer, and here Carrie comments on how she makes her selections:

"The common denominators I seek in photographers across the variety of stock shoots are technical brilliance and spontaneity.

"Business subjects, lifestyle, portraits all require top technicians with great lighting skills. It is equally important that they have an empathy with people, and not just the models, but the crew too… what feeling they capture from people is paramount… it's this combination that captures the moment and gives us 'the shot'."

For the 'Dinner Party' title Carrie sought out photographer Paul Viant:

"It's not often you find a photographer who can turn their hand to anything. In the stock arena it's a valuable commodity… most people tend to specialise."

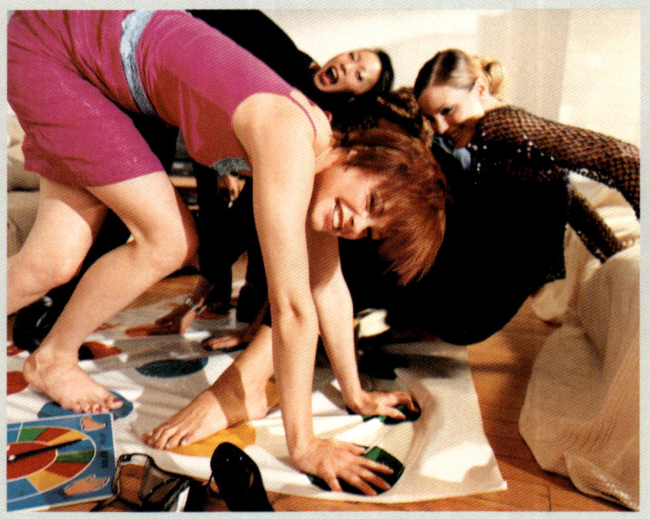

Compositions that show action are highly sought-after.

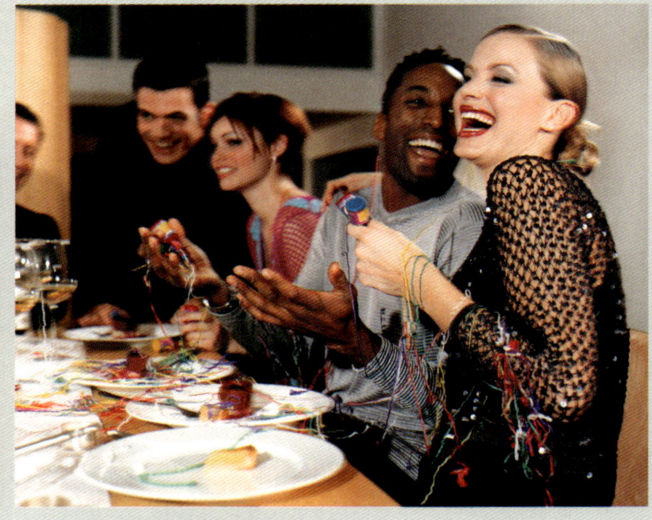

Be careful with props and accessories as they can limit an image's market appeal. For instance, the party poppers pictured here are not used in the US.

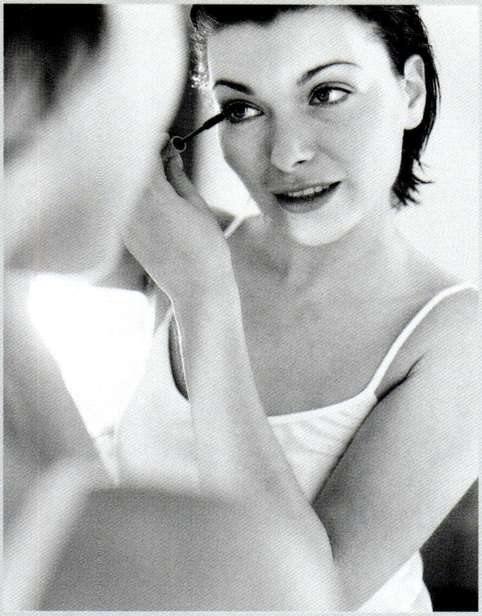

Images like this one that are taken 'in situ' are popular for the editorial market.

The Models

Carrie and Paul cast the shoot over a couple of days and approached mainstream agencies to find models with traditional 'model good looks' in their late twenties/early thirties, deemed to be the right age for the dinner party circuit. Naturally, since the disk would be marketed and sold around the world, the casting had to consider the ethnic balance too.

The Styling and Props

Both aspects were crucial to the success of the shoot and needed to be stylish and aspirational, without being either too distinctive – and therefore risk alienating end-users – or treading the line of being too fashion-led, which means the images would quickly date.

"Sometimes this balance is harder to achieve than styling for an unusual stock shoot," says Carrie.

Colour palette was a big consideration of this shoot. Neutral black and white were chosen for the bathroom scenes while muted blues and grey pastels were used for the kitchen preparation shots. For the dinner party itself, sophisticated and classic red and black was utilised.

The Shoot

The scripting of the shoot was straightforward with the event itself dictating the set-ups. Essentially it followed a classic three act play through real time with a beginning, middle and end. In this instance the beginning consisted of the preparation for the party in the bathroom and 'what to wear' scenes; getting the food ready; then the event itself and the post-party antics like games and dancing.

There was a variety of set-ups from close-ups to small and large group shots.

A fresh and uplifting atmosphere was wanted and therefore the lighting was clean and bright:

"We didn't want to go too moody and dark to allow for greater usage," said Carrie.

Techniques such as motion blur were also used to create movement in the dance scenes and give a sense of energy.

The Results

Because it's an intimate subject, 'Dinner Party' was an ideal title for the 'Voice' magazine series, which showcases individual, personal work from photographers. There is also enough of a variety of shots within the title to span a range of uses.

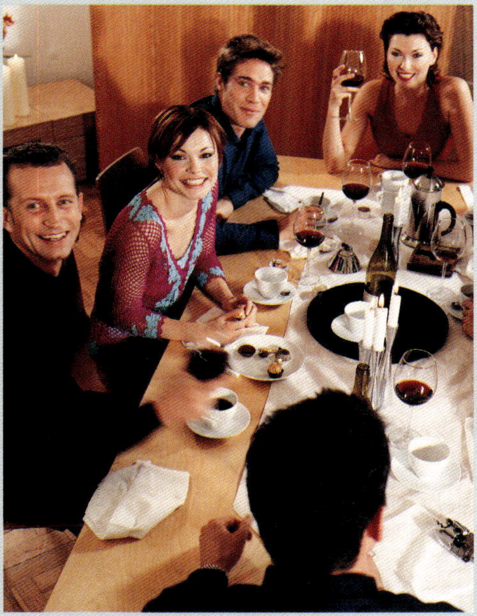

An image like this can be achieved by shooting from a ladder or a landing.

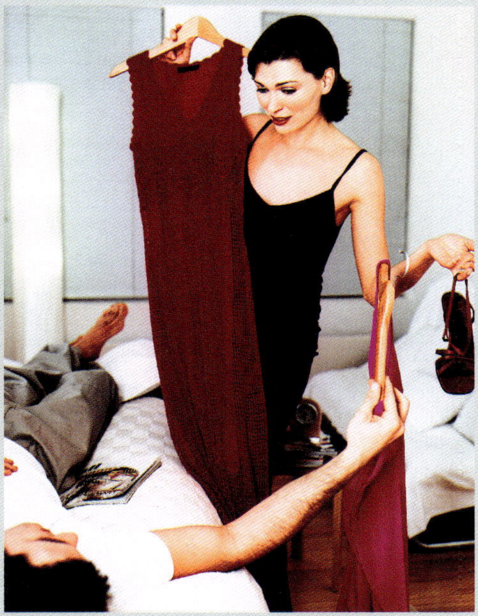

An image rich in magentas and reds is ideally suited for use in text-heavy page layouts.

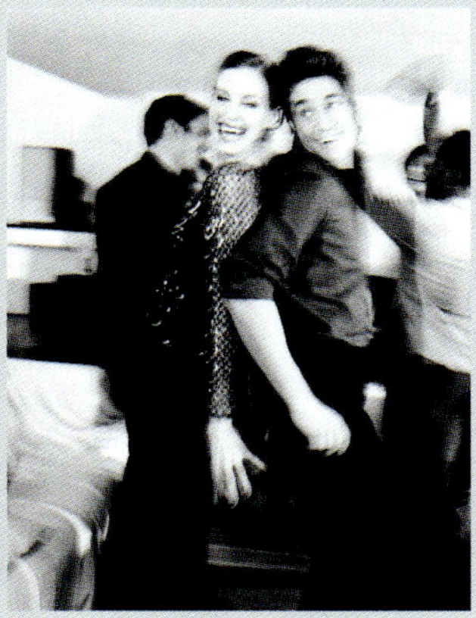

Motion blurs, added post-shoot, create a sense of movement and activity.

How the Image Could be Used

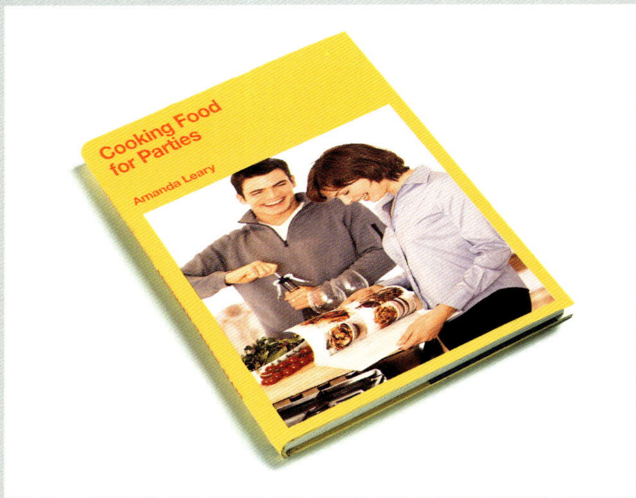

Use 1
Editors seek strong cover images with subjects representing the target market, which this image does perfectly.

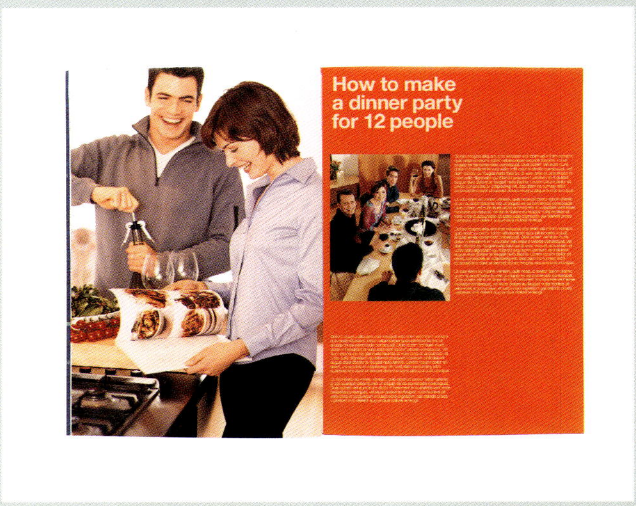

Use 2
The cover image can be used twice – it could also feature in an inside spread.

This playful image is an ideal choice for a lifestyle-driven cookbook.

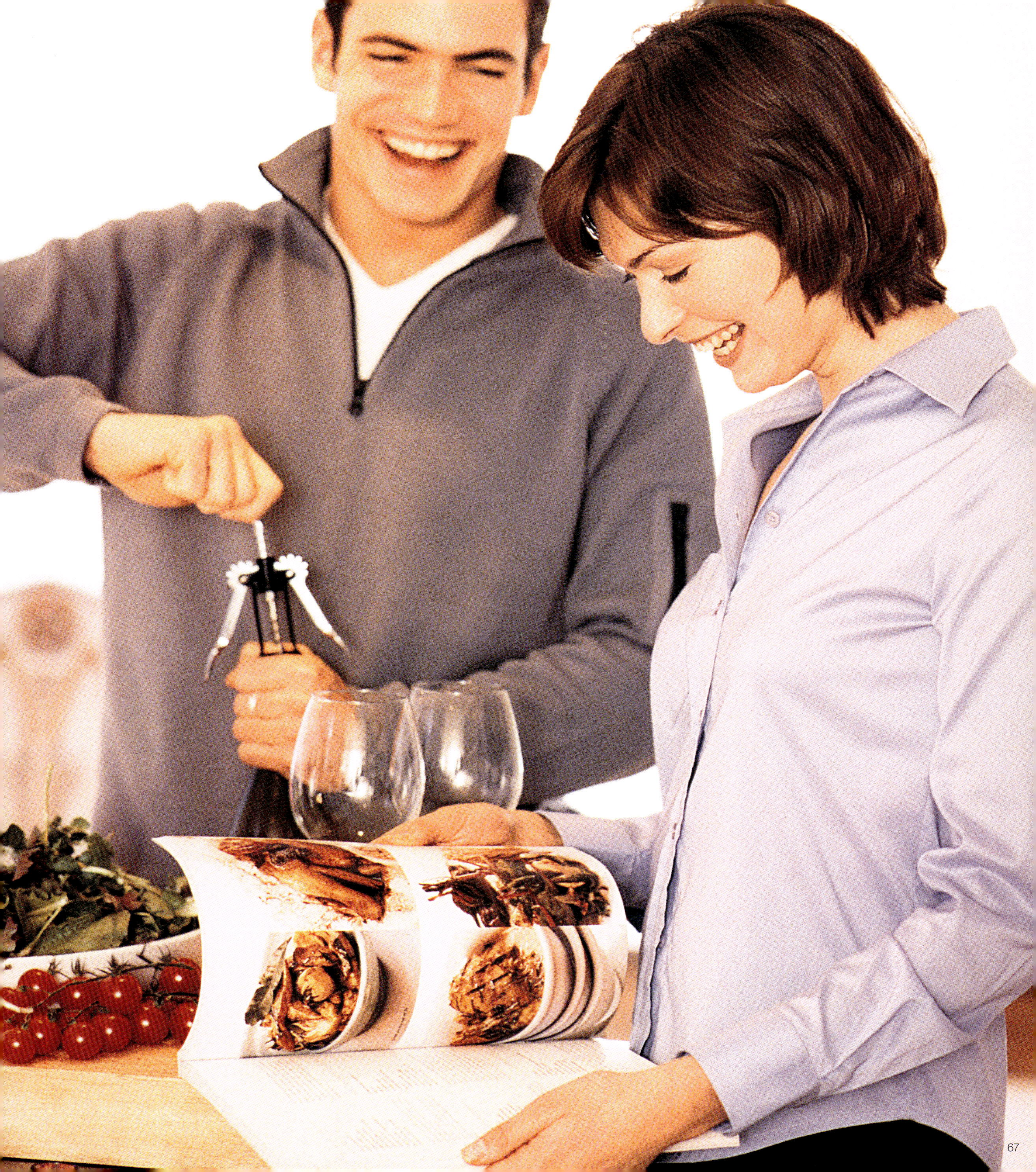

Case Study 5
'A Strange Piece of Business'

The Art Director
Jo Kennils

Also a professional photographer, Jo brings in-depth knowledge of lighting and film techniques to each assignment. Known for giving a wonderful theatrical flair to her subject matter, she is frequently involved in cutting-edge shoots.

The Photographer
Tom LeGoff

A New York-based photographer known for his creative portraiture.

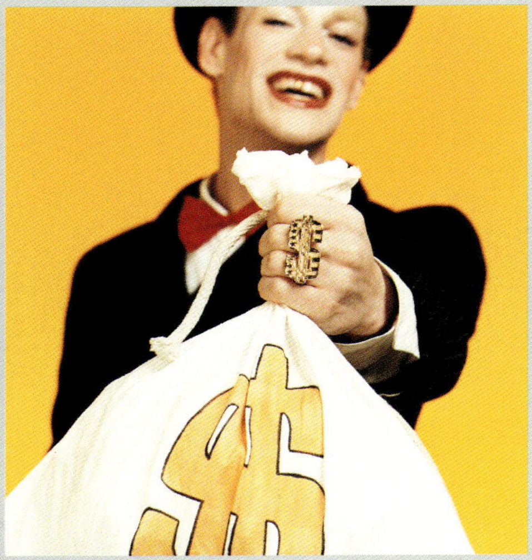

A bright background adds to the iconic appeal of this image.

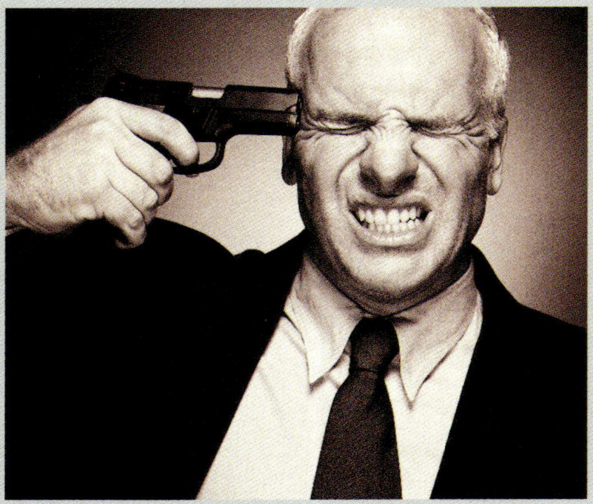

Slightly uncomfortable images are ideal for advertisers since they quickly capture audience attention.

The Brief
To generate a series of conceptual business images with a strong dreamlike quality, to be used across global markets to illustrate a variety of stock themes. These themes centre on the core ideas of 'difference', 'standing out from the crowd' and offering something beyond the usual stock pictures.

The Art Direction
Jo Kennils art directed the shoot in New York:

"It was imperative that the shoot was very tightly scripted, we were working to a very tight time frame in which we had to cover an enormous amount of work. There was no room for deviation! We were certainly not seeking a natural or spontaneous mood but rather one of highly contrived theatre and that requires attention to detail, strong planning and good teamwork. With a good team you can be safe in the knowledge that each element necessary to the shot's success (including location, model, props, styling and photographic technique) will go exactly as planned."

Jo instinctively knew which photographer she wanted to approach to shoot the title – Tom LeGoff, whose celebrity portrait work she had seen in New York:

"Tom works mostly in the film industry and for editorial publications. His strong, classical portraiture was exactly the style I was looking for. I also felt his personality would bring a certain humour to the offbeat situations I wanted to create.

"He is not used to shooting the number of images we needed from each session and he worked incredibly hard through the day to cover the subjects."

The Models and Casting
Tom and Jo didn't use the usual mainstream channels such as model agencies for casting the shoot…

"We needed weird, strange, kooky, bizarre… so we had to look further afield. Further afield was a bar called Botanica in the East Village frequented by a strong cross-section of characters who don't conform to the model stereotype," said Jo.

They managed to find artists, designers, a cab driver and, a particular coup, a number of models who have featured strongly in fashion photographer David LaChapelle's surreal visions. Their final choices also had to meet with the standard stock remit of variety in age and ethnic background.

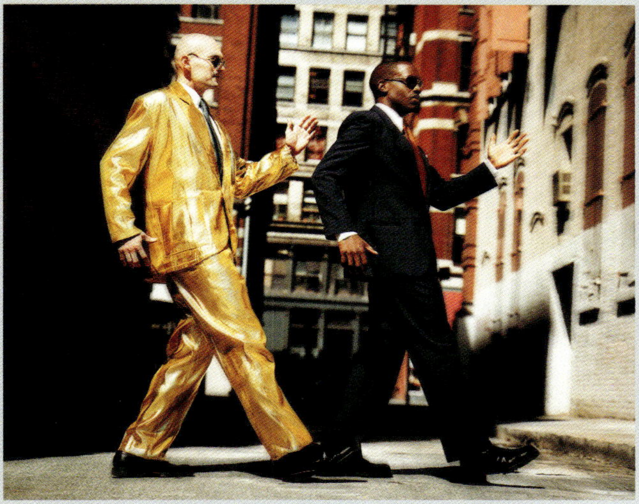

Contrasting models make for a striking look.

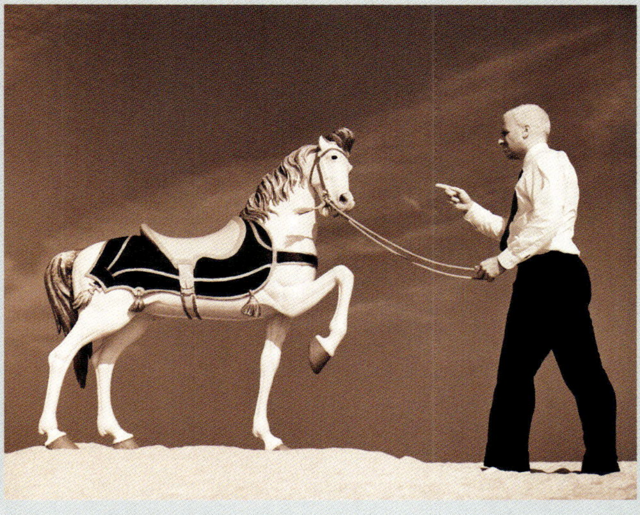

Adding a touch of surrealism gives an interesting twist to the well-trodden business theme.

The Location

Choice of location was another crucial element of the shoot.

A long time was spent scouting for locations and this was made even more complicated by New York City law which demands photographers/film-makers etc. have permits for shooting in certain areas. "The beaches particularly can be a bureaucratic nightmare," according to Jo.

Unable to bypass the red tape in time to secure a beach location in New York surroundings they skipped over the river to New Jersey to shoot the beach scenes.

Another two days' worth of images were shot on New York City's streets and two final days were spent in Tom's studio shooting René Magritte-inspired portraits.

The Props

Tom and Jo painstakingly took trips around various New York prop houses with a digital camera seeking an oversized chess set, 4ft angel wings, prosthetic devil horns, giant beach balls, a truck full of bowler hats and a gun… amongst other things.

The Lighting and Technique

The entire shoot was shot with a medium format camera on a mix of black-and-white and colour film stock. The colour film was pushed one stop to increase contrast and enhance colour, helping to create the slightly strange and surreal mood required for the brief.

The crew took a generator, lights and diffusers with them to the beach. Bright sunlight casts harsh shadows, particularly across faces, but the diffusers prevented this and the end result was a strangely contrived, unnatural light, which once again emphasised the surreal edge.

The Results

"We definitely got what we were looking for at the end of the day. Tom hand-printed all the work himself. He insists upon this level of control, playing with tones and colour to get the best quality prints possible. We are happy to give him this freedom because we totally trust his attention to detail," said Jo.

The shoot also reinforced the importance of getting a good team together. As Jo comments:

"We had a lot to shoot in a short space of time and it was very important to have unflappable people on the crew… there were a lot of opportunities for histrionics but everyone kept their cool, which was great."

The title was launched in a dedicated business catalogue 'In The Black', published in July 2001.

On Location…

Given the strange subject matter, Jo has many anecdotes but one stands out strongly:

"Tom was a lot of fun to work with and I have several memorable moments from our collaboration. Like the time I stood in the middle of the street holding up my hand to stop New York's city traffic at the Holland Tunnel entrance during rush hour. The intention was to provide a gap allowing Tom to shoot an angel walking down the street in a pair of 4ft white feather wings and a night-dress. Faced with huge, angry trucks bearing down on me, I closed my eyes for a split second in sheer fright. The sight of a drop-dead-gorgeous 6ft blond angel in see-through cotton stopped the most hardened of truckers dead in their tracks."

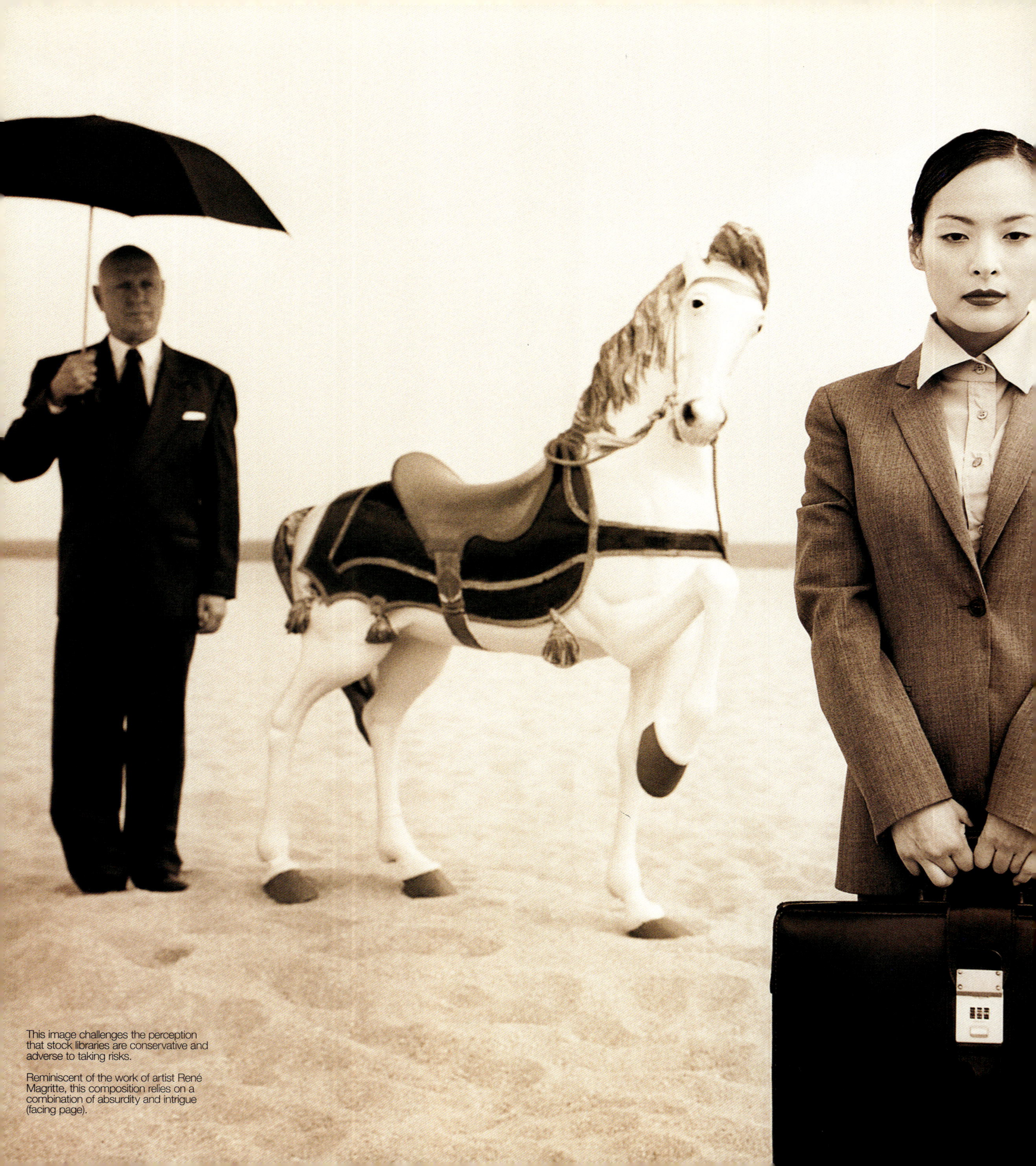

This image challenges the perception that stock libraries are conservative and adverse to taking risks.

Reminiscent of the work of artist René Magritte, this composition relies on a combination of absurdity and intrigue (facing page).

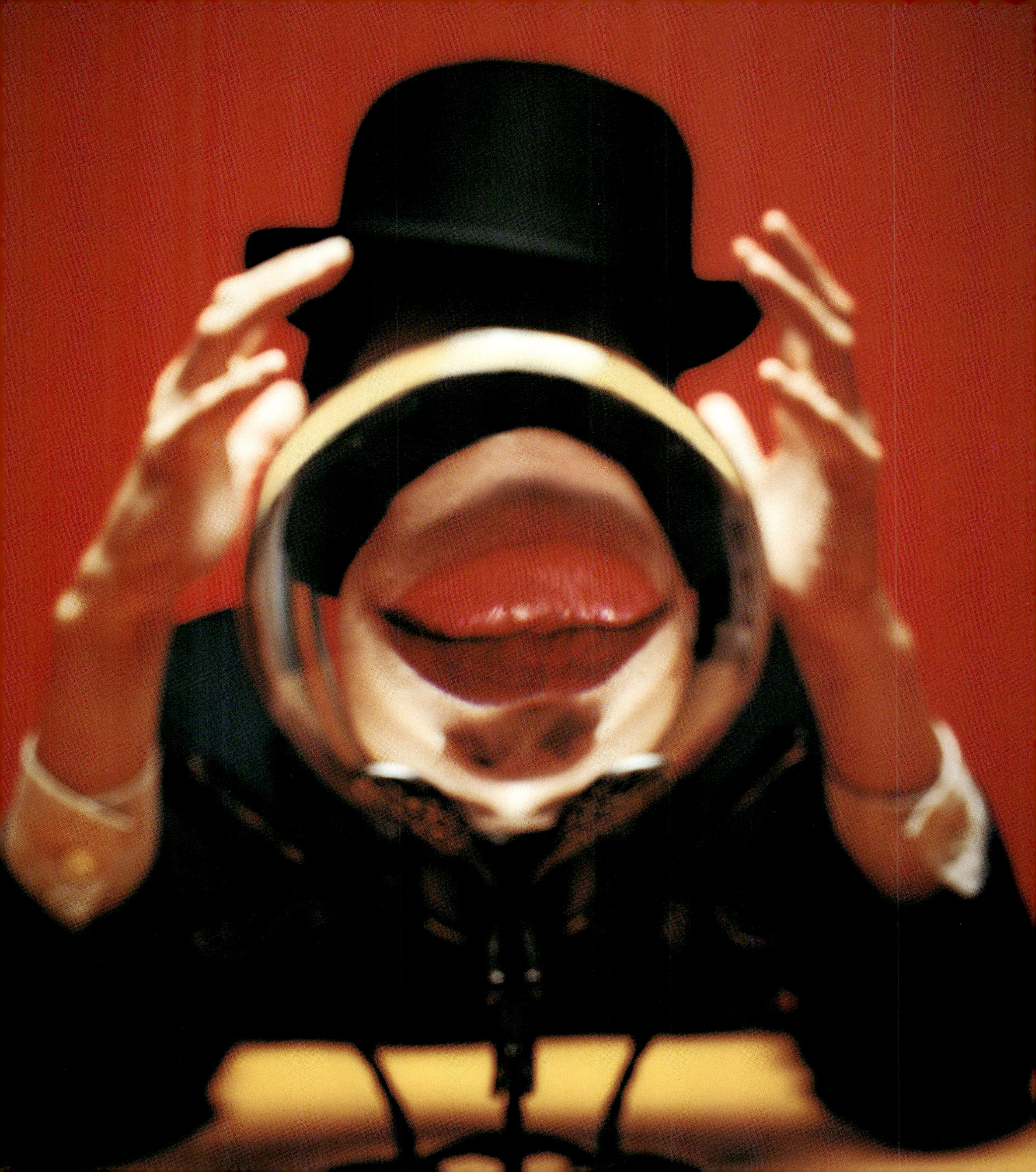

Case Study 6

A Jazzy Shoot

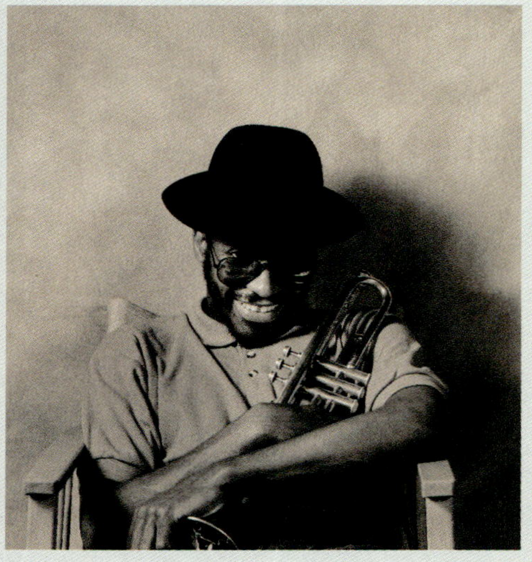

The Photographer
Will Woods

Will is a London-based photographer who is known for his work in the advertising industry. His attention to detail and photographic staging made him an ideal choice as the photographer of a series of images based around the theme of jazz.

Filters, tints and sparkling gold teeth add a sense of atmosphere to the images on this spread.

The Brief
To shoot a series of emotive and atmospheric images revolving around the concept of jazz and jazz musicians. The title of the CD would be 'All that Jazz' and it would feature a compilation of images from different photographers. Will, having skills in both composition and effects, would be responsible for the majority of the disk.

The Location
The shots were done primarily in Will's London studio which he miraculously transformed into a smoky, jazz nightclub by using dry ice, an old piano and a platform for staging.

The Models
A unique combination of professional musicians and models whose faces were intriguing and weathered were used for this themed shoot. The thinking behind this was that musicians could show the models how to hold the instruments naturally – in this case a guitar, a saxophone and a piano – without the images looking too contrived.

The Art Direction
The art direction was provided by the stock agency and it focused on providing reportage style shots – ones you might see in the great jazz books of the last century.

The Styling
Since the shoot was dependent on providing a highly evocative atmosphere, styling was key. Hair was styled in a combination of 1930s' jazz curls, loops and swirls and 1990s' modern dreadlocks and close cuts. Mineral oil was introduced to the 'singer's' wig (overleaf) to reflect lighting and a moustache was added as needed!

The Lighting and Film
In order to capture the moody atmosphere of the jazz world, a variety of lighting set-ups and techniques were used. Smoke machines enabled Will to set the scene by creating a dusky haze to help emulate the steamy, claustrophobic ambience of a jazz cafe; and differential focus was often used to create shallow depth of field and allow the eye to be drawn to the main focal point. This threw distracting backgrounds out of focus but allowed them enough presence to generate a sense of realism.

Lighting set-ups were manipulated to achieve contrasting, high key scenarios to mimic actual live jazz events. Will used a mixture of fast and slow film to span the range of finishes from high grain to sharp. A variety of tones were also used in the printing.

The Results
Produced last year, these images have been popular with those wanting to evoke a period of time or feeling of yesteryear. The beauty and composition of the shots have made them an agency favourite, with many of the images framed and placed in the office.

On Location...
At one point in the shoot the art director was very discouraged by a silvery reflection which kept appearing in the sample Polaroids. Hunting for what seemed like an eternity, she finally found the culprit – one of the musician's metal shirt buttons. Several pieces of electrical tape later, the problem was solved and the shoot continued.

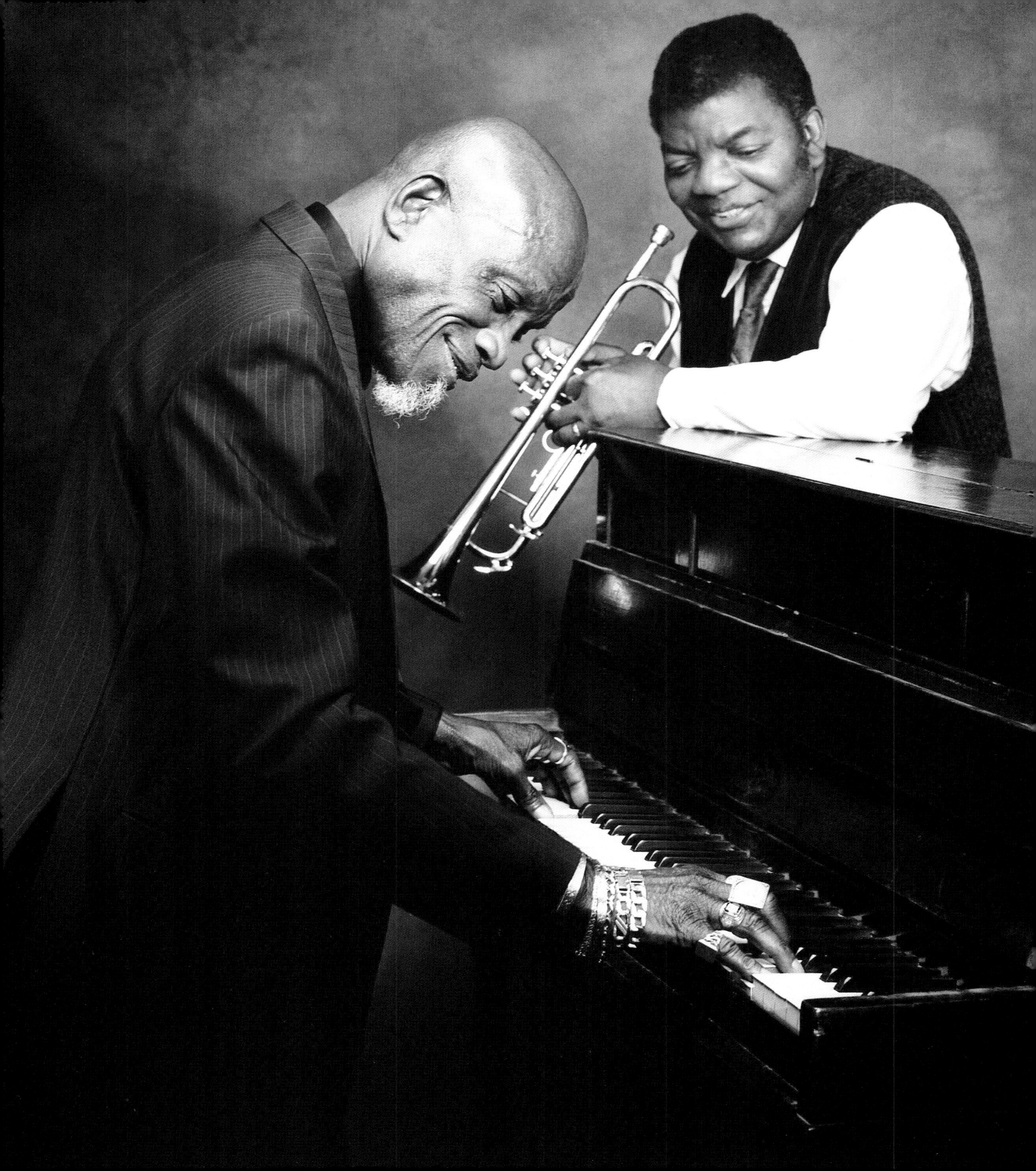

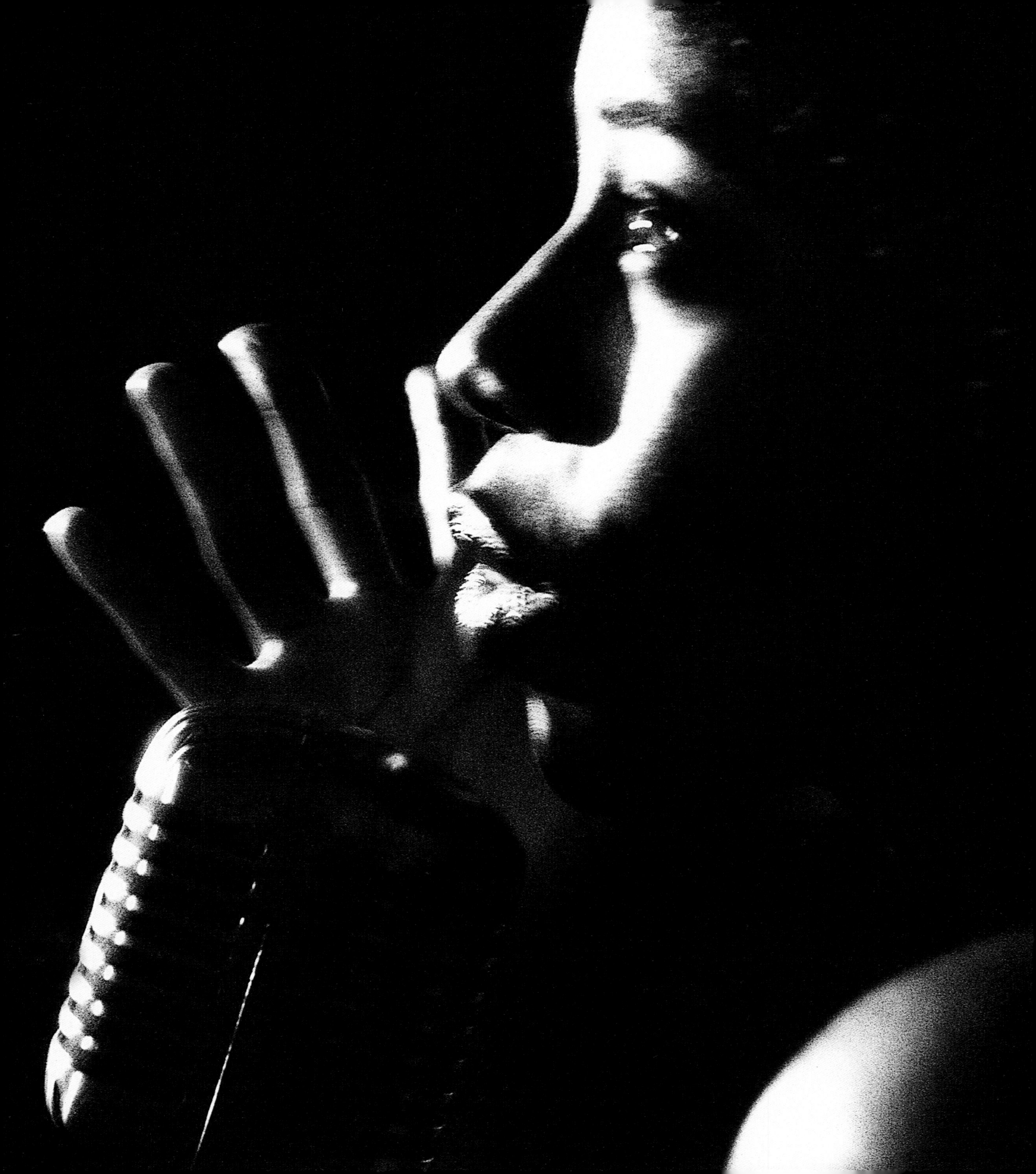

How the Image Could be Used

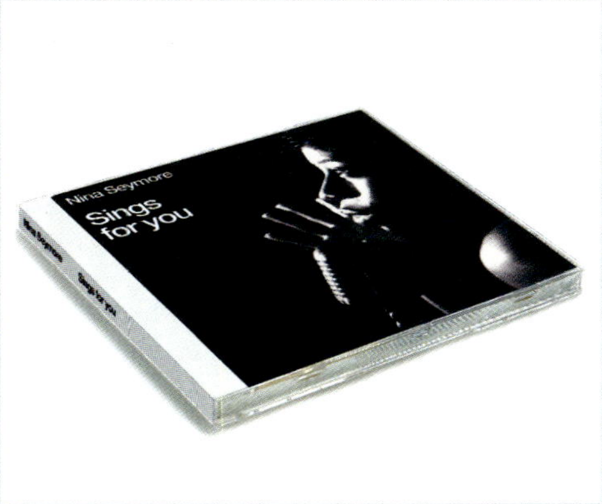

Use 1
This image is great to use as the cover of a CD, as royalty free images are a cost-effective choice when print runs are high.

An image like this with natural room for text is ideally suited for advertising and large-scale posters.

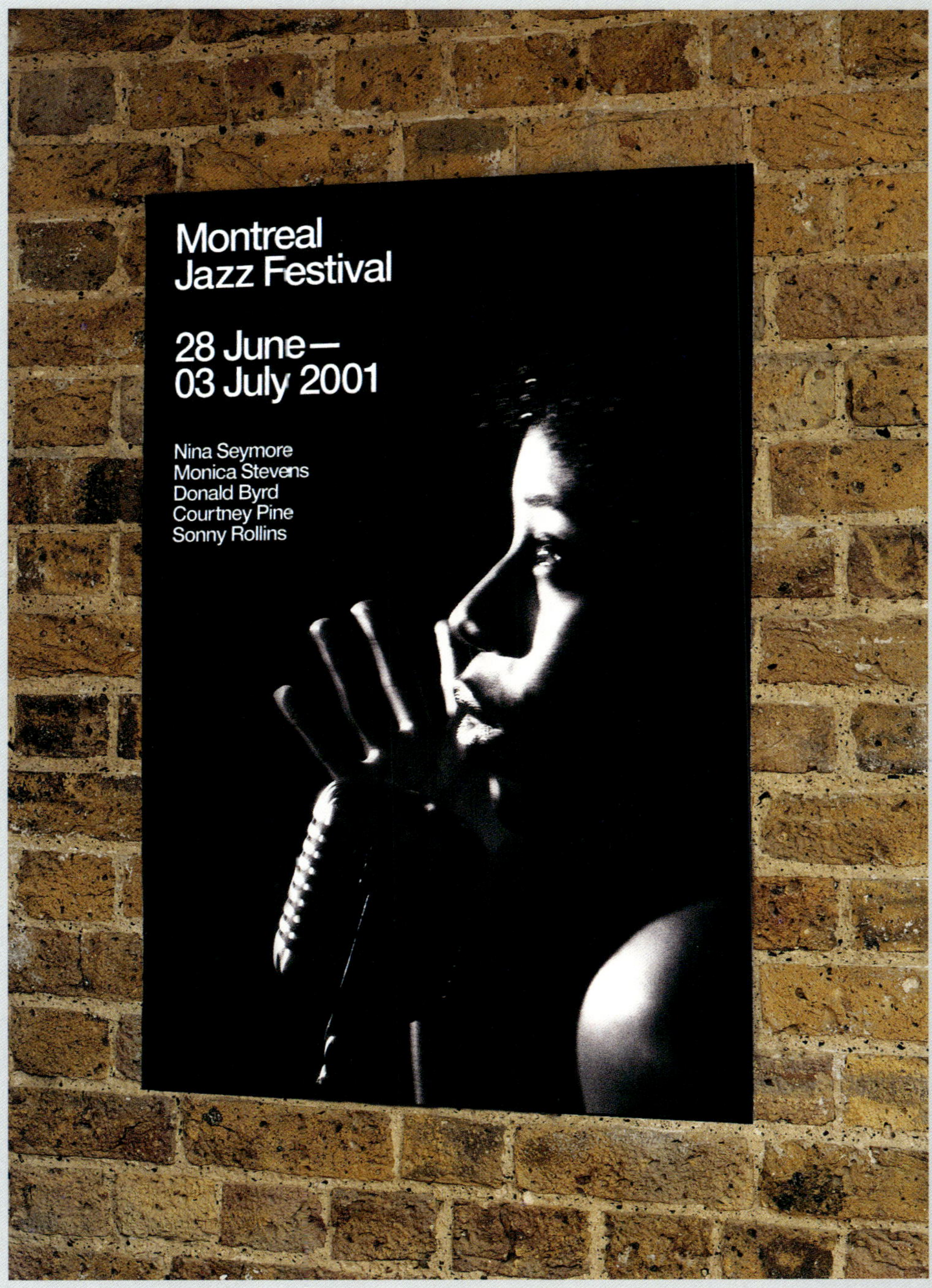

Use 2
Using the image again in poster format, would ensure a fluid and consistent 'brand' identity for the CD launch.

Case Study 7
Photographing Children

No doubt you have heard the saying never shoot with children or animals... both can turn a shoot upside down!

Children have however always been important stock subjects with demand especially from the editorial and advertising sectors. Images of children tug at the emotions of adults: there is an old advertising maxim that if you put a child and a puppy in the advertisement, the product will sell! While animal photography isn't covered in this book, here is some advice as to how to get the most out of photographing children for stock.

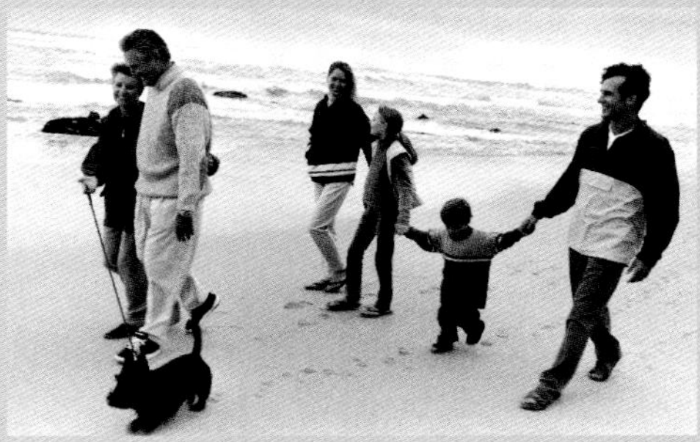

A group setting is ideal for children shots, since not being the main photographic focus is less nerve-wracking for a child.

Photographic Direction
Some of the strongest stock imagery of children features the child in his/her own natural, uninhibited, inner world, revealing their individuality and way of being. To truly capture this essence requires a skill on the part of the photographer to communicate what they want and expect from the child – all in a manner the child will not only understand but respond to. Often this will entail gently coaxing and cajoling the child in a fun and indirect way rather than literally telling them what to do. The natural reaction of very young children is to instinctively respond "I don't want to!" or just plain "No!".

Some of the best photographers of children are those who are able to quite literally see the world as a child does. Often, these photographers will have children of their own. They are able to be playful and direct them in a manner and with language that will put them at ease.

Sometimes the brief will demand a considerable degree of play-acting – in many ways a natural habit for role-playing youngsters who with sympathetic direction, can often pull this off more convincingly than experienced adults. Using props like colouring pads, paints and playground equipment will allow for natural reactions among a group of children, and will often yield the best photographs.

Be careful however. While they may not be unsuccessful in terms of sales, some child stock shots can veer heavily toward the contrived and will usually be regarded as too aesthetically 'cheesy' by the more discerning libraries.

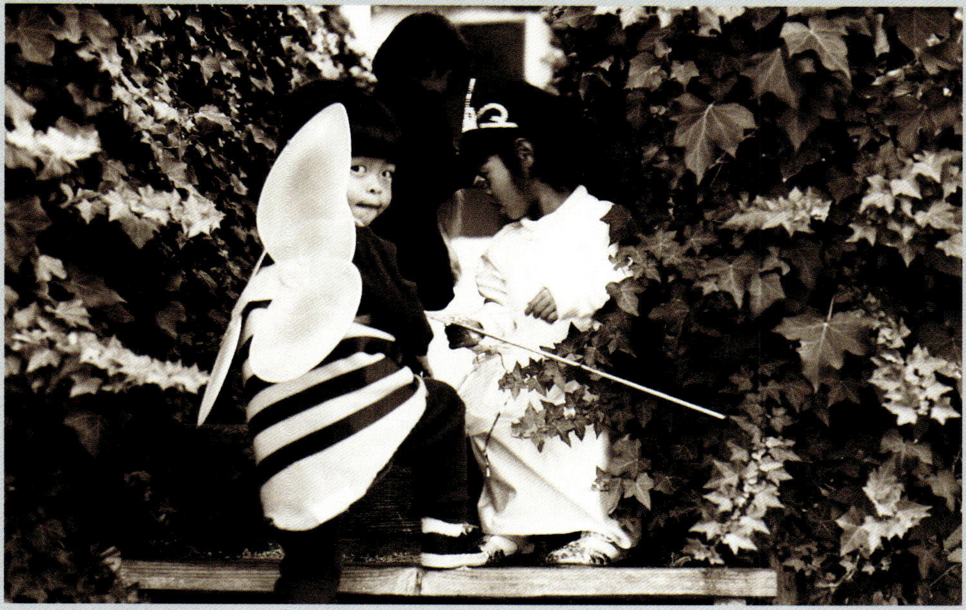

Secret glances captured by the camera are strongly emotive.

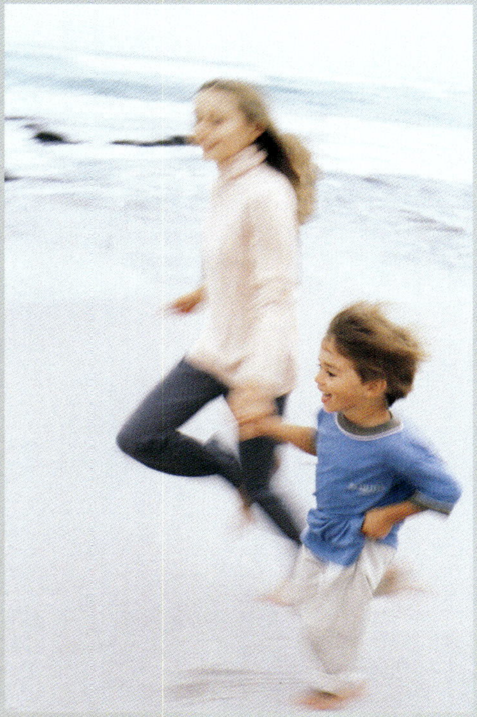

Focusing on the boy's smile strengthens this image.

Child Models
Child model agencies do exist, and many photographers use them. During castings and on shoots, babies and young children will always be accompanied by a parent and/or guardian. Having a known adult around them whom they trust will also help them feel more secure in a possibly quite frenetic shoot environment.

It is wise if shooting with babies or young children (and model agencies will usually suggest this) to book more models than actually needed. This will act as a back-up if one/or more of the children don't cooperate on the shoot. On occasions, valuable shoot time can be spent trying to coax them to cooperate which may in turn mean running overtime and bumping up costs from other models, hair and make-up, stylists etc.

Bear in mind also that babies and children can only work an hour or two at a stretch by law (check this with the model agency). This can impact on your shooting schedule if you are not aware of the regulations.

Try Babysitting!
Quite often photographers will use children they know; friends of their own kids for example, with whom they will already have a degree of interaction. The child will feel familiar and comfortable in their presence.

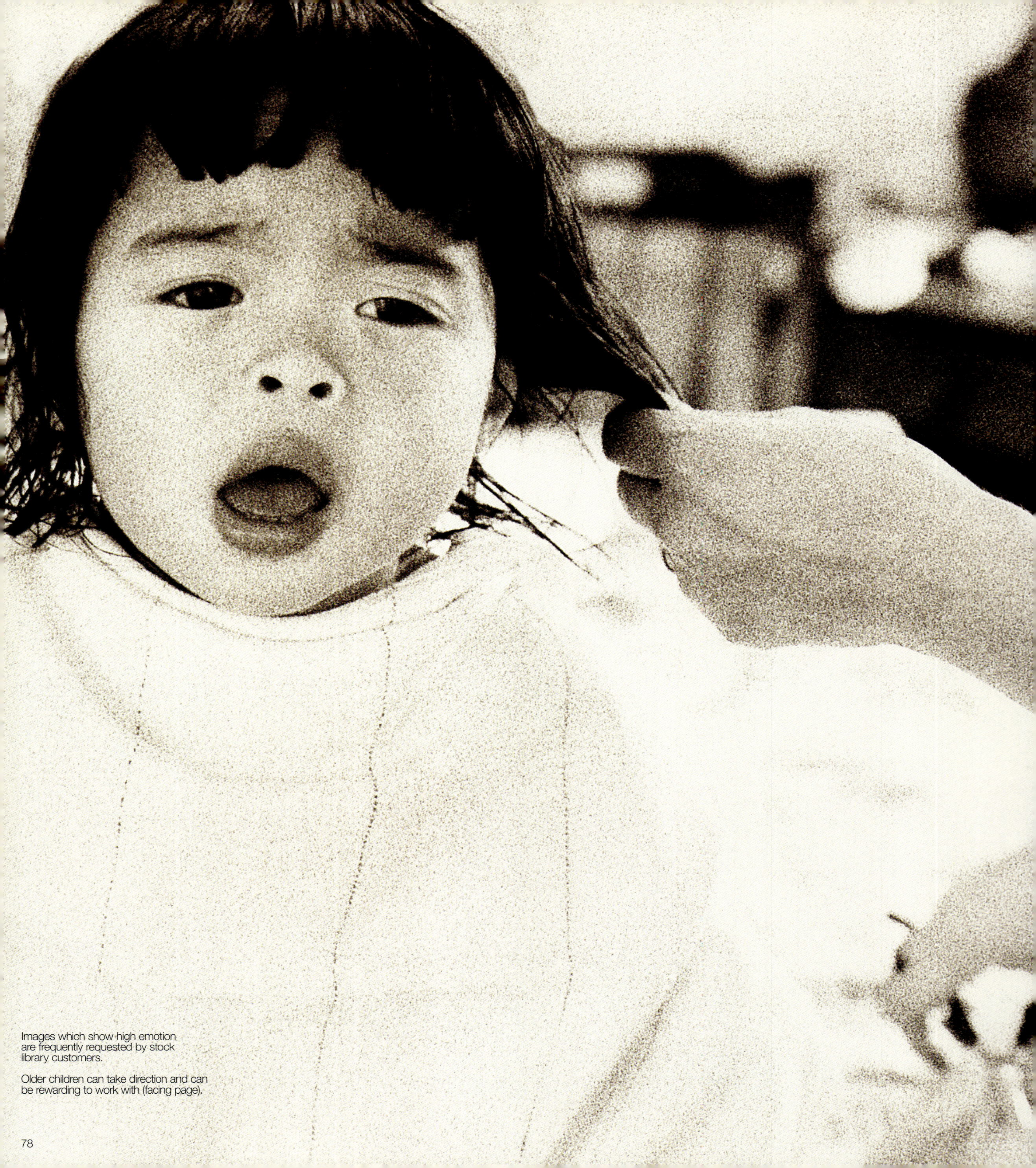

Images which show high emotion
are frequently requested by stock
library customers.

Older children can take direction and can
be rewarding to work with (facing page).

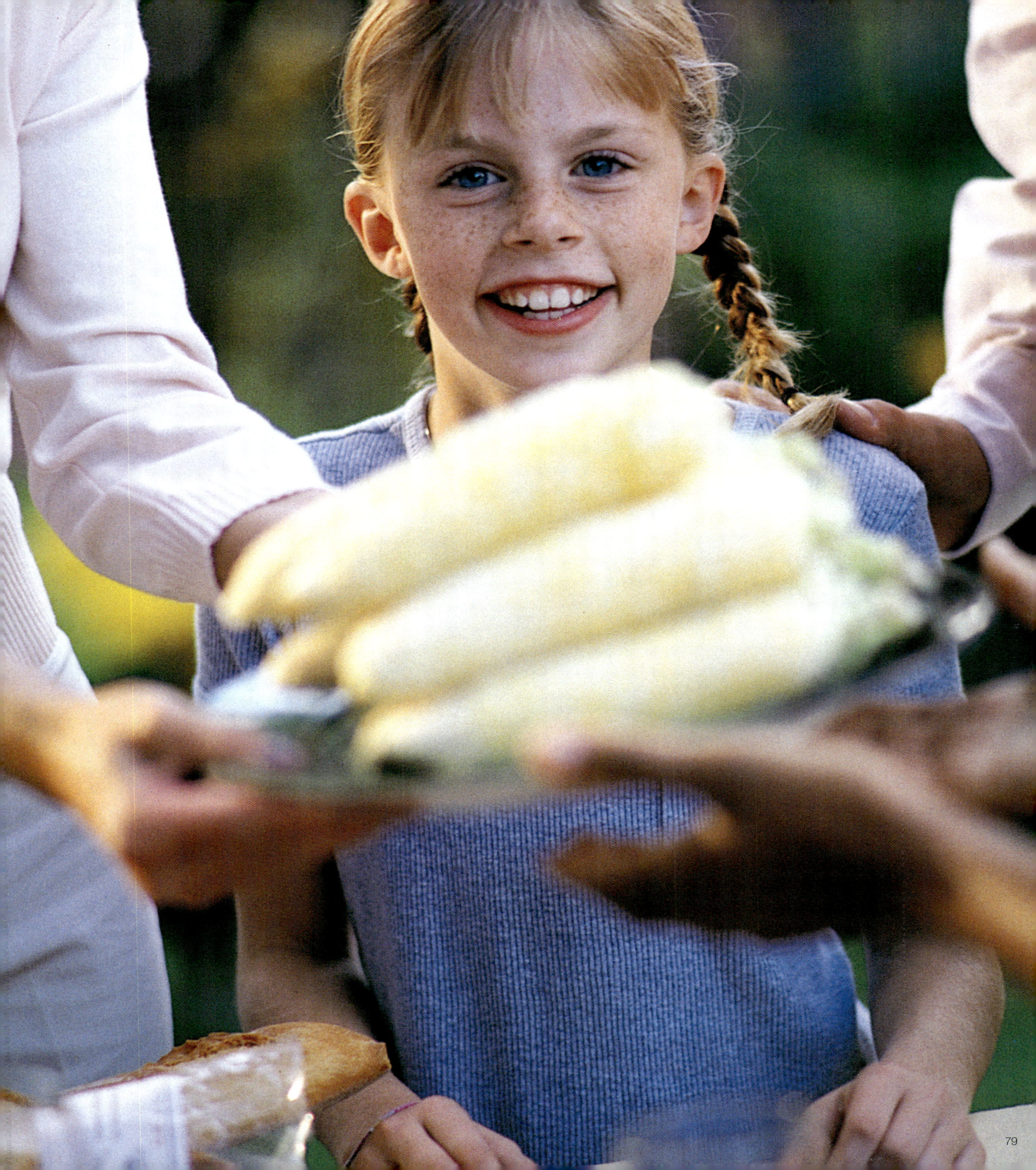

Case Study 8
Medics on the Scene

The Photographer
Brendan Byrne
A UK-based photographer known for his meticulous attention to detail.

The Brief
To generate a 100-image medical themed title featuring reportage styling, which would highlight both surgical and Emergency Room situations.

Authenticity was one of the key characteristics the library wished to capture on this particular shoot, while at the same time considering the need for the title's global appeal. Given this brief, a considerable amount of research time was taken to accurately style hospital rooms, staff and medical props.

The photographer Brendan Byrne comments, "In general I create and control every aspect of my images. I would never walk around hoping and looking for images or scenes and snap something on the off-chance.

"I think of the images I want to create first and then find all the precise elements I need to create them. I will define the area and the look I want to cover then begin to pre-produce it over many weeks. If I can't get exactly the right locations, wardrobe or props, I'll build them or have them made."

Talking generally about preparing for a shoot Brendan comments, "Research into your subject will provide reality. I prepare on an average of four days for every one shooting day. Get your production ironed out beforehand and it will free you to concentrate solely on your photography on the shoot day. Before you take any stock picture you must ask yourself as many questions relevant to your image as you can, such as:

'Would a woman in Paris like my wardrobe choice? Would an Arab in Dubai wear these western clothes to a business meeting? Would two Japanese business men actually shake hands at a meeting in Tokyo?'

"Always bear in mind different countries' idiosyncrasies... for instance, What does the road look like in my picture? In the US they have a yellow stripe down the centre – this rarely happens in Europe... normally it is white. Australians, Japanese, South Africans and the British all drive on the left, so any street scenes shown would need to be carefully considered.

"If shooting interiors, what are the size and shape of the windows of this house and what are the door handles like? Each country has very different decor style in reality.

"With regard to styling... you have to ask yourself what do people really wear to do this job? For instance what colours and what styles do you use to convince the local market in Brazil to buy your image? It's very easy to assume or worse, guess, and be totally wrong.

"On this shoot we found that doctors who treat older children in the UK rarely wear medical white coats. It's deemed too scary. Which way round should you push a trolley bed? Exactly how many people in an operating team and where do they stand? Make sure you know everything before you shoot."

Finding the right locations for this shoot was especially challenging not least because it required the authorisation of hospital authorities and staff, and availability vied with real-life emergency situations which caused scheduling problems for the hospital and the photo team.

The angle of the camera (rigged up on the end of the trolley) almost beckons us to be part of the team, and the motion blur adds to the sense of urgency.

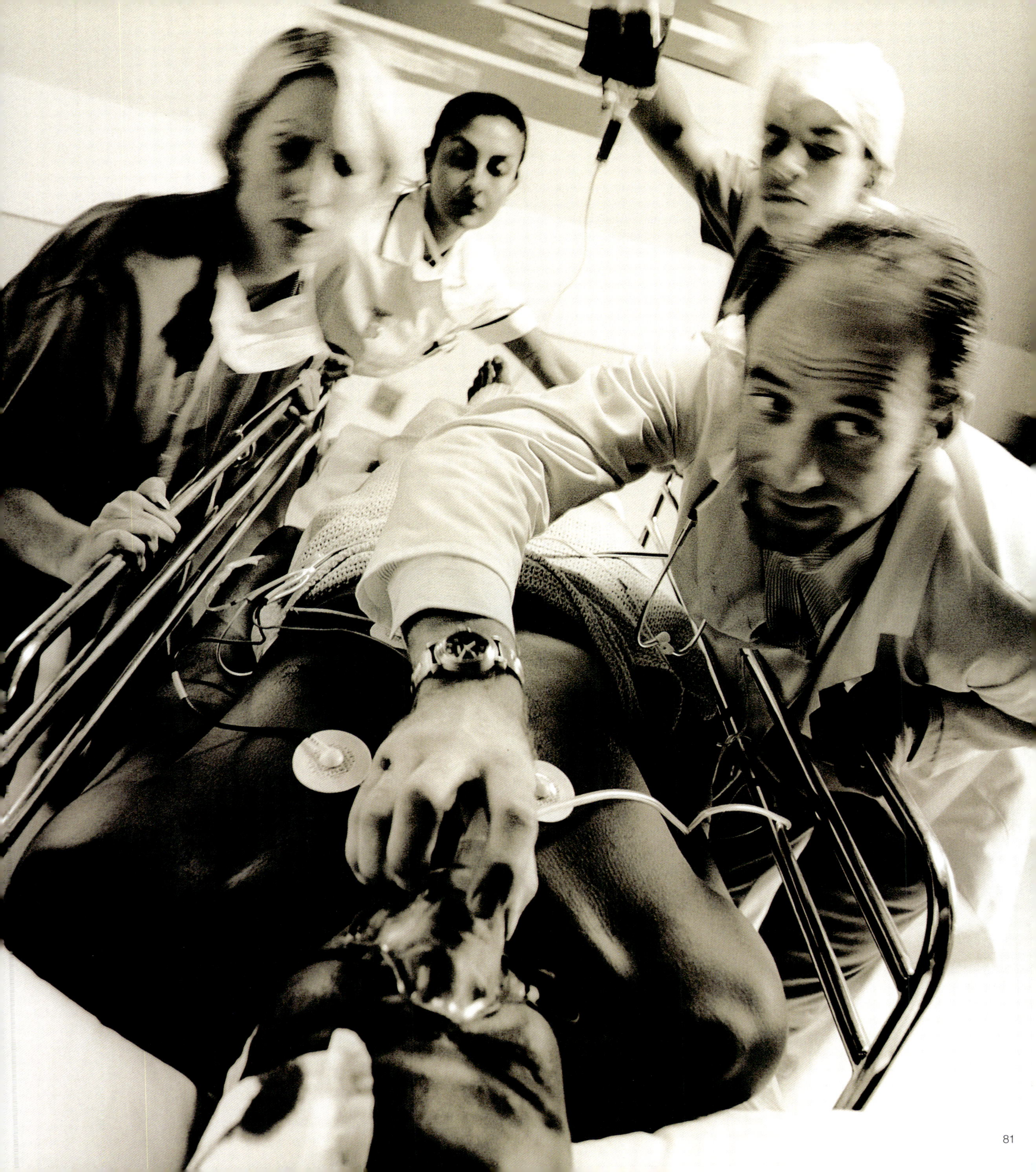

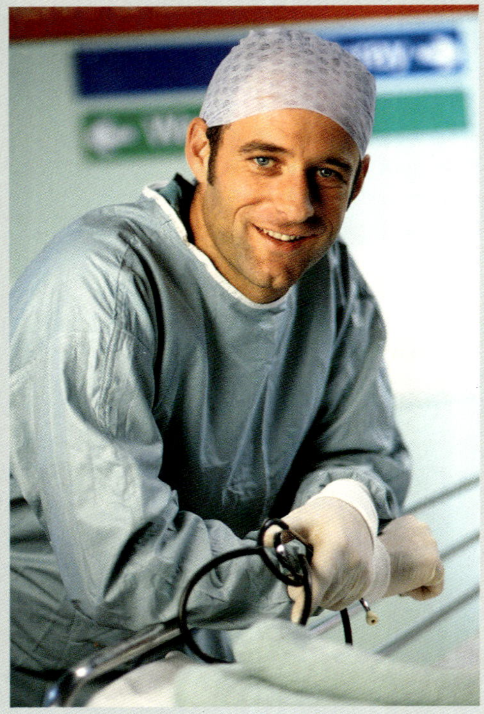

The portraits, which all too often can be stiff and unyielding in stock shoots, show the subjects to be natural and responsive.

The Pre-production

A real operating theatre was eventually found for the surgical scenes, but following an intensive reconnaissance and then logistical production problems at the locations, the decision was made to build sets in which to shoot the corridor, intensive care, emergency room and ward scenes. Brendan's team was able to construct and prop highly convincing compact and versatile sets in his studio.

High production values also mean being prepared to invest, as Brendan explains: "I often spend something like the equivalent cost of a new car on a one-day stock shoot because I firmly believe that only the highest production values and the best production help are acceptable... and they are both expensive. I usually have about six production people working with me on each shoot day and they are kept very, very busy. To my eye, any production short cuts or compromises stick out like a sore thumb on the lightbox later."

The Casting

Casting is also something Brendan is prepared to invest a lot of time in:

"To get the right social and ethnic balance is critical. To find ten people who I like, we will hand-pick 100 to 150 people from six or seven model agencies, then get them all to come to the studio for a photo casting. We will then narrow it down steadily, making families of casting pictures, tweaking and changing the balance until each group looks and feels right. Once I have the actor group on set I try to get the required ideas and mood right in the actors/models' heads before I shoot a single frame."

During the shoot, a newly born baby was required for a birth scene in which it is shown in an incubator. Rather than taking the easier option of casting a slightly older one-month-old, he sought out a woman who had had a baby three days previously and got her cooperation to bring in the baby. There were a few nervous moments during a shot of the model holding the baby, as she had never held a newborn before!

The Shoot

The shoot itself took place over the period of a couple of months and took a total of five shooting days. The level of pre-production certainly bore out Brendan's conviction that it would pave the way for highly productive and trouble-free shoot days.

In fact the only instance where there was a slight hitch in events involved a child model who had performed well in casting, but came to the studio and decided she didn't want to perform in front of the camera. Despite her mother and Brendan coaxing her, she simply refused to participate. Time ticked away as she edged towards a tantrum. Brendan waited patiently as the model in the scenes with her was able to take the child's thoughts away from the immediate task in hand by chatting and playing with her, and happily her efforts yielded plenty of great shots.

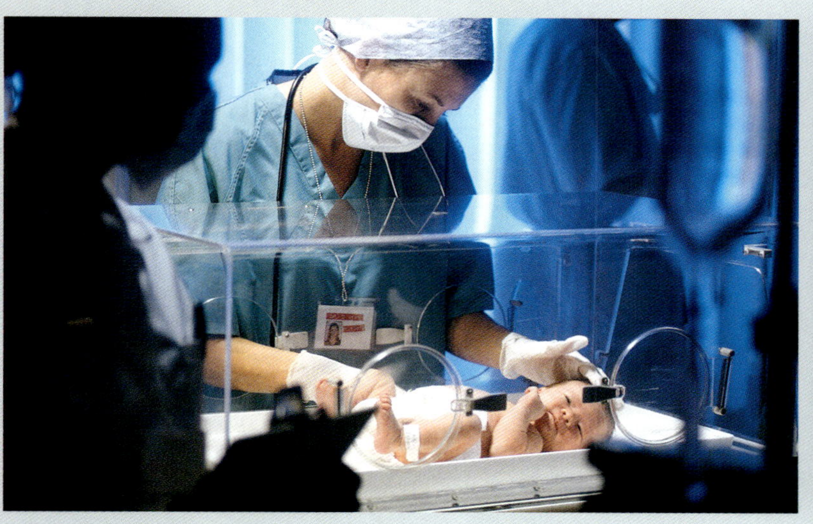

Lighting is used to great effect here to highlight the focal point of the image (the baby) whilst also allowing the peripheral elements of the image a presence.

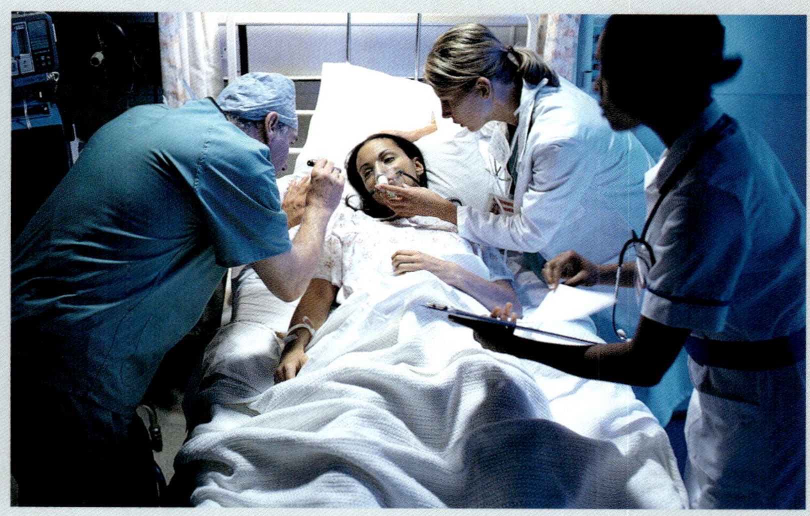

Lighting is utilised here to reinforce focus on the woman in bed with the oxygen mask, while there is less emphasis on the doctors attending her, and the nurse to the right is thrown out of focus and is in partial darkness.

The Lighting and Technique

Flash and continuous source lighting were used together and separately. Warm and cool lighting were mixed in the same scenes to give depth or to accentuate an action or area of interest. Differential focus was also used to subdue busy backgrounds and foregrounds leaving the eye to fully focus on the main message of the image. All light sources were used sympathetically throughout the shoot to give a strong sense of atmosphere. Camera motion blur was also used to create a sense of urgency and documentary style.

The Results

A very successful shoot, not least because of its planning! It yielded a high ratio of winning shots and amply filled the gap in the library's medical series for a strong, reportage emergency room title.

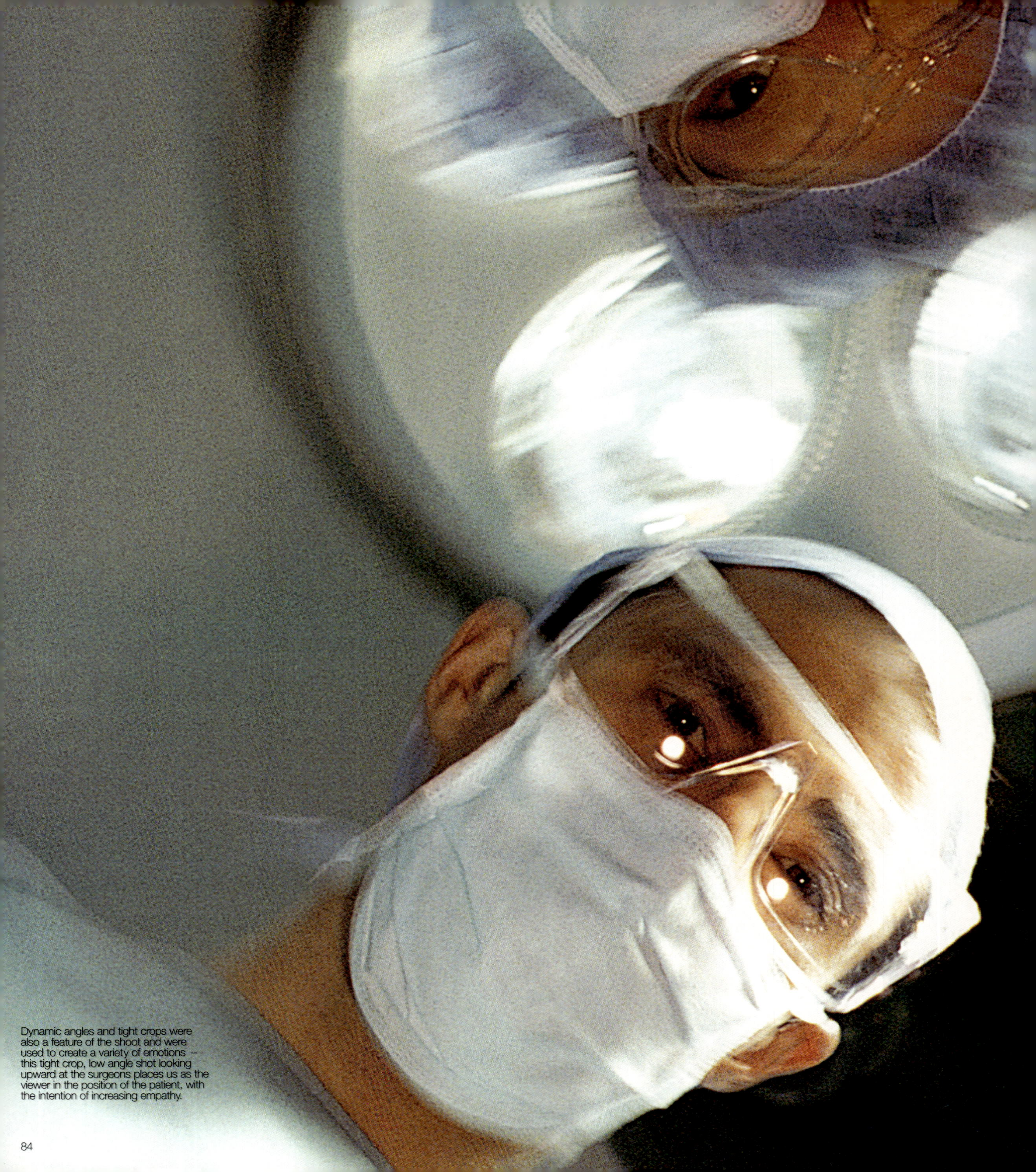

Dynamic angles and tight crops were also a feature of the shoot and were used to create a variety of emotions – this tight crop, low angle shot looking upward at the surgeons places us as the viewer in the position of the patient, with the intention of increasing empathy.

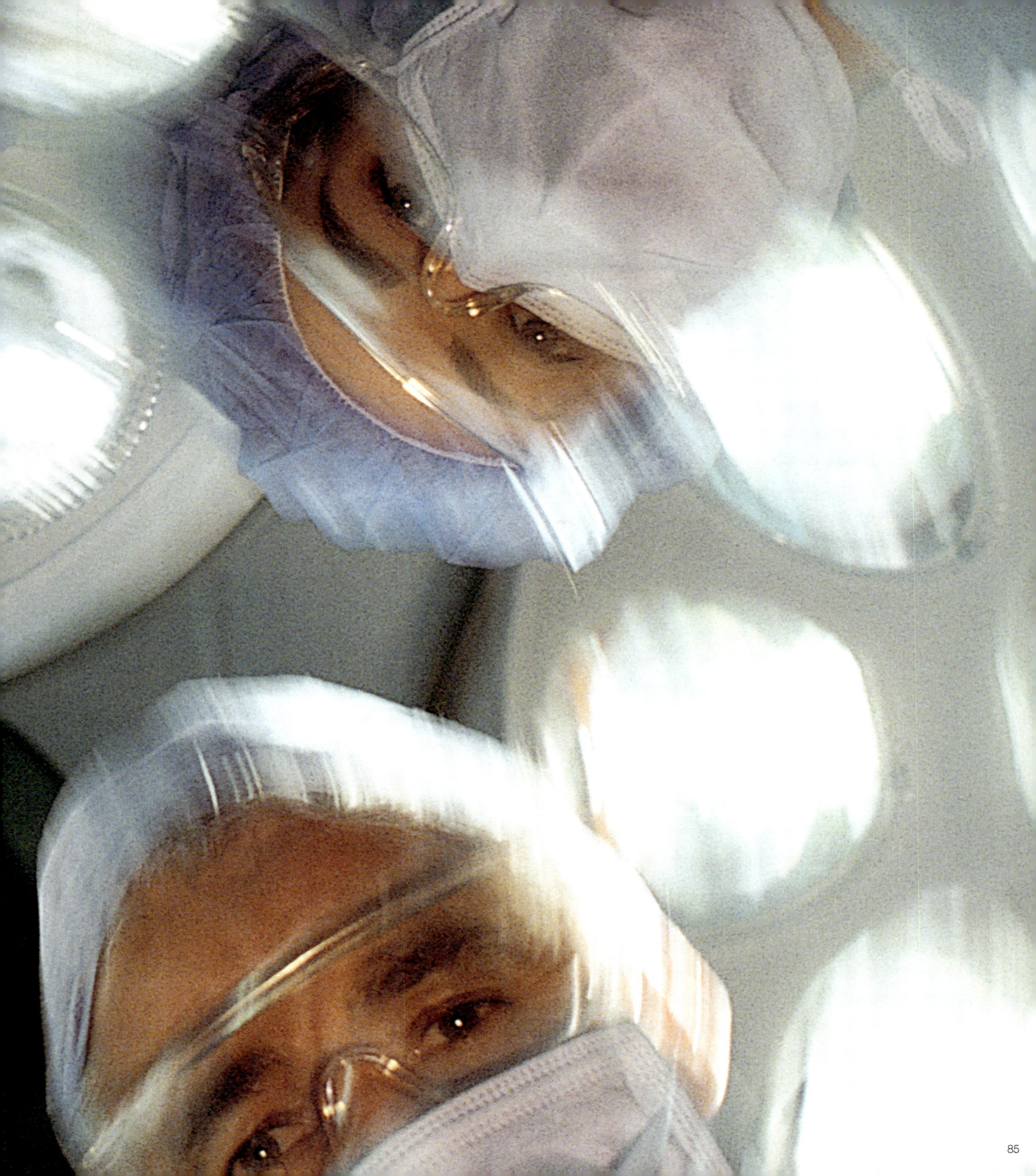

Top Ten Photographers' Tips

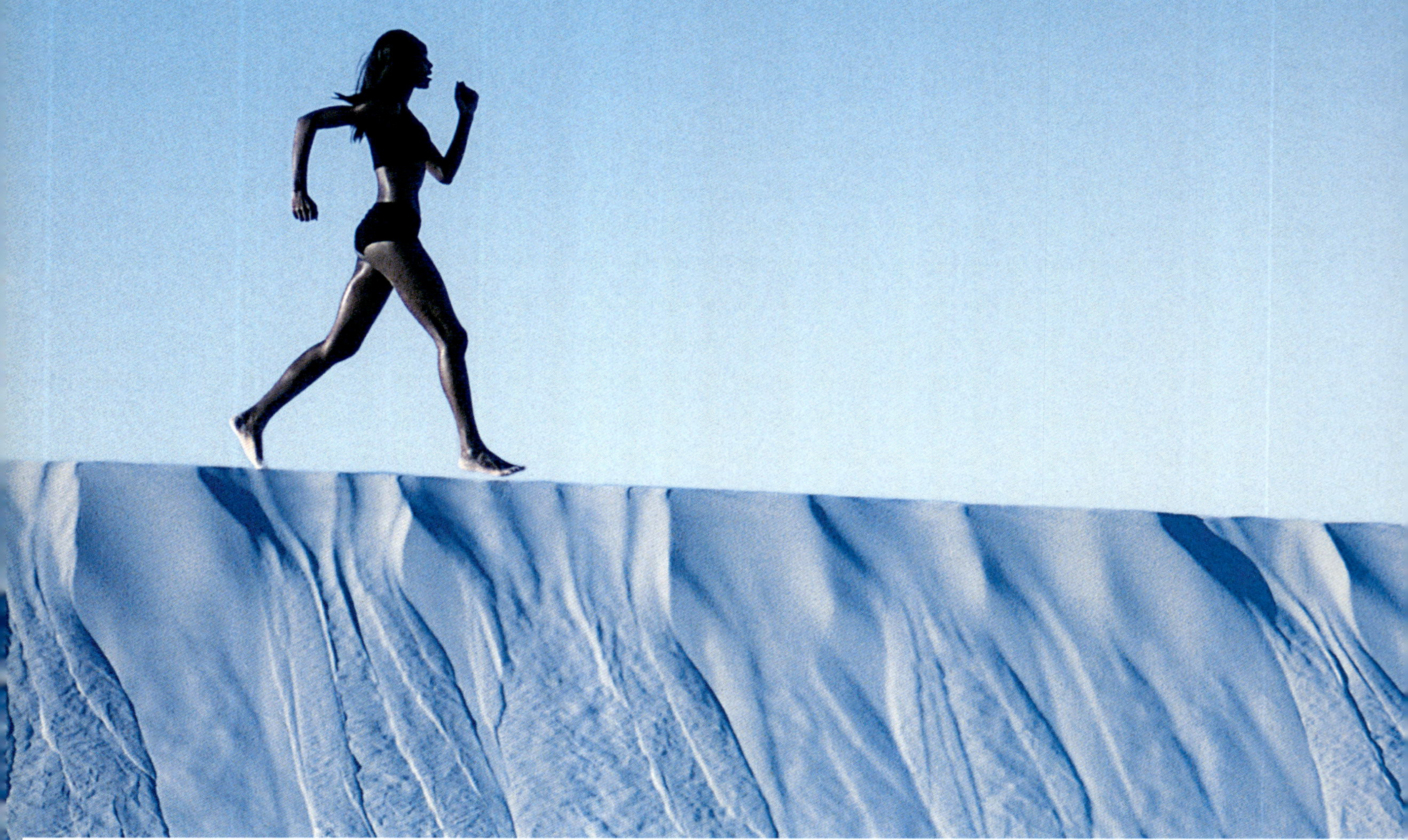

1—Prepare and research before you shoot
This is vital to the success of the shoot. Know your subjects, whether it be business, industry or lifestyle. This will yield the degree of detail which will achieve the necessary sense of realism and authenticity.

2—Be prepared to invest
Working in stock is essentially a partnership, both emotionally and financially. Many libraries will expect the photographer to invest in funding their own shoots. Those prepared to do this are often seen by the library as taking the industry seriously and making a commitment to achieving results.

3—Develop a strong photographic style
Experiment. Look at the current trends in advertising, editorial and of course stock! Some libraries have a list of aesthetic or style likes and dislikes. This may include considerations such as Likes: dynamic angles, shallow depth of field etc. to Dislikes: no focal point and poor composition.

4—Build a network of contacts
This can include anyone who will help you achieve the results you may want, from a set builder to a group of reliable and suitable models, stylists and assistants.

5—Target and get to know the library or libraries you wish to work with
Speak to the art directors and buyers/acquisitions teams. Usually less available to photographers are the image researchers who are at the front line in terms of dealing with client briefs so have a strong knowledge of what sells and who will be the people who ultimately pitch your images for a brief... they too will have their favourites!

6 — Learn from your mistakes
Don't be too disheartened if your first edit doesn't have a high hit rate. Learn from it... speak directly, if you can, to the edit team and find out why they accepted certain images and rejected others. Understand their process and put your point of view across too without being defensive.

7 — Be flexible
Some libraries will be very specific about what they wish to shoot – others are open to photographer ideas. Offer your opinion and ideas and show them you are able to think around a variety of subjects and problem solve.

8 — Be prepared to travel
And often for a period of time. Many shoots demand overseas travel to sunny climates like South Africa and Miami. These may be for lifestyle shoots that require you to be away from home for anything from a week to two months and more.

9 — Be organised
Stock shoots demand high levels of organisation, frequently over a period of time. You will be dealing with model castings, budgets, shoot planning and often travel plans – if it doesn't come naturally to you, get help.

10 — Don't expect immediate returns
Working in stock is an investment. It usually takes upwards of one year to see royalty returns on images. It will depend very much on how long it may take for the library to publish the catalogue your work is in. This is still the prime marketing tool for images. Increasingly, however, the company will be able to launch images through the web a lot quicker than print.

Chapter 5
Understanding Your Creative Options 88 – 117

Literacy

One of the underlying truths of stock photography is that 'cheesy' pictures sell. As a photographer, you may rebel against images featuring waxen models with perfect teeth hugging children with neatly combed hair on a spotless beach, however, this type of imagery is aspirational and fulfils a huge commercial need. But wait, be honest with yourself – if you were shopping for a holiday in Florida and saw a lovely tanned couple against an azure blue sky – wouldn't that be more appealing than a couple with winter-white skin against an overcast skyline?

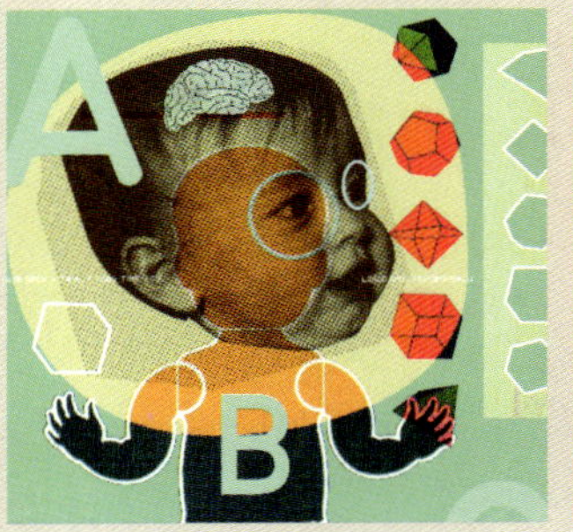

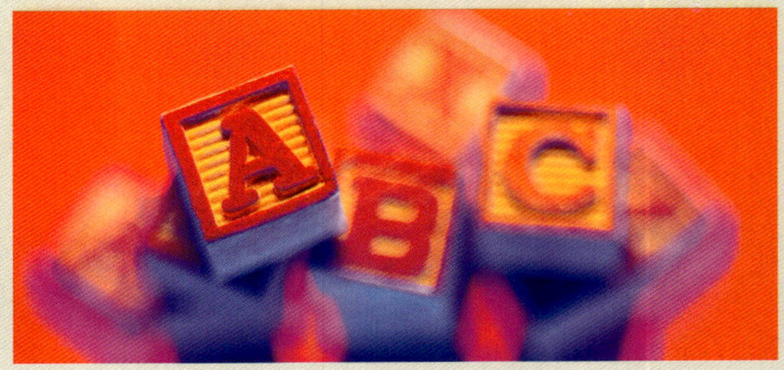

Images 1 and 2
These brightly coloured images won't date quickly. Primary age students respond to bright hues and these images would more than likely be used for students in their early educational years. Interestingly, Image 2 would also appeal to the corporate brochure market as it evokes the concept, 'It is as easy as A,B,C', which is a common theme in business marketing.

As an artist, you might be strongly questioning at this point whether or not you want to enter this industry, but don't despair. Stock agencies are taking more and more risks by accepting and shooting what they call 'natural' or 'reportage' style images. Real life captured through your lens is now considered a commercially viable option. Customers are now requesting these types of images, and where there is demand there will be work.

To illustrate how stock agencies explore different themes and concepts, this unique chapter focuses on a set subject and shows the variety of images available to the customer. When possible, we've included notes as to how the image was taken, trends we see for this subject matter, and comments from stock professionals. It just might make you view the stock photography industry in a whole new light.

The well worn image of education and learning is two children – normally a boy and girl – looking at the globe. Imagery today, however, has to fit in with new concepts of education. Teachers are now more relaxed in the classroom and children are as often picked up from school by Daddy as well as Mum. This shift in society brings changes in the ways in which we perceive education.

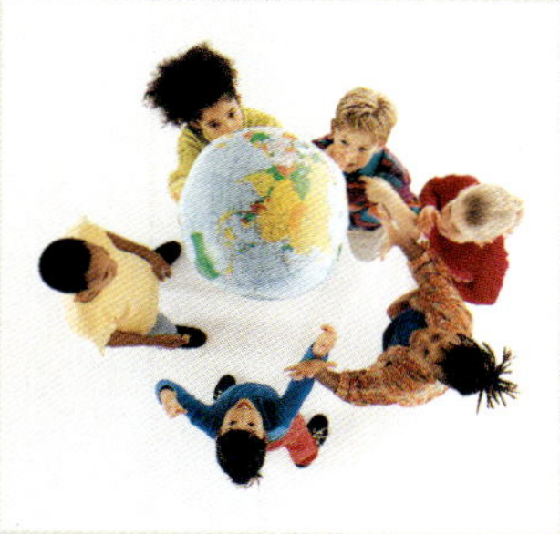

Image 3
This image takes a slightly more contemporary twist on the familiar globe in education theme. Firstly, the group of children is culturally diverse and the angle is from above rather than straight on. The theme probably requested by the art director was, 'We've got the whole world in our hands'.

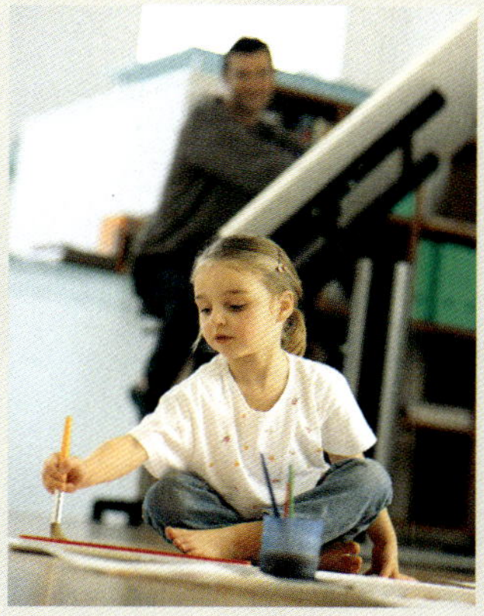

Image 4
The composition of this image is different to the others shown for this section. Note a father working in the background – rather than a mother, say unpacking groceries (the 'norm'). The visual of the father working from home also speaks of the changing nature of work lifestyles.

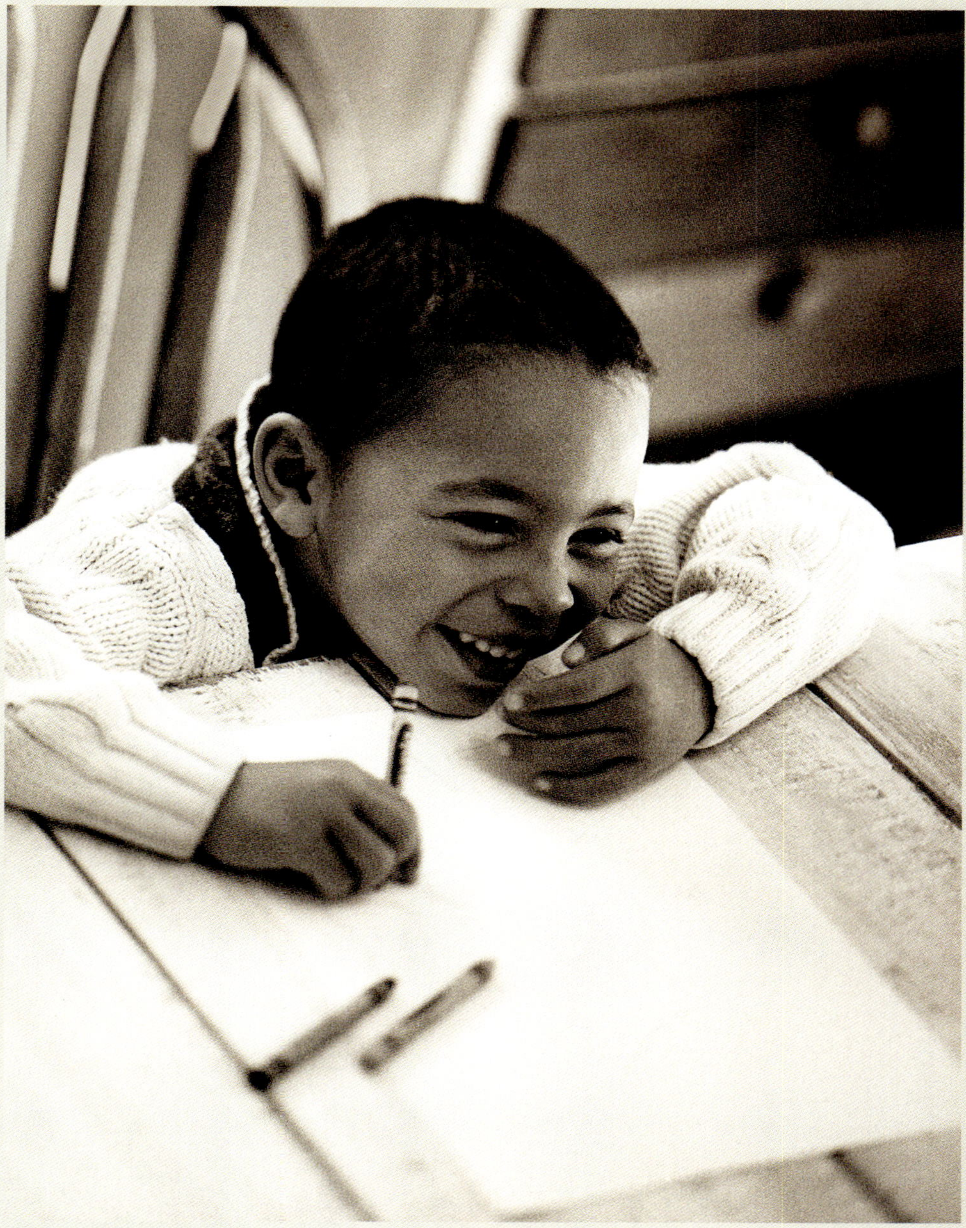

Image 5
This emotive image is far more like a personal image than a stock one – it is true that photographers are sometimes chosen on the strength of their 'off-hours' shooting. The use of toned, black-and-white imagery is appealing to corporate clients and advertising agencies.

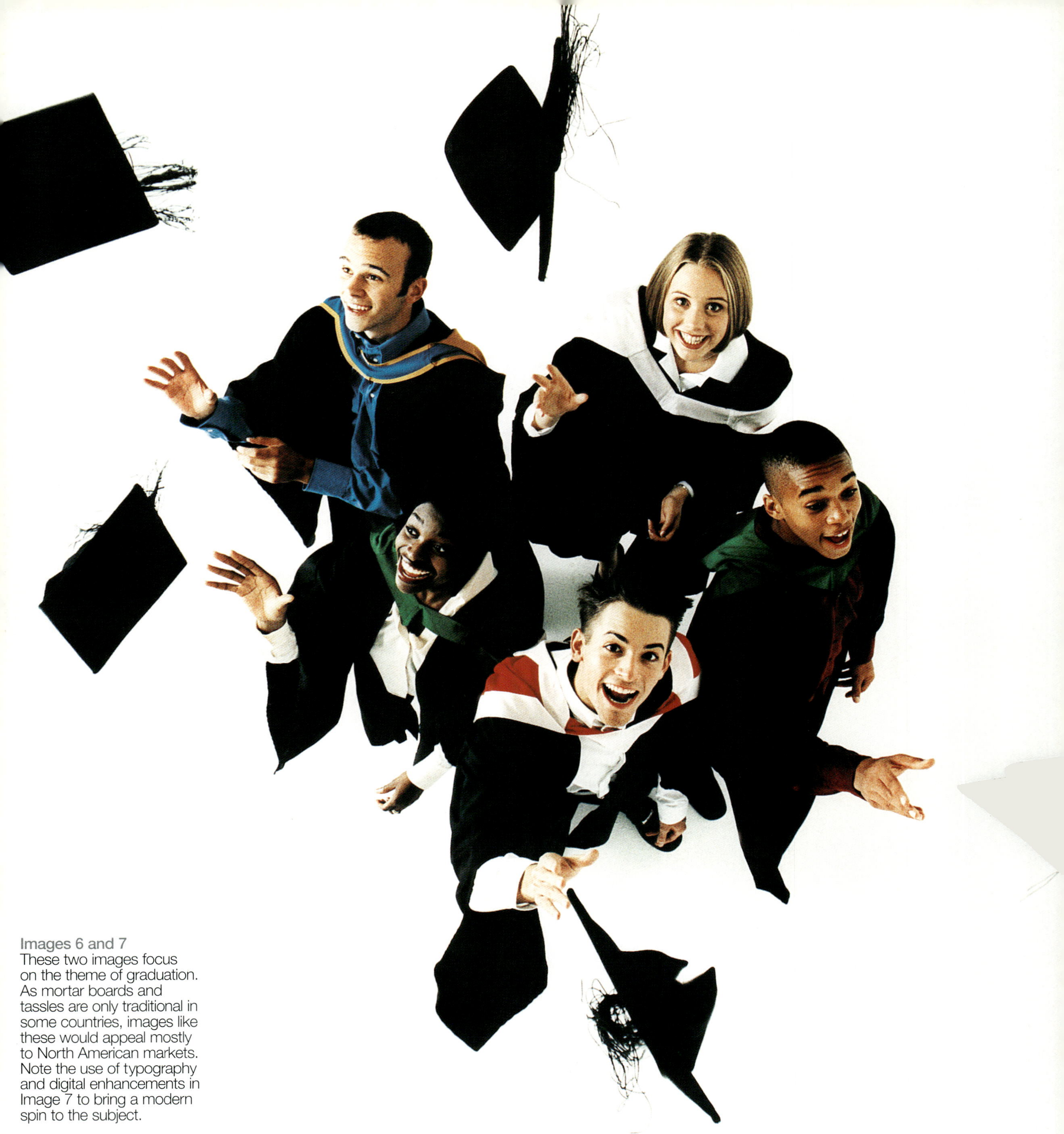

Images 6 and 7
These two images focus on the theme of graduation. As mortar boards and tassles are only traditional in some countries, images like these would appeal mostly to North American markets. Note the use of typography and digital enhancements in Image 7 to bring a modern spin to the subject.

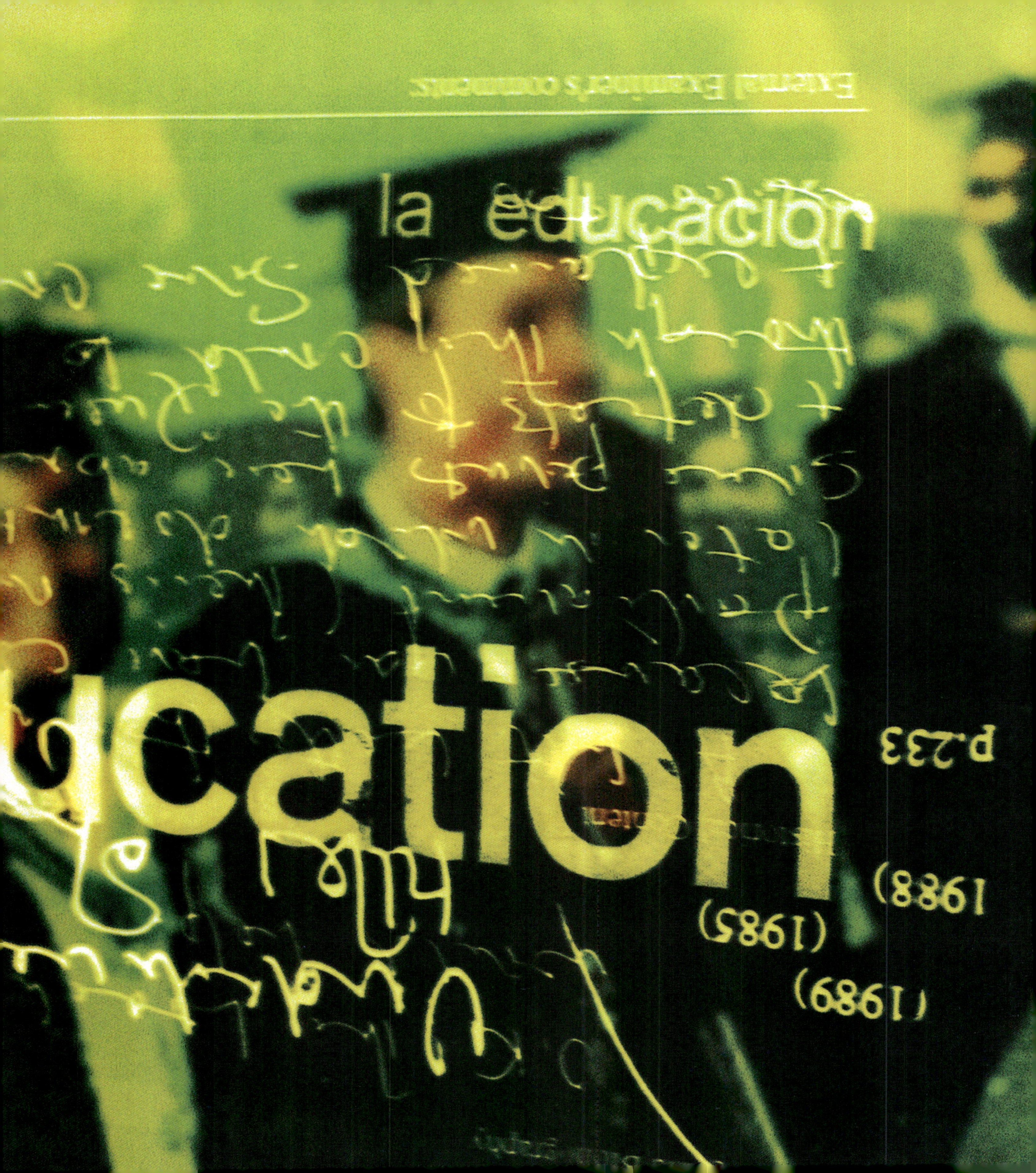
la educación
ucation

Senior Lifestyles

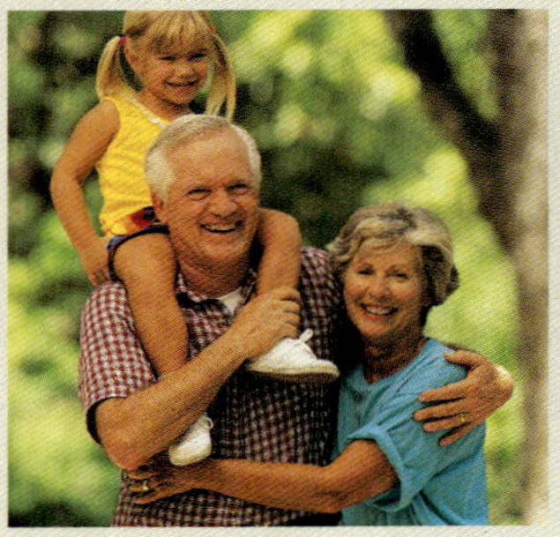

Image 1
Bright colours and the multi-generational theme make this very commercial image ideal for brochures. To contrast this conventional composition and theme, compare with Images 2 and 3.

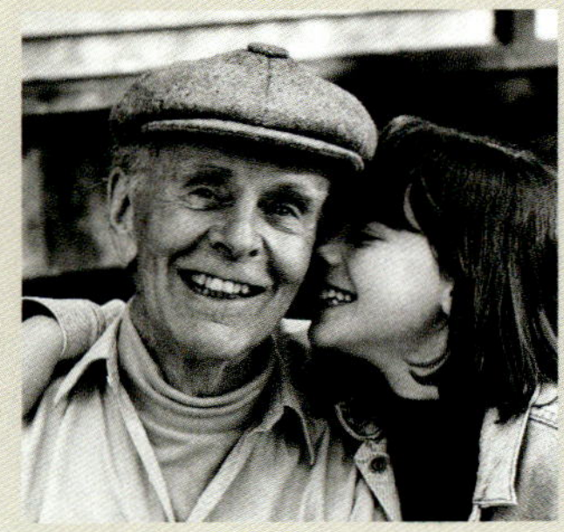

Image 2
This shot was taken more recently and this is reflected in the looser styling and more 'natural' looking models. In fact, these are not professional models at all but friends of the photographer.

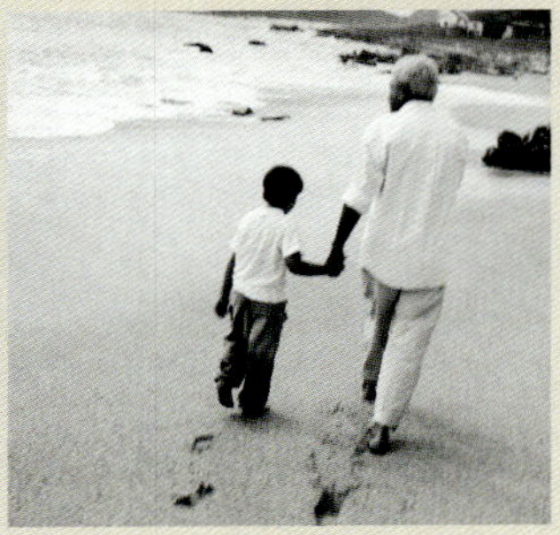

Image 3
This very contemporary image has movement in the foreground and a reportage feel. Note the use of slightly matching clothing, which responds to today's fashion climate of clothing stores like GAP which cater for all age groups.

Images of senior citizens have always played a big role in stock photography, under what is classified as lifestyle imagery. Changing demographics mean that more and more of the population are surviving into later life, causing a huge surge in the images needed to promote retirement homes, healthcare products, consumer goods and more. Grandma and Grandpa no longer appear in a rocking chair – they are out there enjoying the best years of their lives.

Interestingly, the underlying message of all the images is vitality and healthy living. The bottom line is that although images of truly aged seniors exist in stock, the commercial emphasis, as expected, is on the active older sector.

The examples here range from the classic grand-parents with grandchildren shots to the eccentric and humorous and all those in-between.

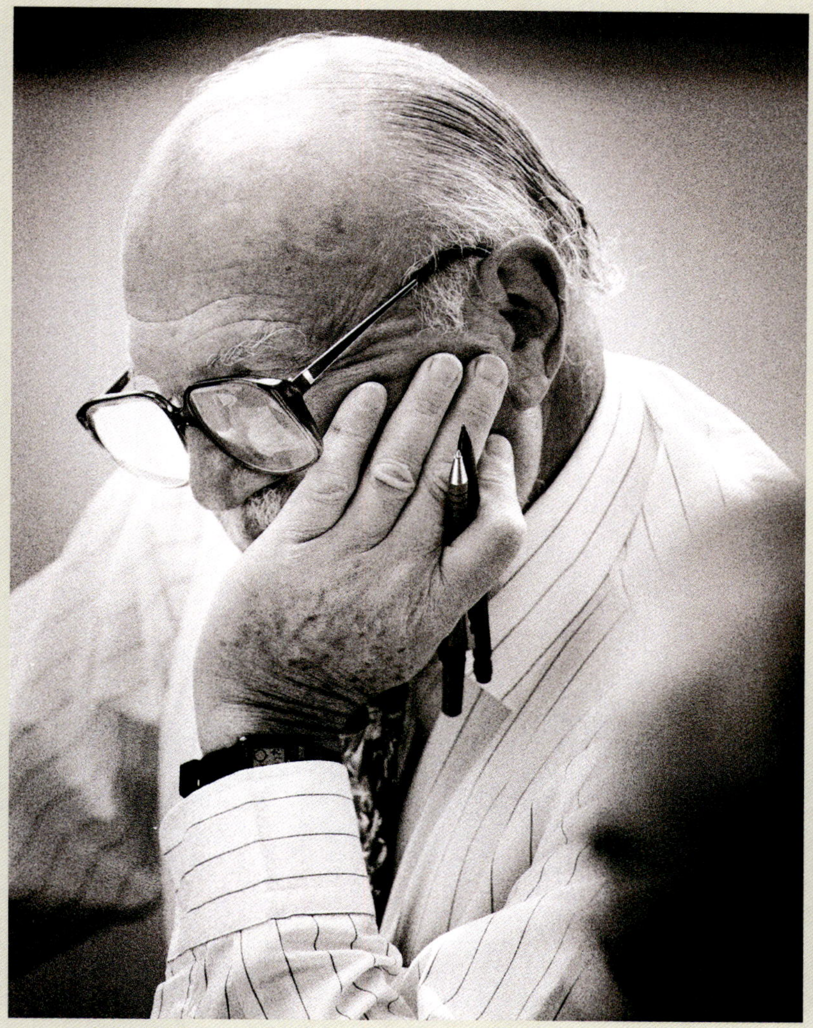

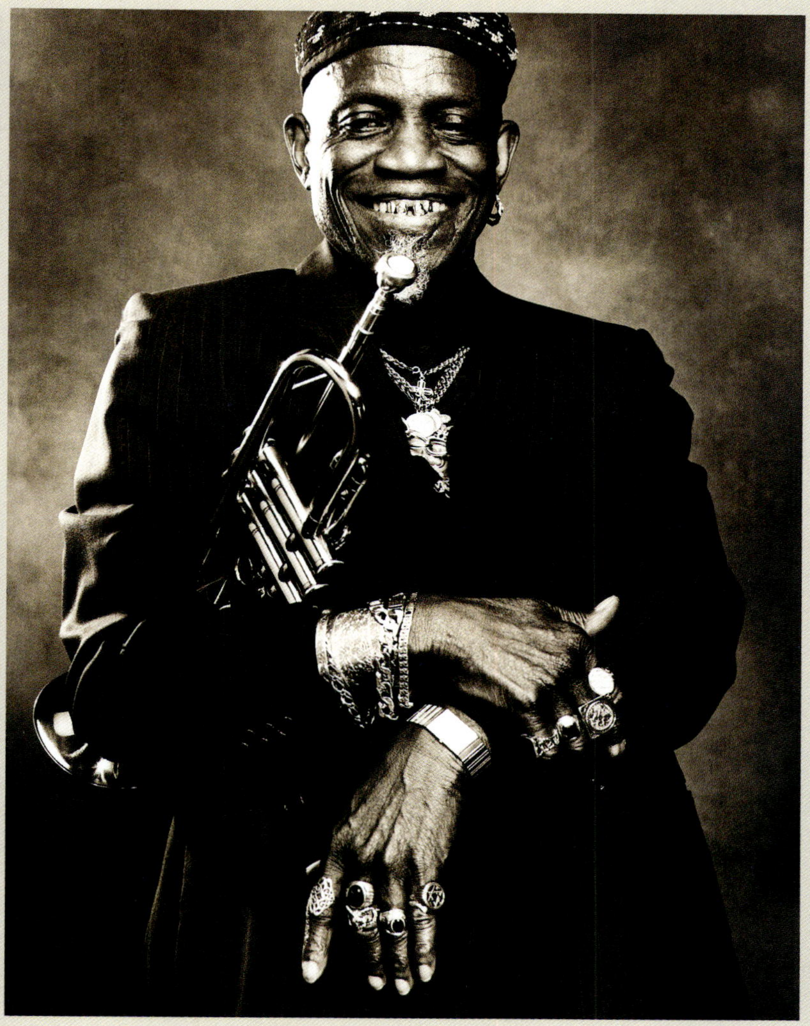

Images 4 and 5
These images, while very different, represent the trend towards showing the important role that older people have in the fields of both work and play. The shot of the jazz musician, with his golden accessories and teeth, is evocative of atmospheric, smoky clubs, while Image 4 truly captures a businessman in deep thought.

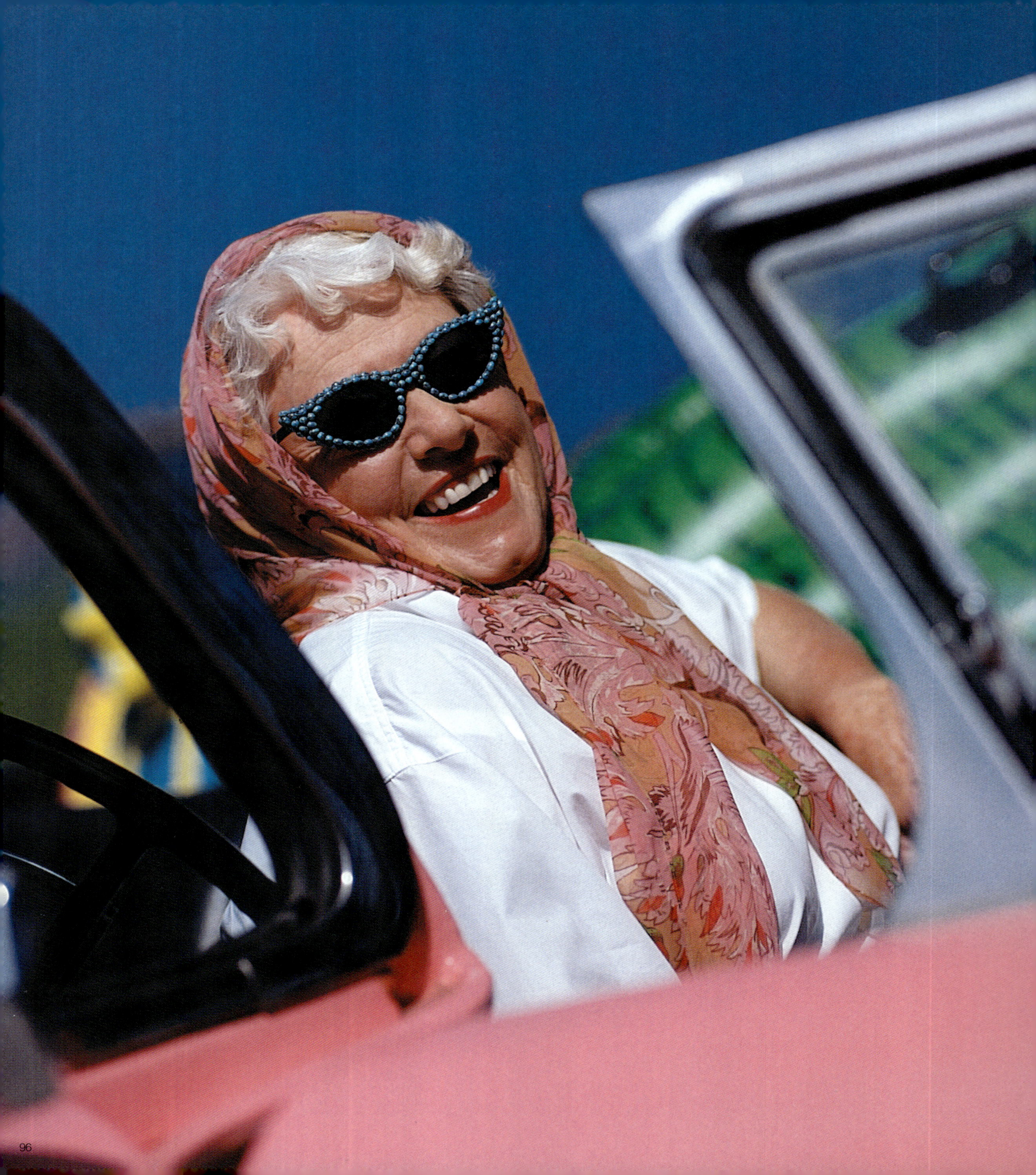

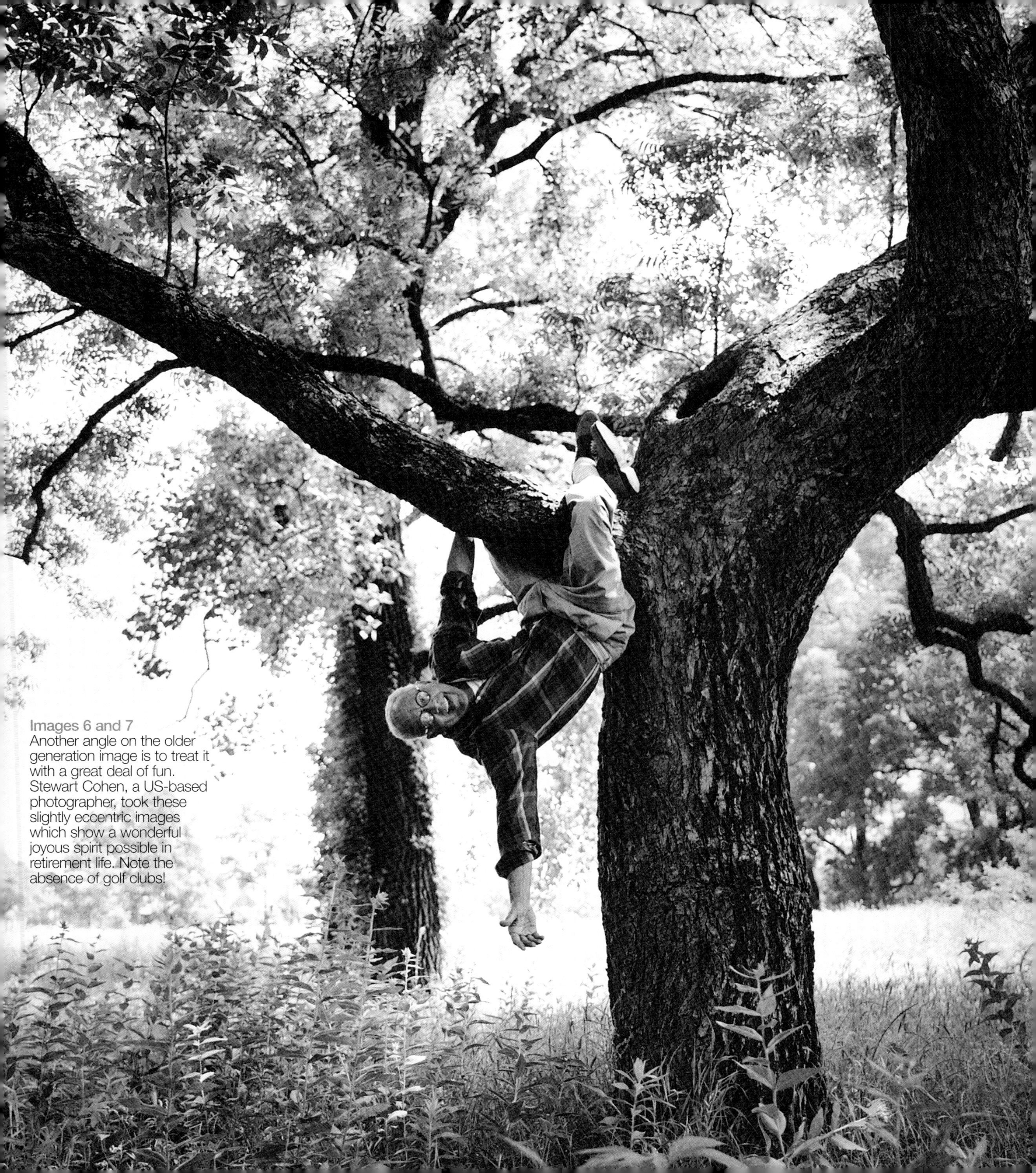

Images 6 and 7
Another angle on the older generation image is to treat it with a great deal of fun. Stewart Cohen, a US-based photographer, took these slightly eccentric images which show a wonderful joyous spirit possible in retirement life. Note the absence of golf clubs!

The Winning Spirit

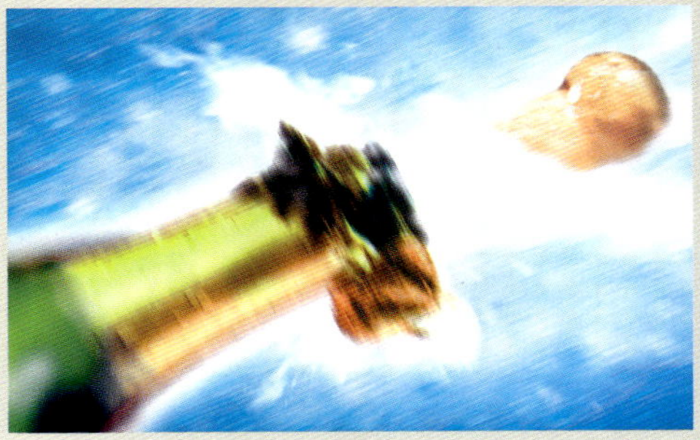

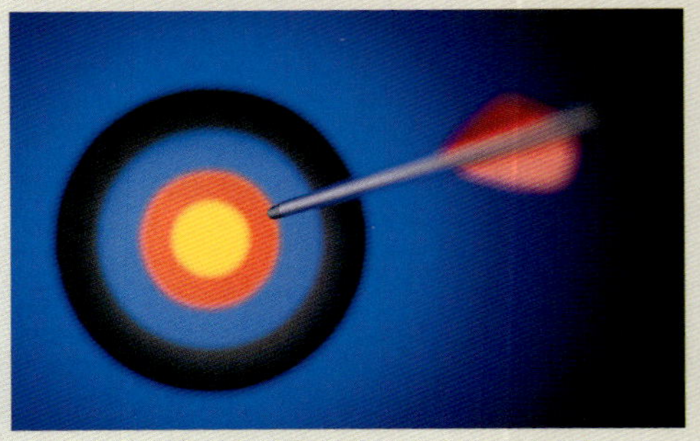

Images 1 and 2
These two 'iconic' shots quickly communicate the theme and more than likely will be used for direct-mail campaigns and corporate invitations.

Another popular concept, or what is called in the industry 'conceptual theme', is that of 'the winning spirit'. Used frequently for business brochures and annual reports, the representation of winning, the winner or team cooperation is highly commercial.

While sports figures crossing finishing lines might be your first thought, the stock trade continues to explore this theme – both in reportage action shots and highly-coloured iconic compositions.

You'll notice in this set of images that the theme is clearly communicated in rather simplistic images, however it is the styling that makes each of these pictures different. Notice the use of blurs to indicate movement and energy and the bold cropping – both hallmarks of today's stock requirements.

Image 3
Contemporary styling makes this image appear very modern. The photographer uses filters and a slow shutter speed to get the blurred appearance shown. Note the use of relatively 'universal' models. Are they Hispanic, North American or European? The intended ambiguity of the models' nationality allows scope for sales in all these regions.

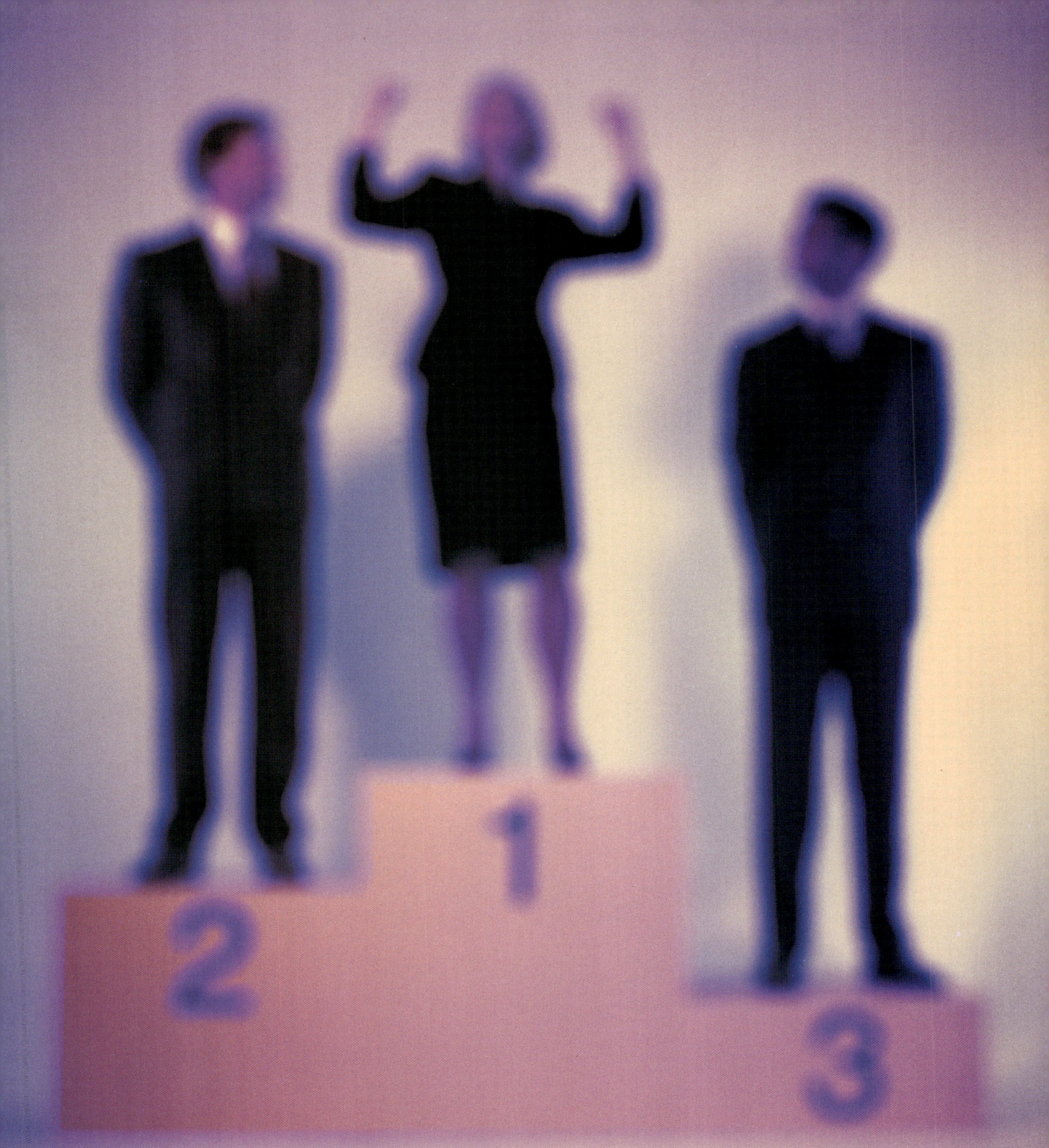

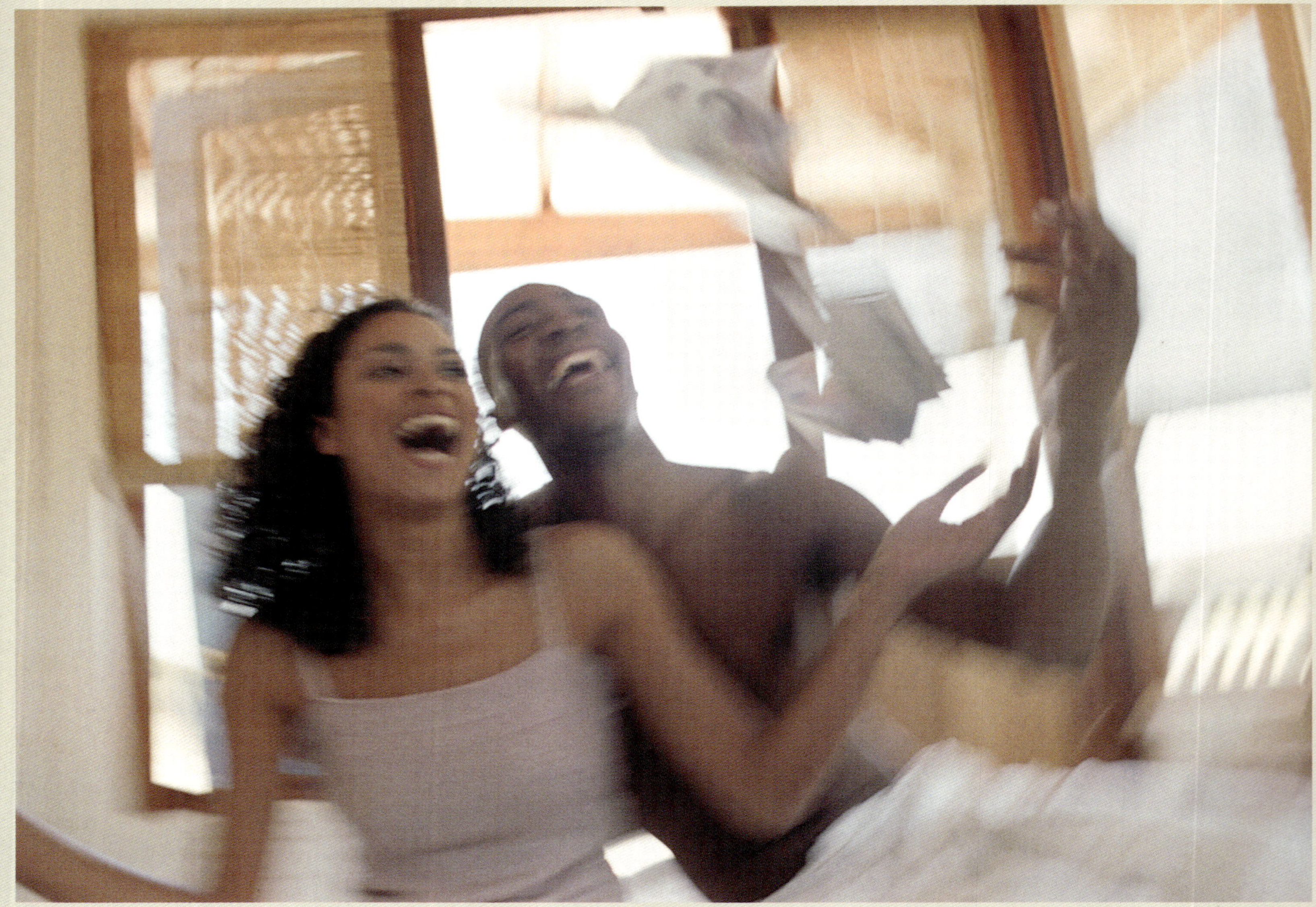

Image 4
This image is certainly a refreshing take on this topic. It explores a couple's win over household finance – a traditionally difficult subject in which to inject creativity!

Image 5
The use of sports imagery goes hand-in-hand with the 'winning spirit' theme. This shot uses the power of direct eye-contact to make its bold statement.

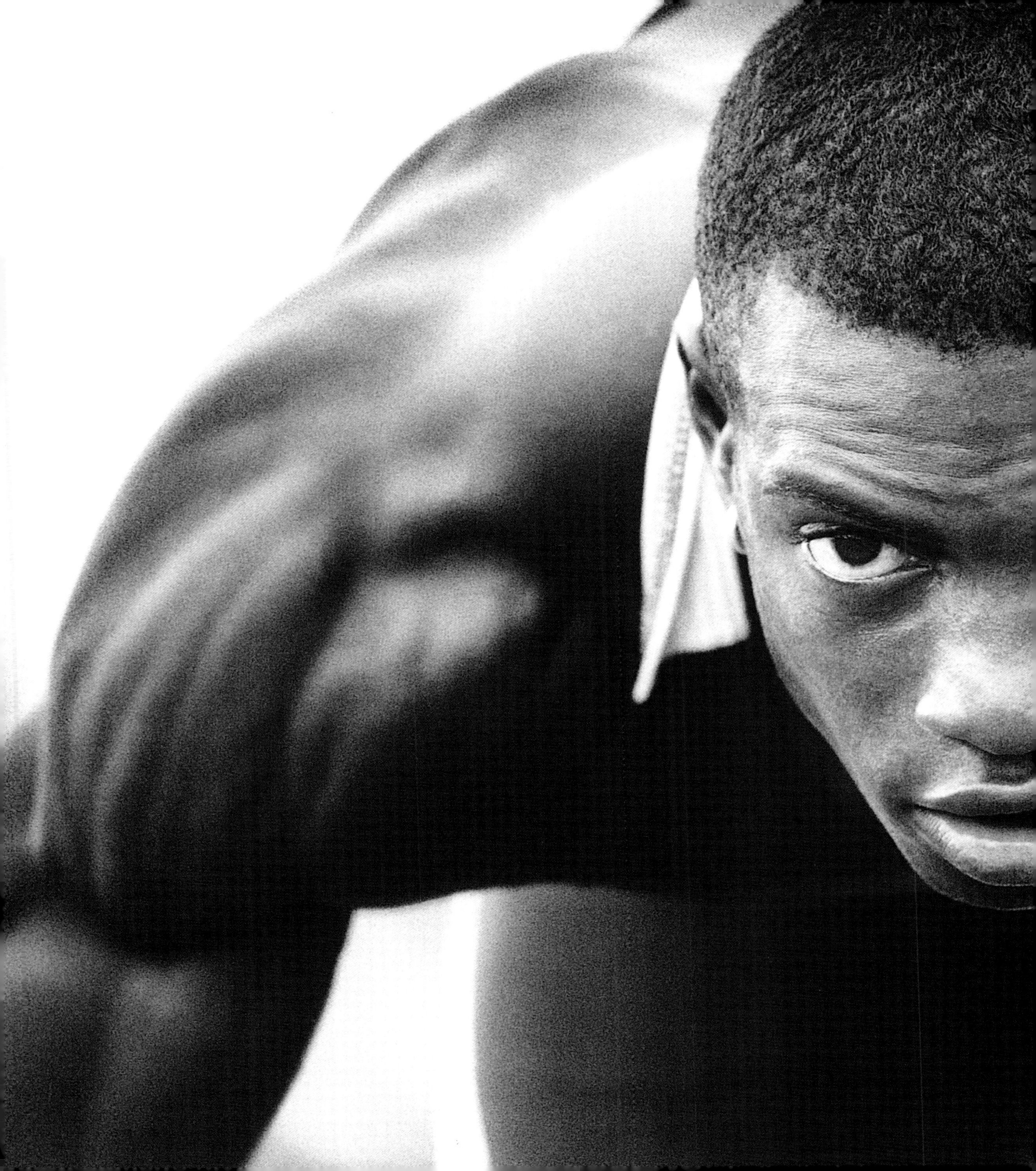

Global Business

The common phrase, 'the changing face of business', conjurs up, amongst other things, mobile phones, internet technologies and computers. And, while the phones have become slimmer and the computers more colourful, it is the actual faces of the people within the meetings that have gone through the biggest revolution.

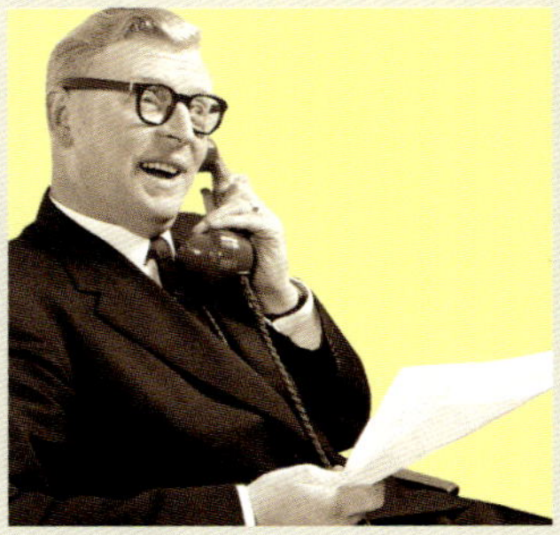

Image 1
While this average businessman image has been 'coloured-up', the overall look and feel is retro in nature. Note the size of the telephone's mouthpiece and his clothing – clear indications of which period the image is trying to capture.

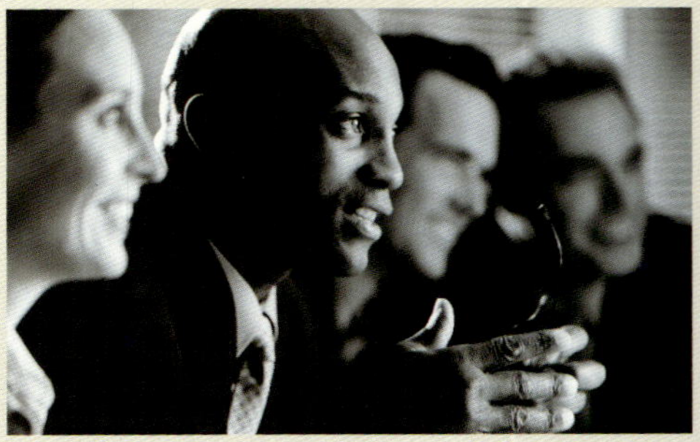

Image 2
While this image is in black and white, the overall composition is modern. Note that the meeting participants are in profile and look relaxed. The photographer has captured the essence of a 'true' business meeting without the stiffness seen in Image 1.

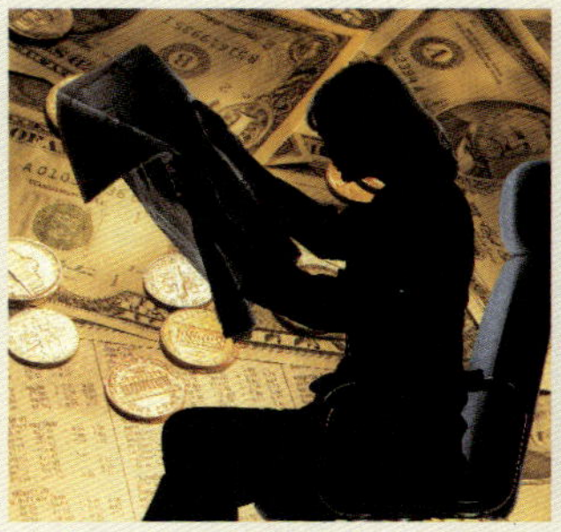

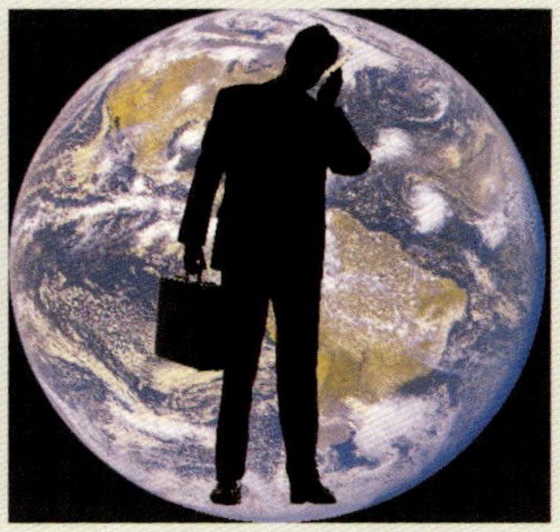

Images 3 and 4
In the late 1980s and '90s, photographers began experimenting with compositing elements and backgrounds with pictures of business people. These early shots show the concepts of high finance and global business.

Image 5
The composition of this photograph with the model's body slightly distended and cartoon-like was popular in the 1990s. The actual way to achieve these results is for the photographer to stand on a ladder.

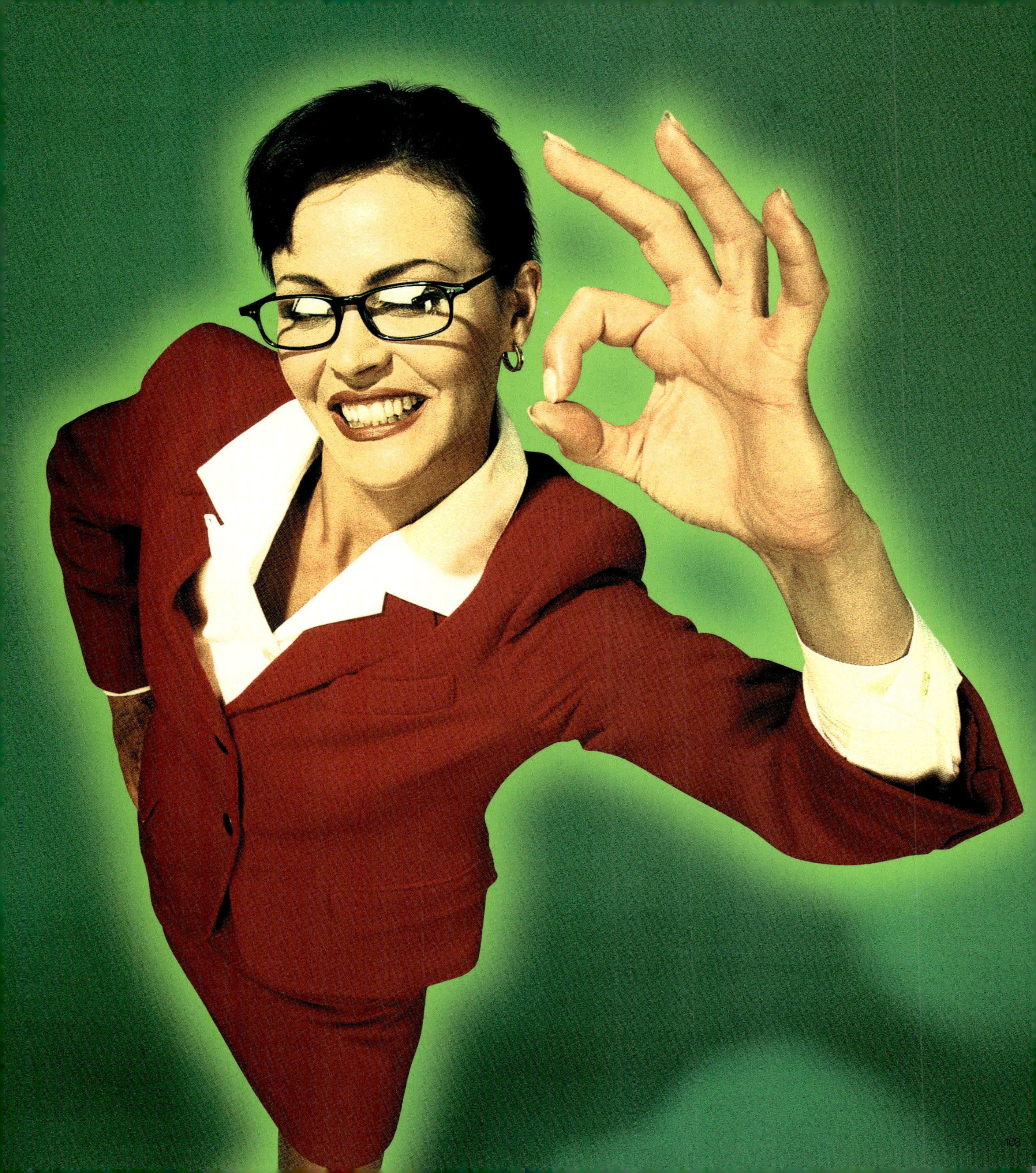

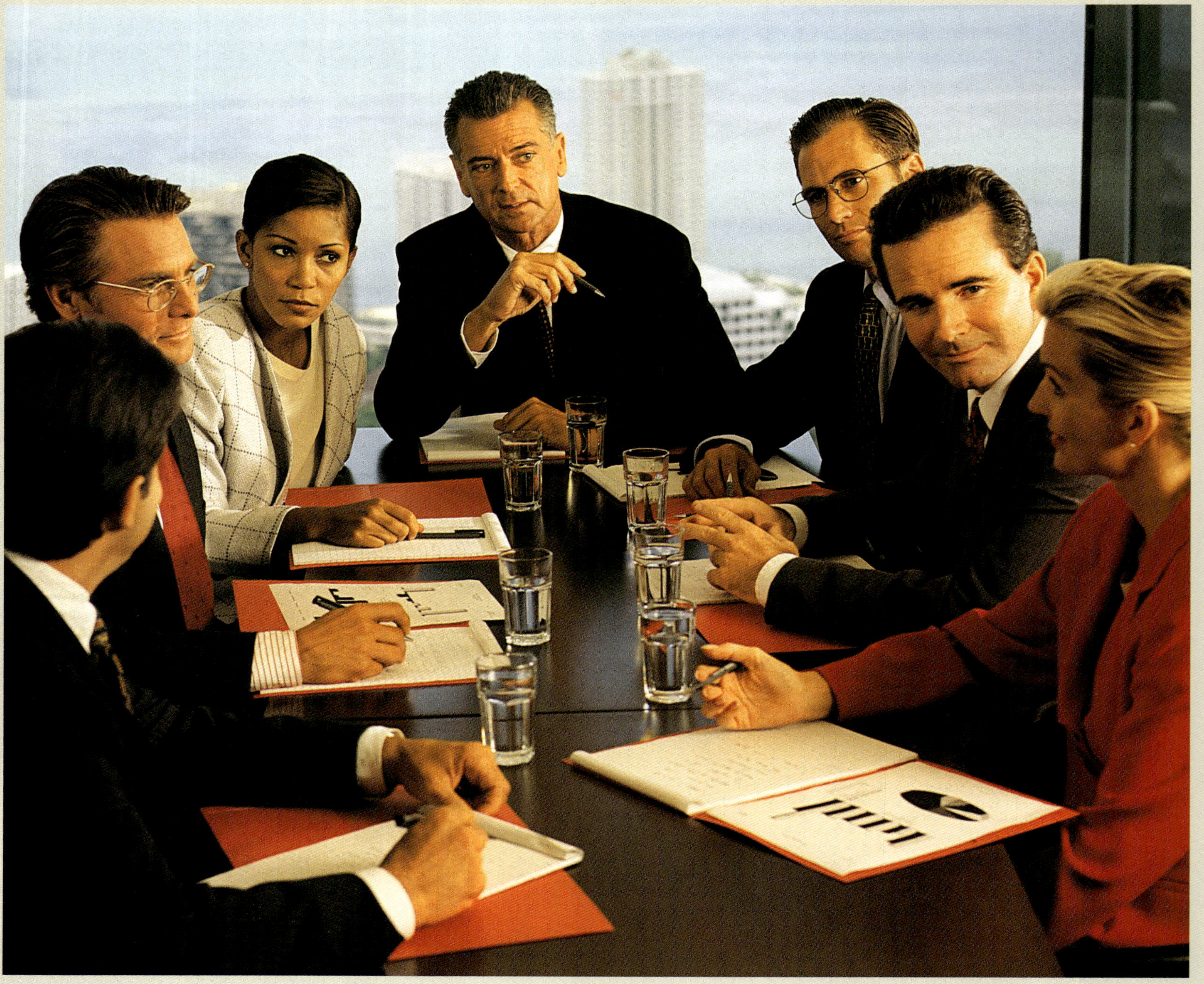

Image 6
Office meetings and conferences are popular subjects since they can be used both in corporate literature and for the hospitality industry. Larger hotels have discovered the profitability of conference planning and are heavy purchasers of this type of poised, rather safe shot. This shot, which now seems a little tired, was extremely successful when released since it had the right ethnic and sexual mix, styling, colour palette, look and feel.

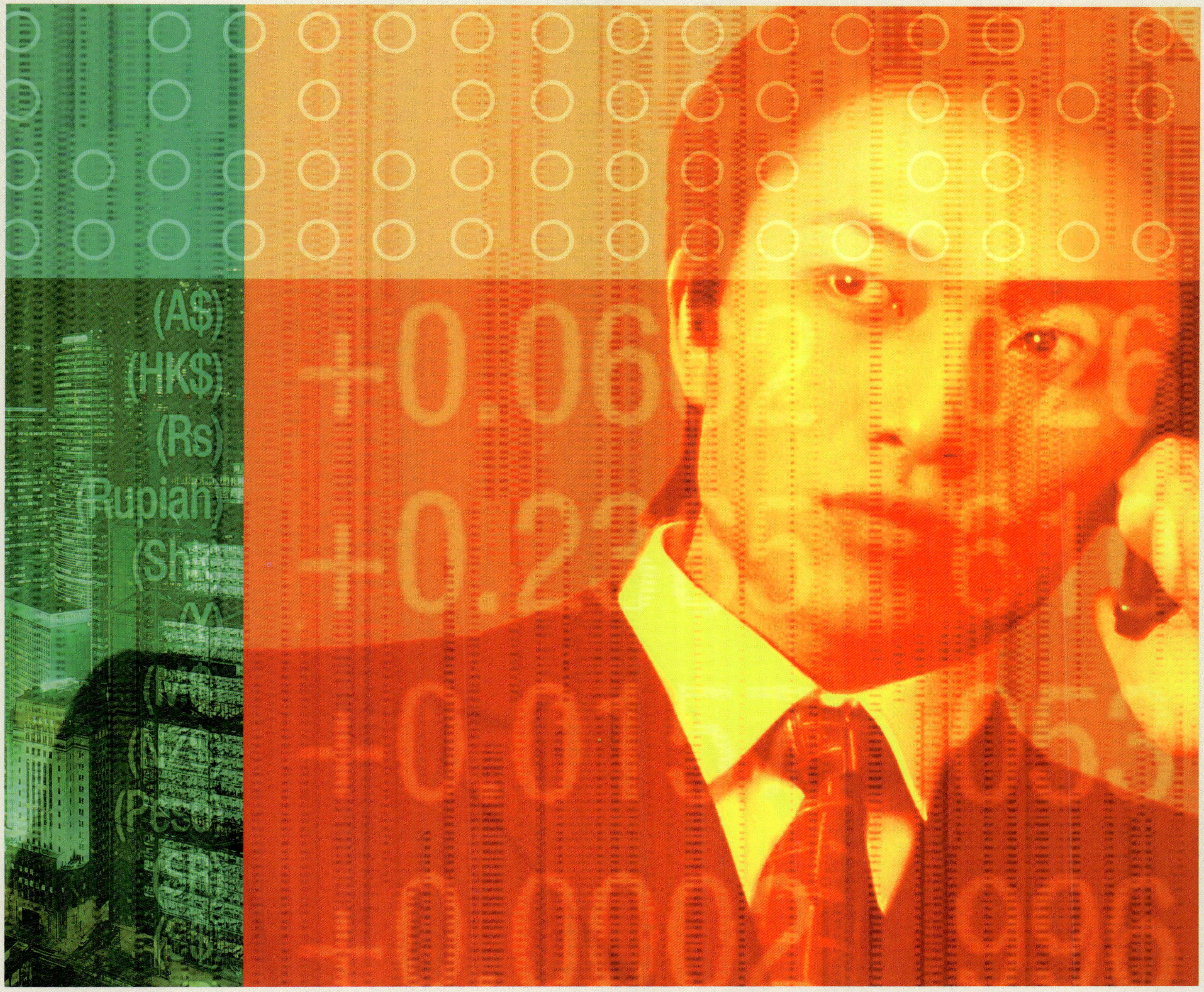

Image 7
This much more recent image also speaks to the concepts of high finance and global business like Images 3 and 4, but it is far more sophisticated. This effect, created in Adobe Photoshop, combines modern graphic design with imaginative cropping in a multi-layered form. Often, for this type of image, a photographer will work in conjunction with a graphic designer to ensure the best possible result.

Young Lifestyles

Portraying a certain demographic, such as people aged 18–35, can prove quite challenging to a photographer. If you yourself are not within that age range, your images run the danger of reflecting only how you 'perceive' that group to appear.

In essence, it is rather like an older person giving a teenage grandchild a gift that they think is hip – the recipient will smile and relegate the gift to the back of the closet! Ideally, for shooting lifestyle-based imagery for the youth market, you may want to consider using a stylist who is aware of trends or even have the models themselves give you feedback.

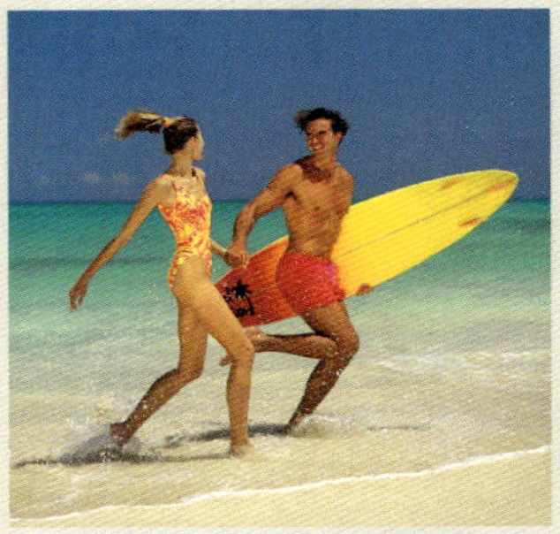

Image 1
Until a couple of years ago, this type of image was considered *de rigueur* for the holiday market, and to be truthful, that has been one of the reasons why stock photography was considered a poor relation to commissioned shoots. This image, with its smiling happy bronzed people on the beach still has its uses, but to today's audiences, the composition and saturated colouring make it appear dated.

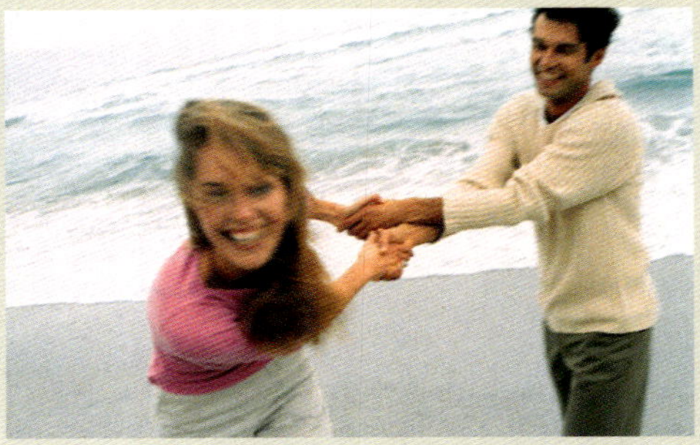

Image 2
Contrast this recently taken image with Image 1. Note the more relaxed composition, clothing and cropping. The pastel hues and direct glance by the model are both contemporary features.

Image 3 (below)
This image follows a similar style. Shots taken in bars, pubs and restaurants are normally far more posed.

Image 4 (right)
There are always requests for more 'natural' looking models. This image answers that brief by providing a relaxed atmosphere with sophisticated lighting.

Images 5 and 6 (overleaf)
Contemporary images tend to be reliant on tight cropping and less formal body language.

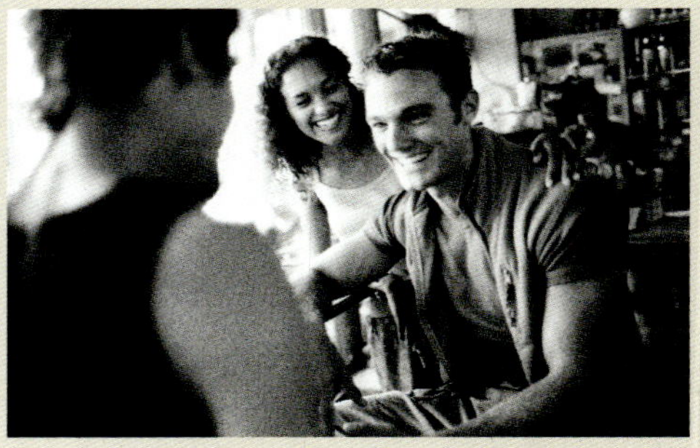

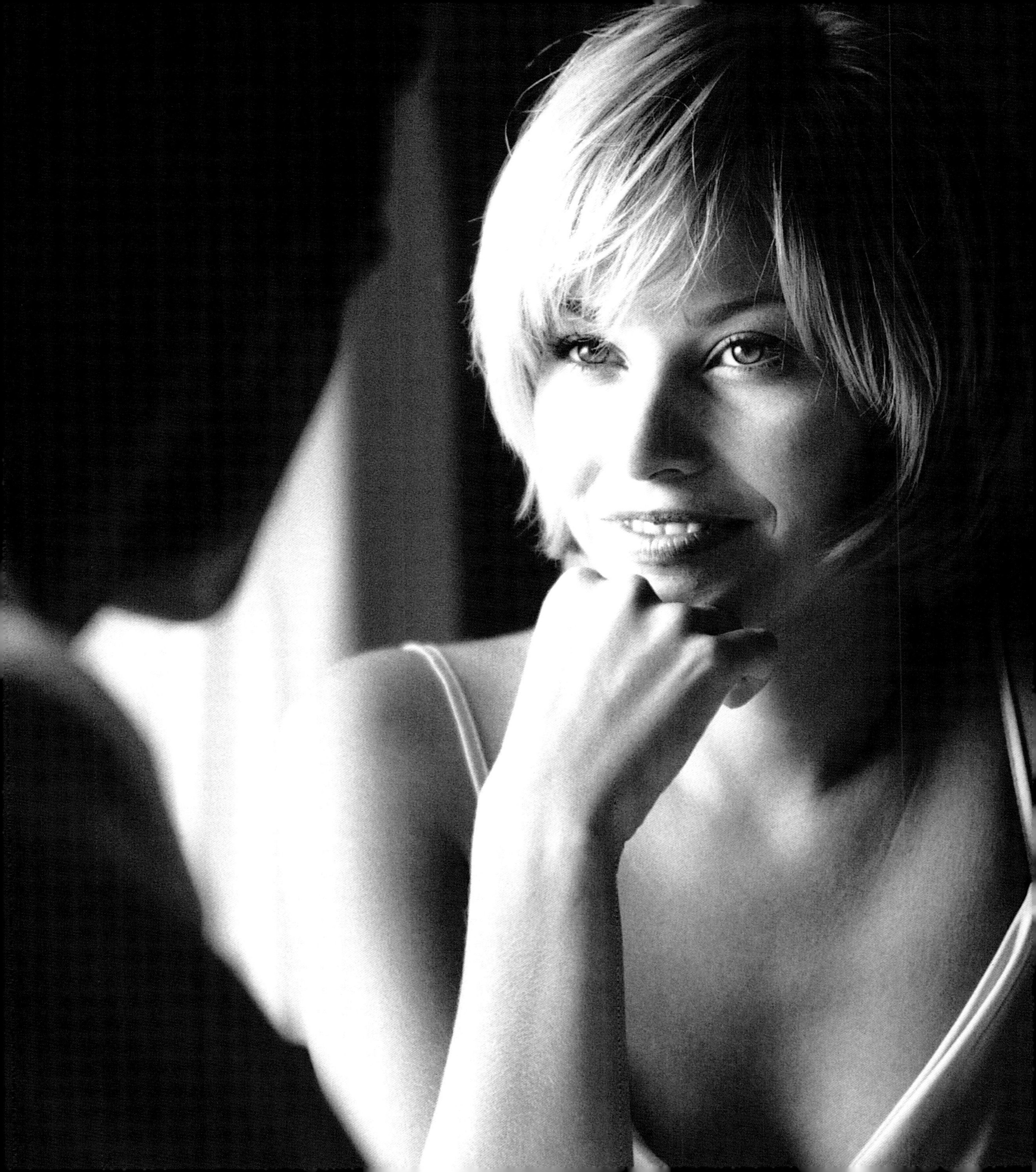

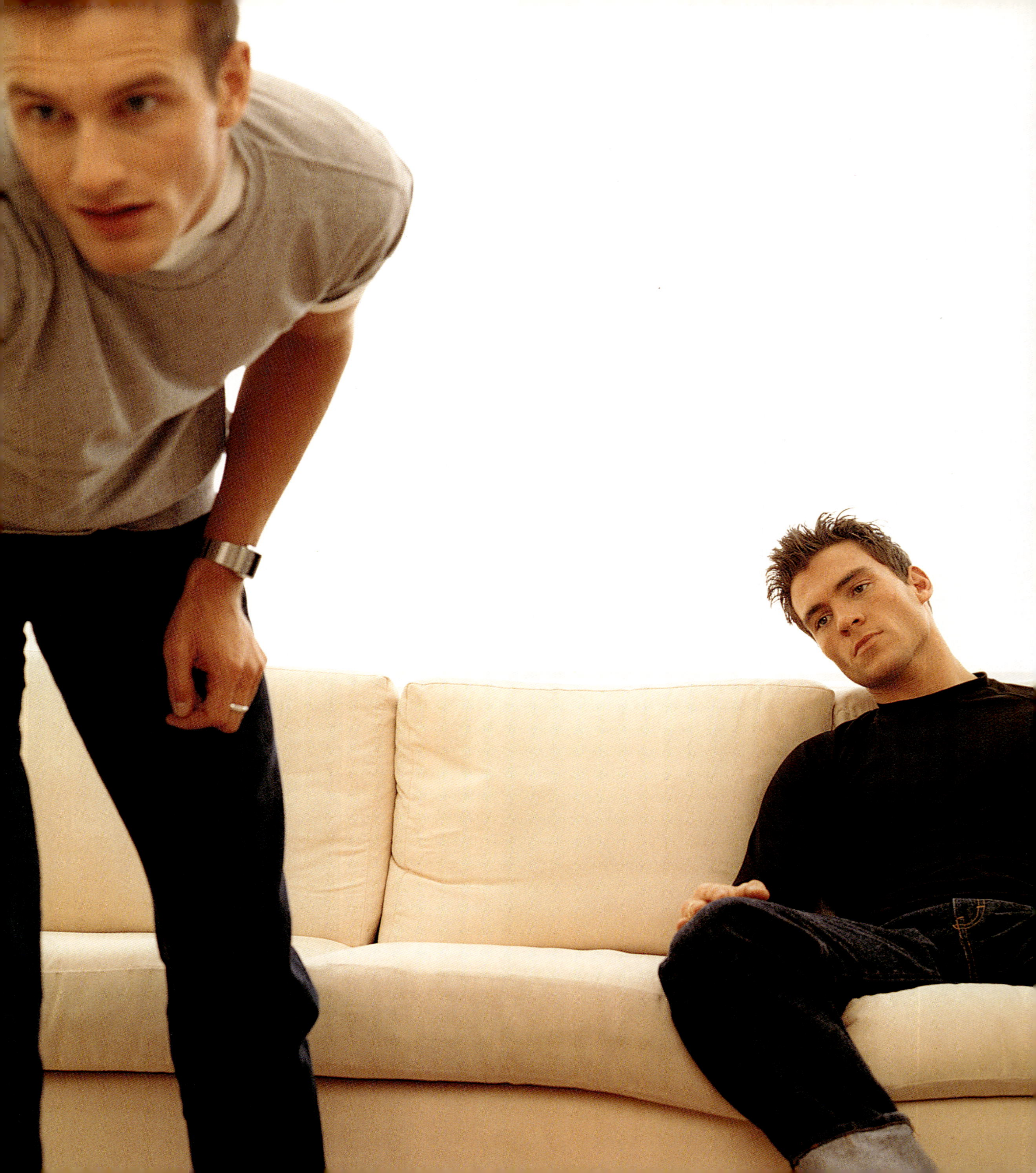

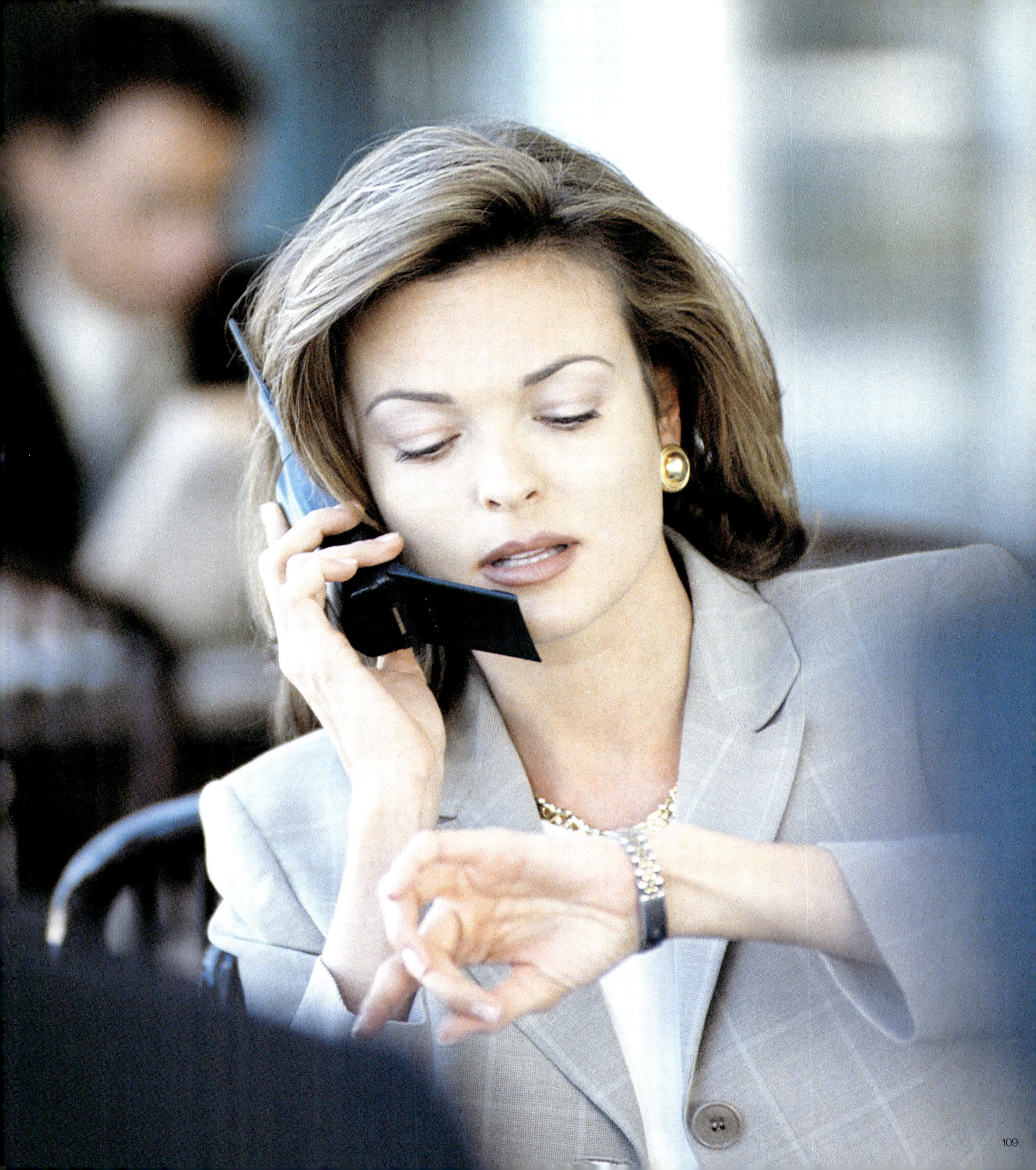

Healthcare

The subject of people's health is a popular stock subject. On a literal level, images of stethoscopes, doctors and pills are used to describe procedures, services, etc.

On a conceptual level, these images are used frequently to describe more complex ideas such as 'curing what ails you' and 'taking care of oneself'. It is this range of requirements that make healthcare an enduring theme for the stock industry.

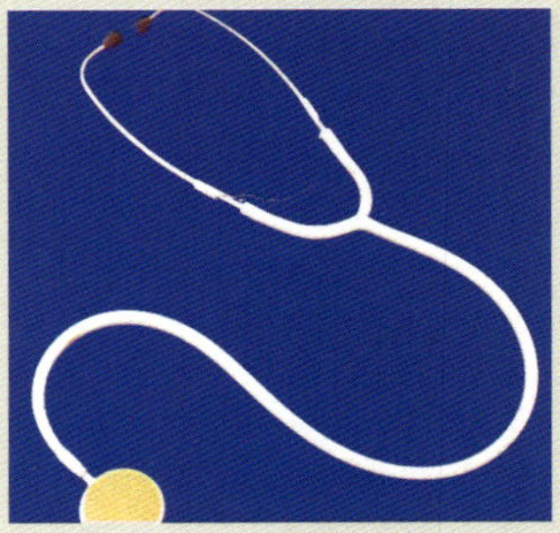

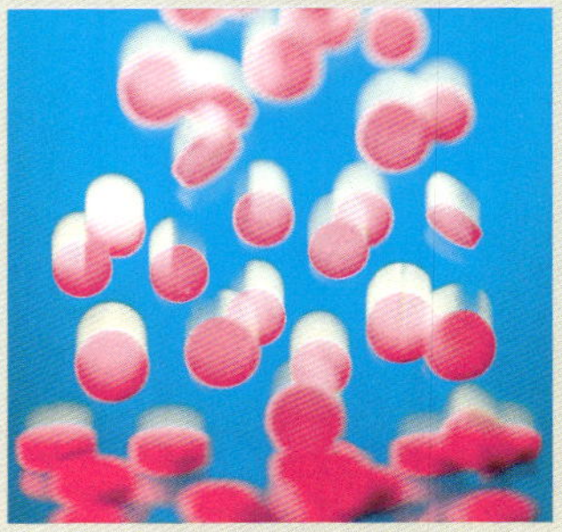

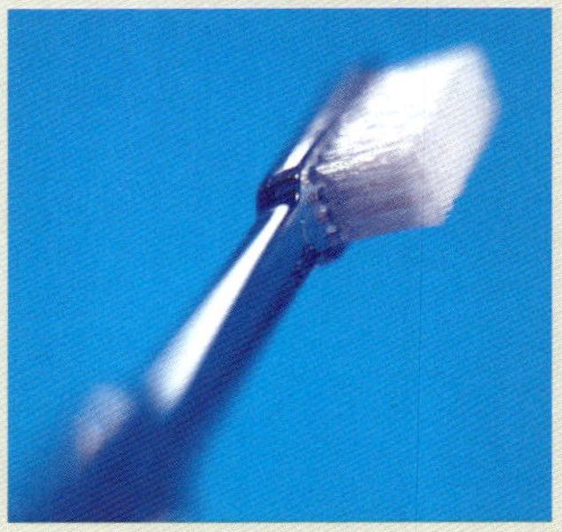

Images 1, 2 and 3
To give people's need for medicine and healthcare a more friendly face, some photographers have created iconic, colourful images which treat things such as stethoscopes, pills and toothbrushes as graphic items. The fields of bright colour available in these shots mean the images lend themselves to type treatments which work well on solid tones.

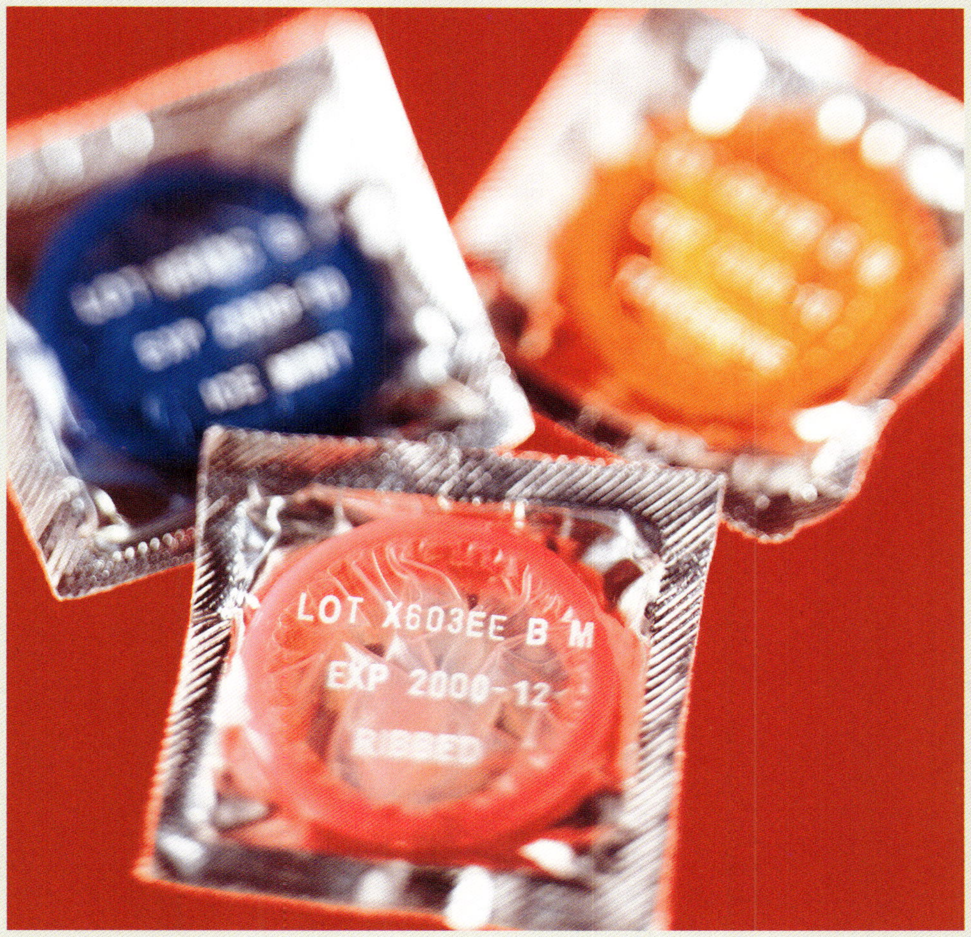

Image 4
In the 1980s the AIDS epidemic was gaining media attention and with it came the call to show 'protection' in advertising. Showing contraceptives until this point was limited to the outside of the boxes of the Pill and condoms, and the actual product wasn't shown.

Advertisers needing to get their message across quickly – and with a degree of shock value – began using images of condoms. Since a condom package is actually a 'circle within a square' the images and compositions were quite iconic in nature. To add to the friendly tone, bright colours were added to further enhance the shape of the product.

Image 5 (overleaf)
This image shows a conceptual approach to women's health. The superimposed clock may be interpreted as reproductive time, or even time left after an illness has been diagnosed.

Image 6 (overleaf)
This shot is once again a conceptual way of portraying women's health, and its bright orange colour is optimistic. The circles can represent the effects that illness can have on someone's life and family.

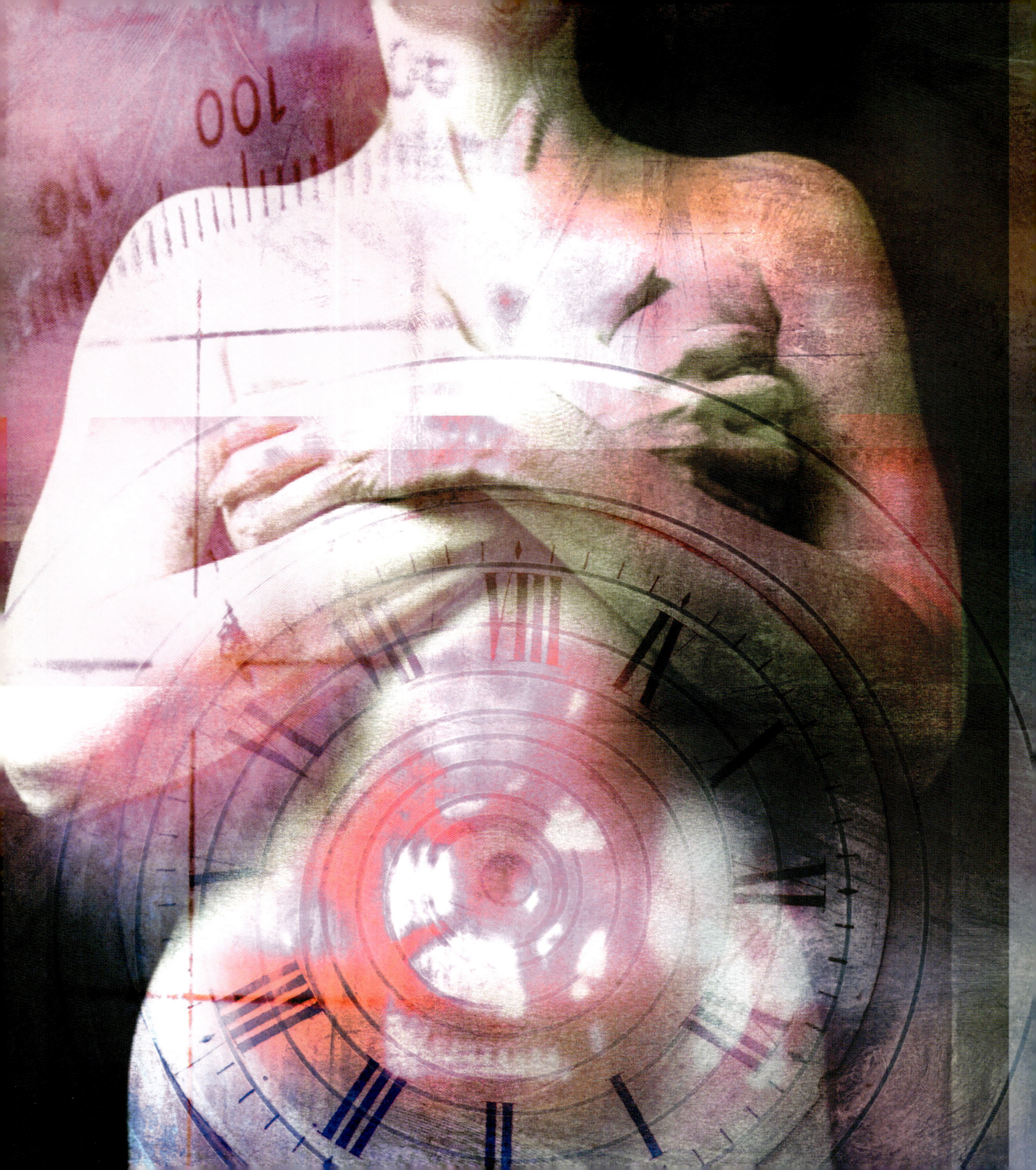

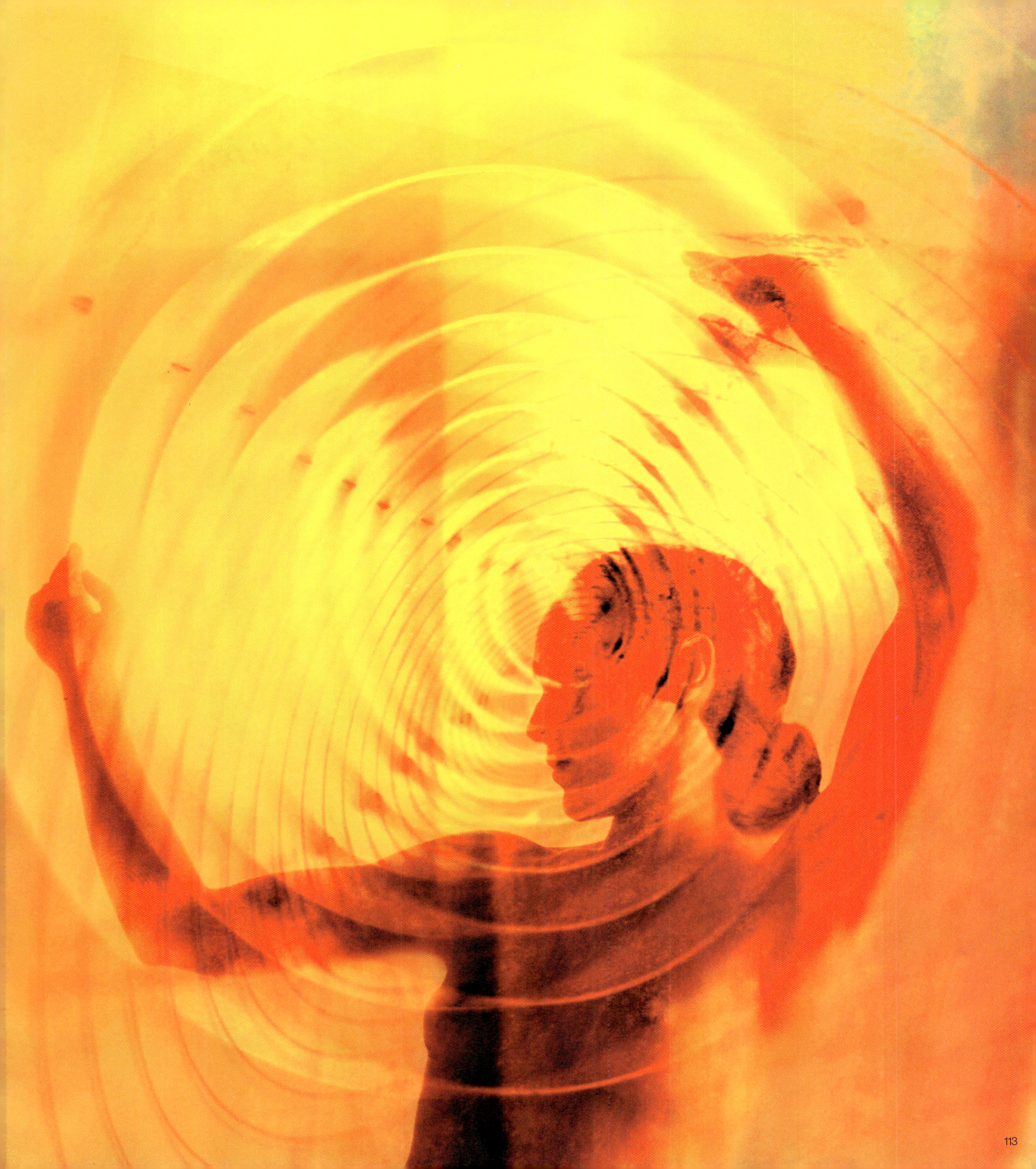

Portraiture

Adding a human face to an advertising campaign immediately gives a warmer edge to any product or service, and when a single person is shown, he or she represents how a company views itself. When an older man in a suit is shown, for example, that could mean 'credibility'. If a young person in streetwear is featured, the company might be portraying 'vitality' and 'energy'. This wide need for images is a perfect market for the stock photographer.

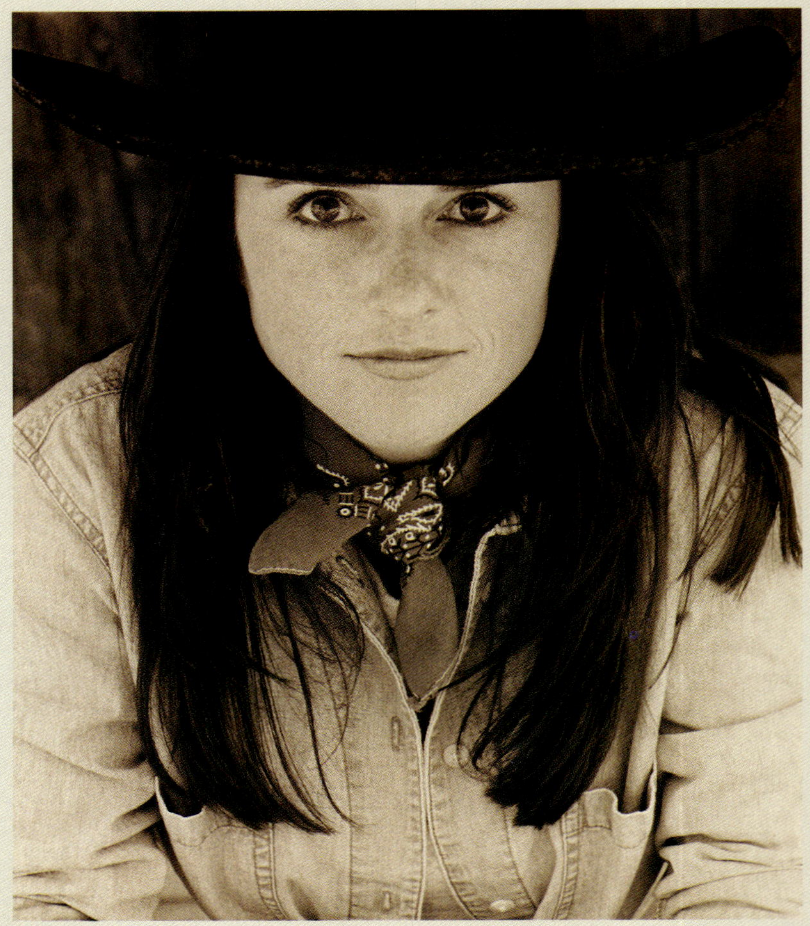

Image 1
Given the Western wear theme, this image will have limited commercial appeal, however, the strong cropping and textures coupled with the model's piercing glance make the image a powerful one.

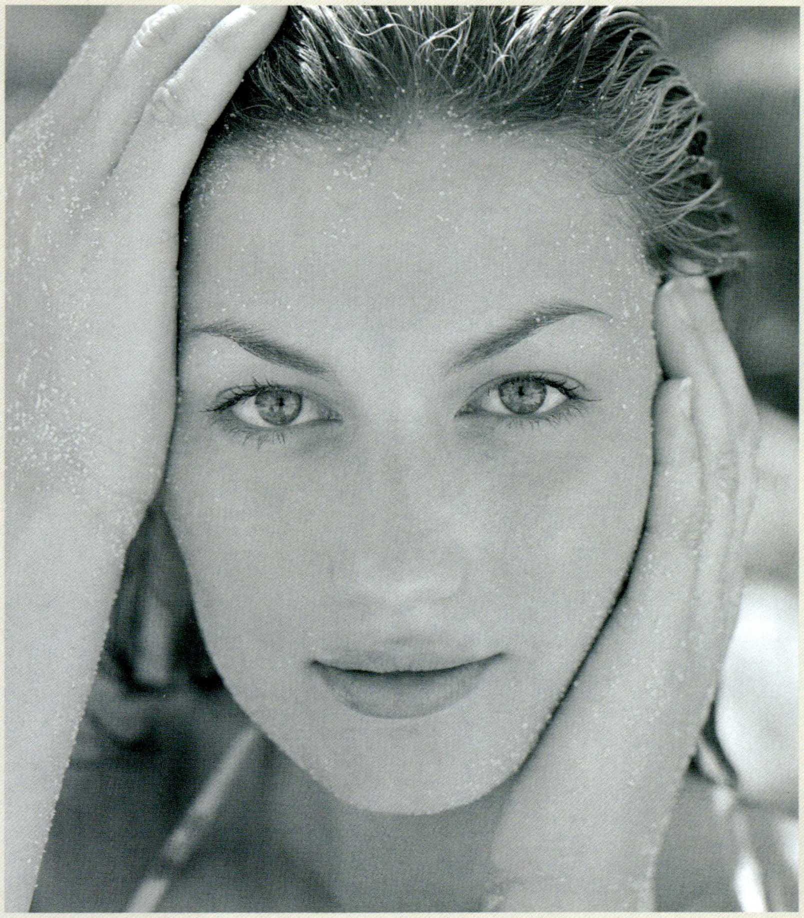

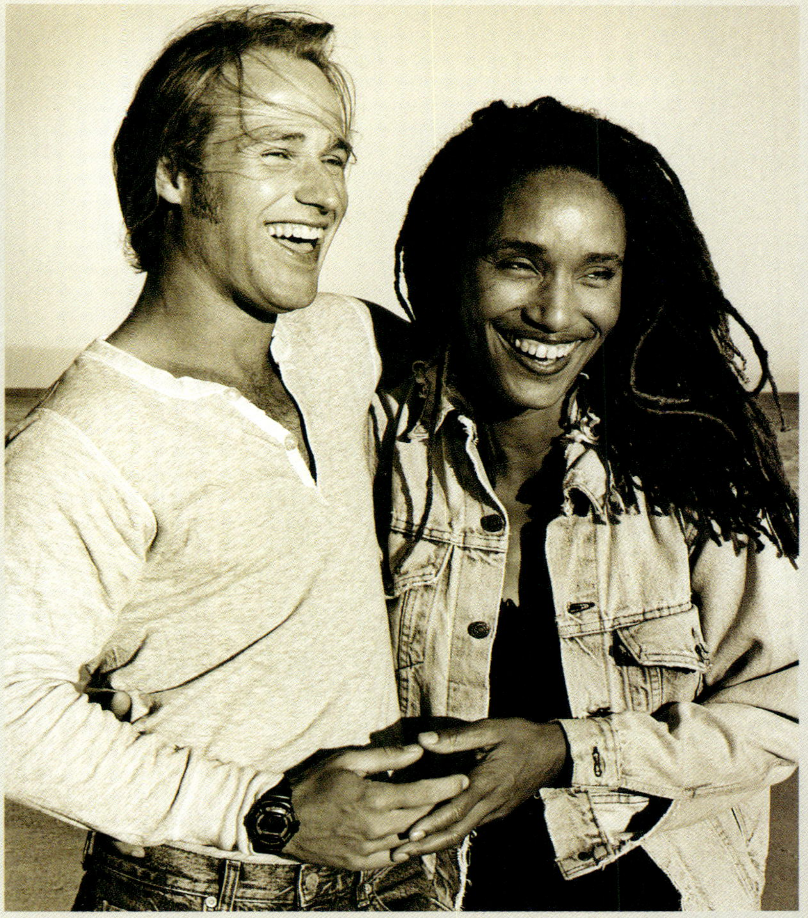

Images 2 and 3
A common theme for people portraiture is 'healthy living' or 'vitality'. The image on the left, of a model with her hands formally arranged would be ideal for illustrating the essence of well-being. The image on the right, given the male model's running watch and carefree pose, also speaks of a clean-living lifestyle. Inter-racial couples also figure more prominently in stock photography now – another example of how stock photographs can sometimes reflect today's social demographics.

Image 4
This unposed image was captured at a wedding and conveys the theme of shyness. The viewer's inability to see the child's full face adds, rather than detracts from, the composition.

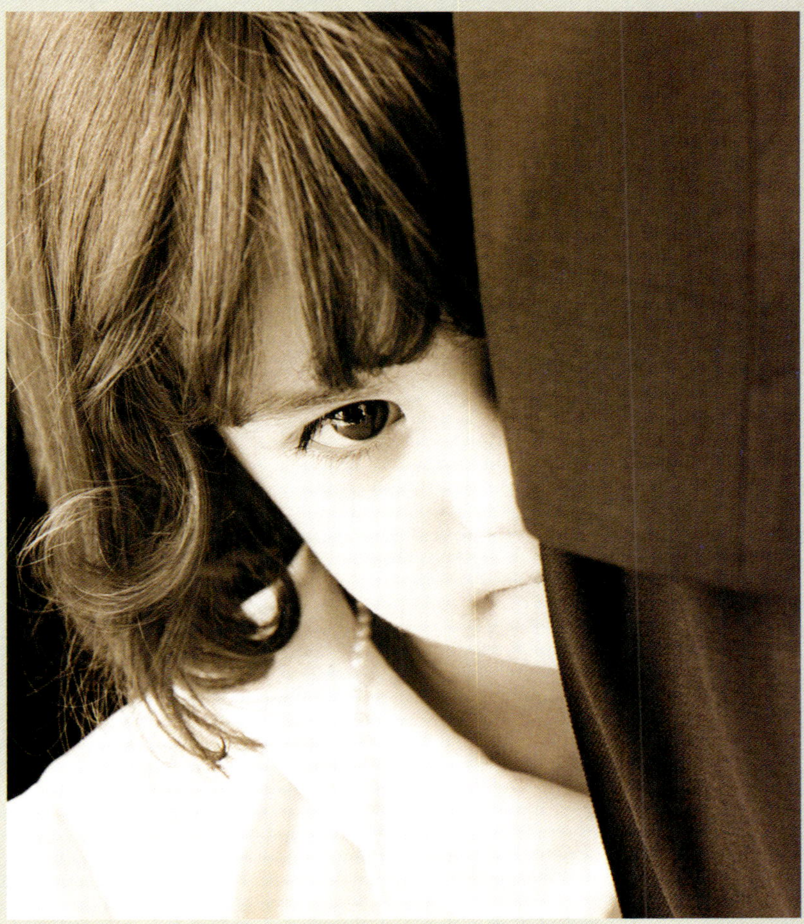

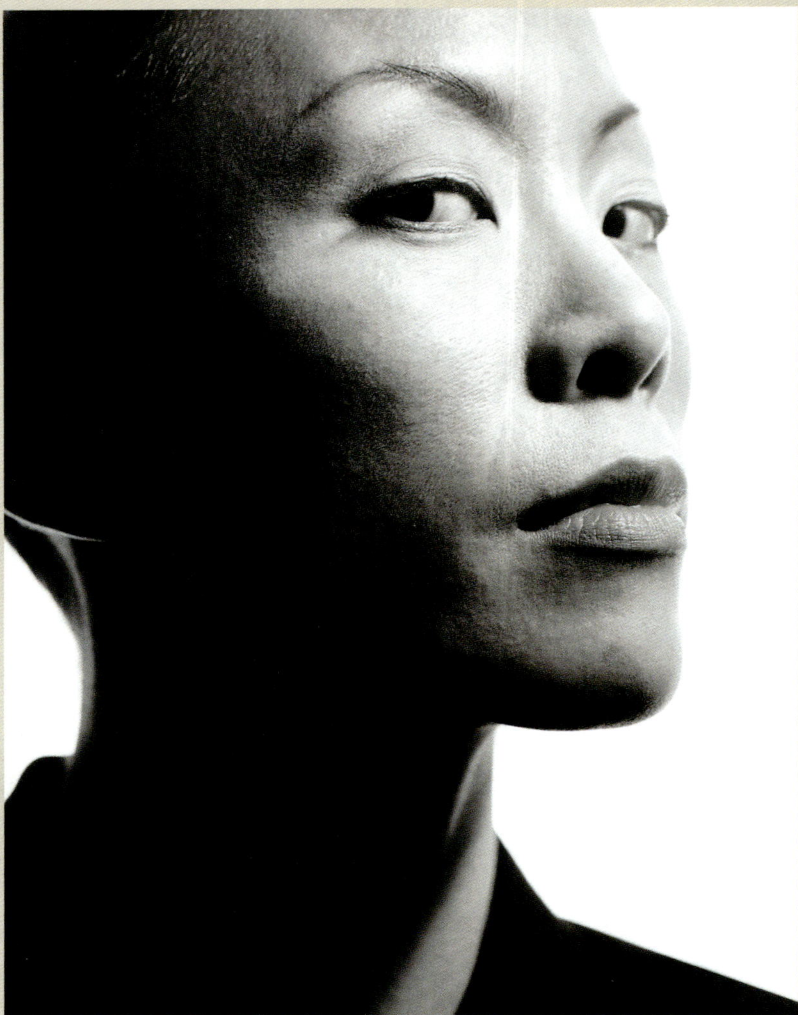

Image 5
The use of white space outside the crop of this image is ideal for magazine pieces which need clean, clear areas for the addition of text. This thoroughly modern shot pays homage to photographer David Bailey's work, at the same time as adding a bit of mystery. Is it a man or a woman?

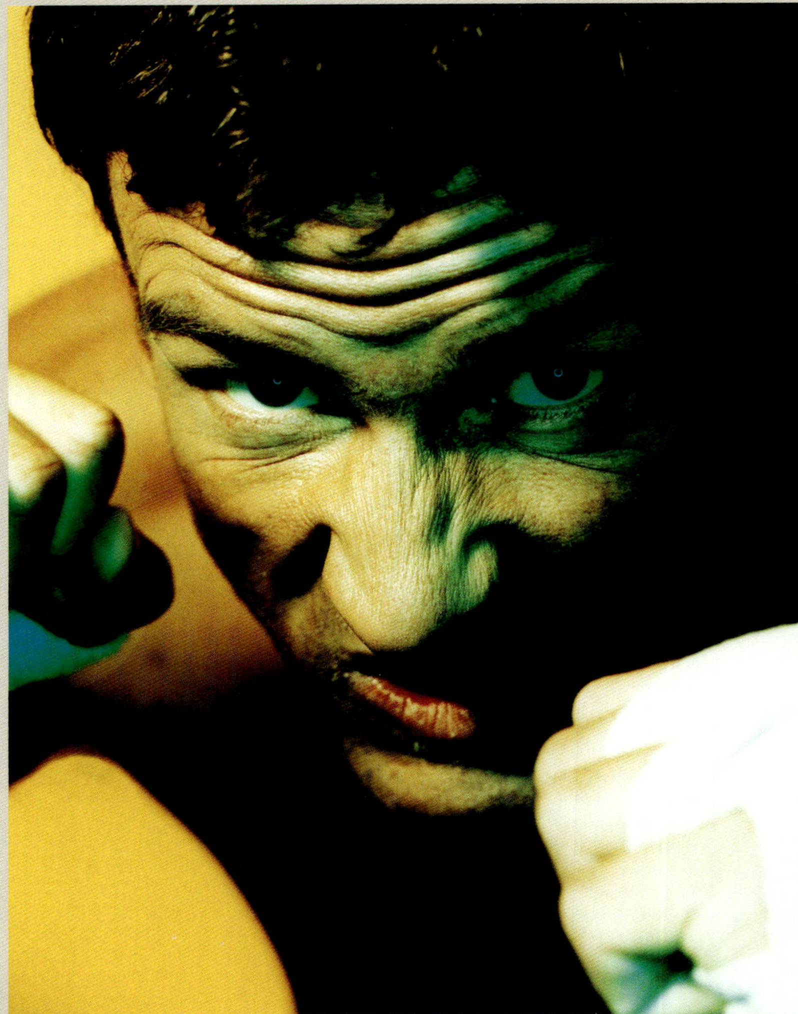

Image 6
Another image with attitude, this boxer is belligerence personified. People portraiture that inspires clearly recognised emotions is more commercial. This image, for example, can represent anger, strength or frustration.

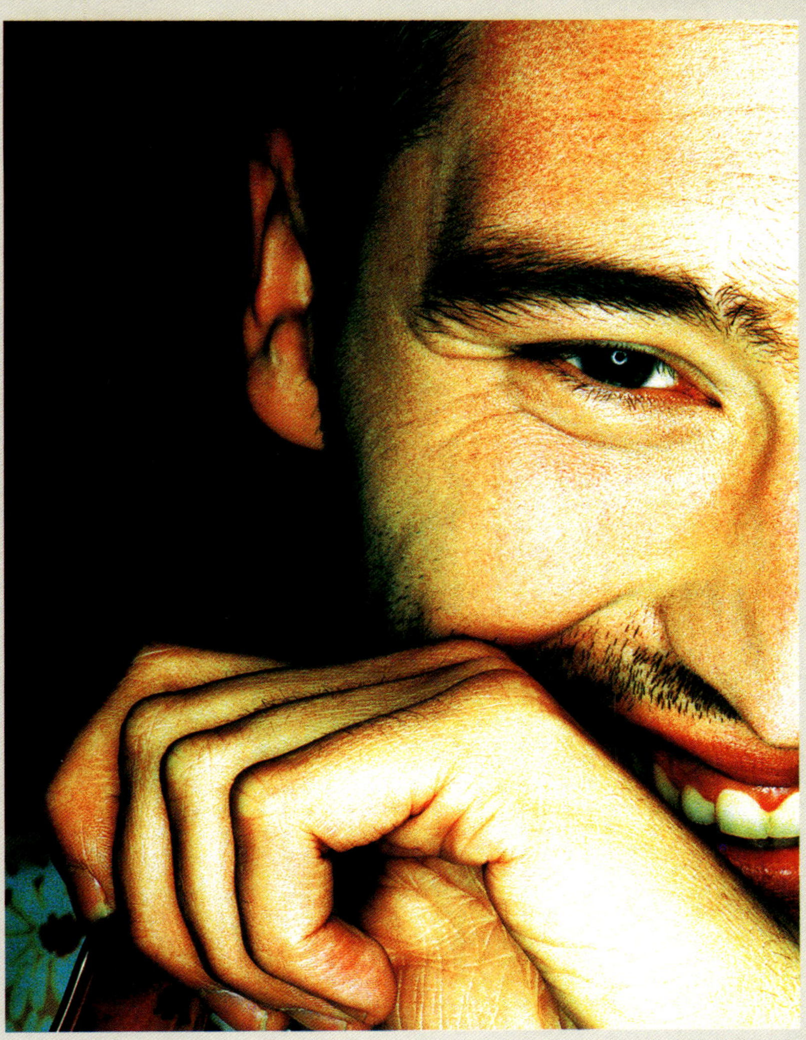

Image 7
Like Image 4, the tight cropping makes this shot more interesting. The model's ethnic-blend look and styling make this image ideal for the music industry or any youth culture company.

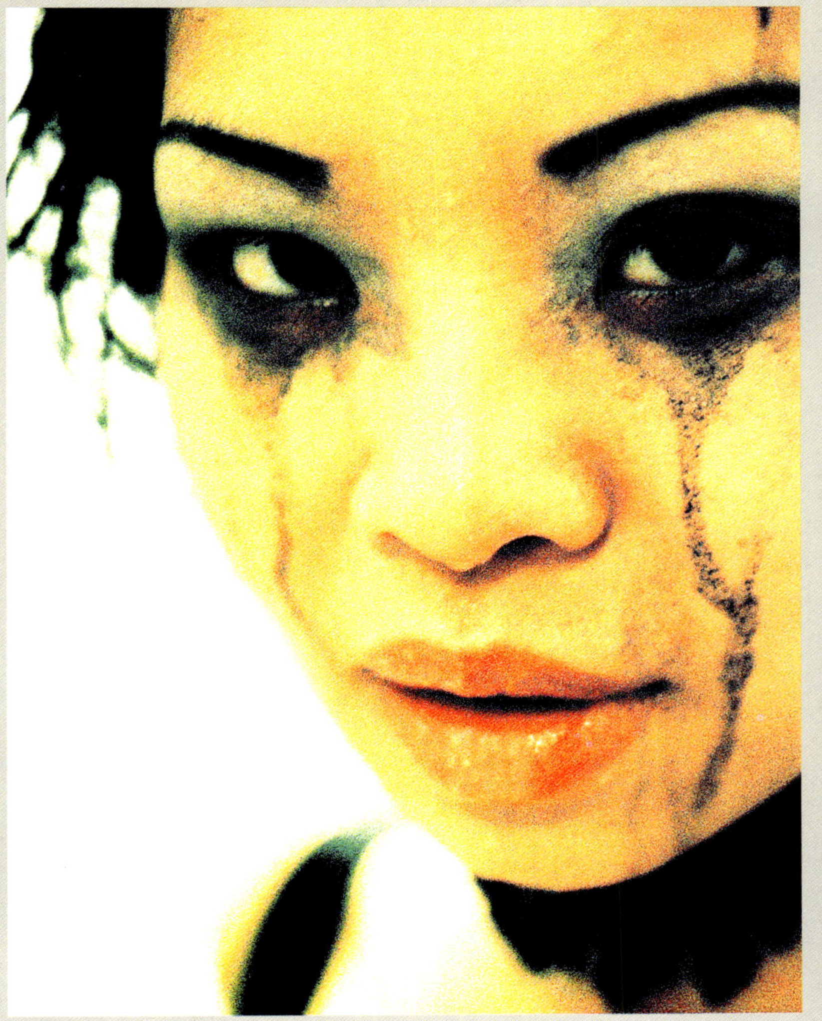

Image 8
Although the majority of customers seek aspirational images in which people are smiling, there is still a requirement for images that are evocative of less pleasant circumstances. This image could represent anything from date rape to drug abuse.

Chapter 6
Future Trends in the Stock Industry 118 – 129

The Zeitgeist of Stock

Historically, it has always been a strong feature of stock to mimic its successes and to provide the buyer with fairly obvious, and at times, stereotypical image solutions. Thankfully this feature is slowly being eroded by the more forward-thinking libraries who are giving photographers the ability to explore more varied subject matter and styling.

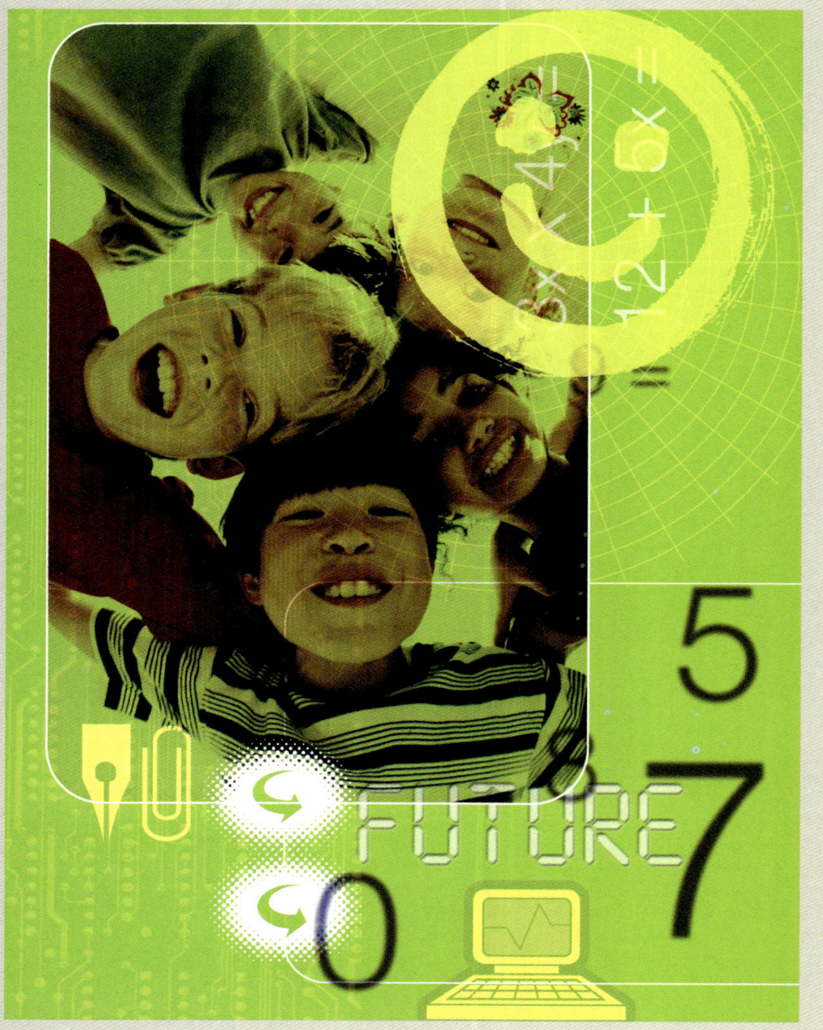

It's impossible to say exactly what stock will look like in five or ten years time. The current signs are that aesthetically there is a shift towards being more 'of the moment' in respect of photographic style, subject matter, model choice, lighting and styling, which conflicts somewhat with the generic mantle stock photography has always held. If this trend continues, it may impact on the longevity of the images that are considered good standard stock. In turn, the libraries will increase the turnaround of images, bringing them to market faster.

As the industry matures both the quality and originality of the photography are increasing. New life is constantly being injected into established stock themes. This process generates entirely new concepts – thus stock photography goes on to reflect the thinking and concerns of the day.

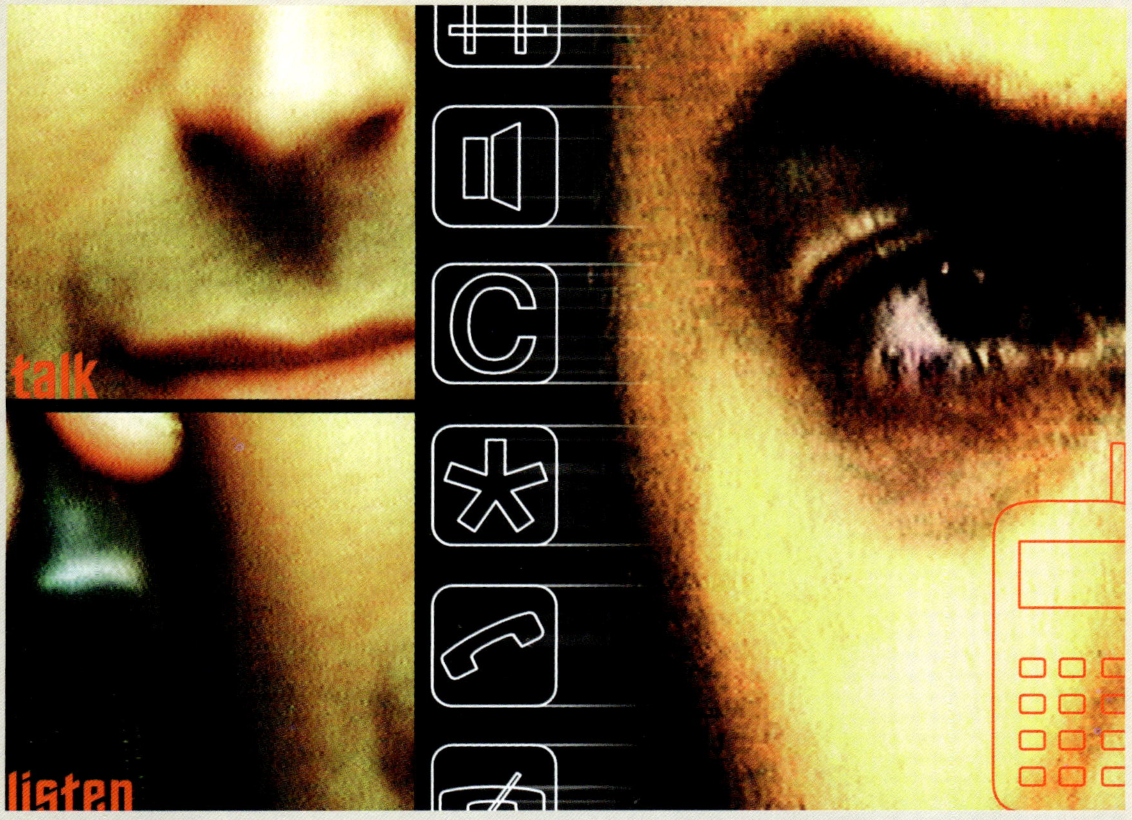
talk
listen

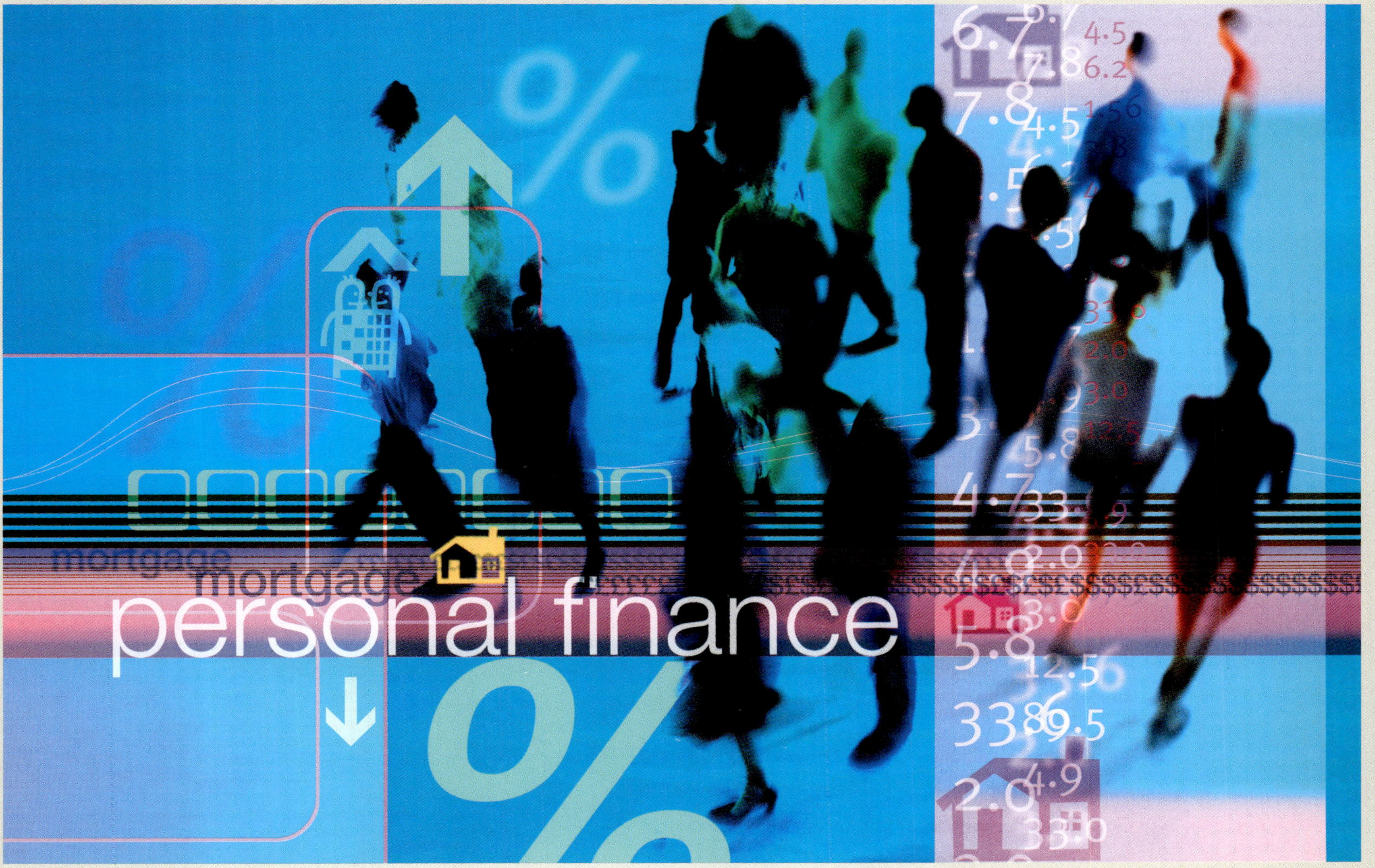
mortgage
mortgage
personal finance

Design Driven – and Leading the Design

The library which is currently pushing aesthetic boundaries is Tony Stone, whose dynamic and fresh approach to content mark it out as a trend-setter. Often, the images will look startling, even 'raw', but the styles are soon emulated by the advertising and design communities. It is an interesting twist that stock may soon drive design – rather than the other way around.

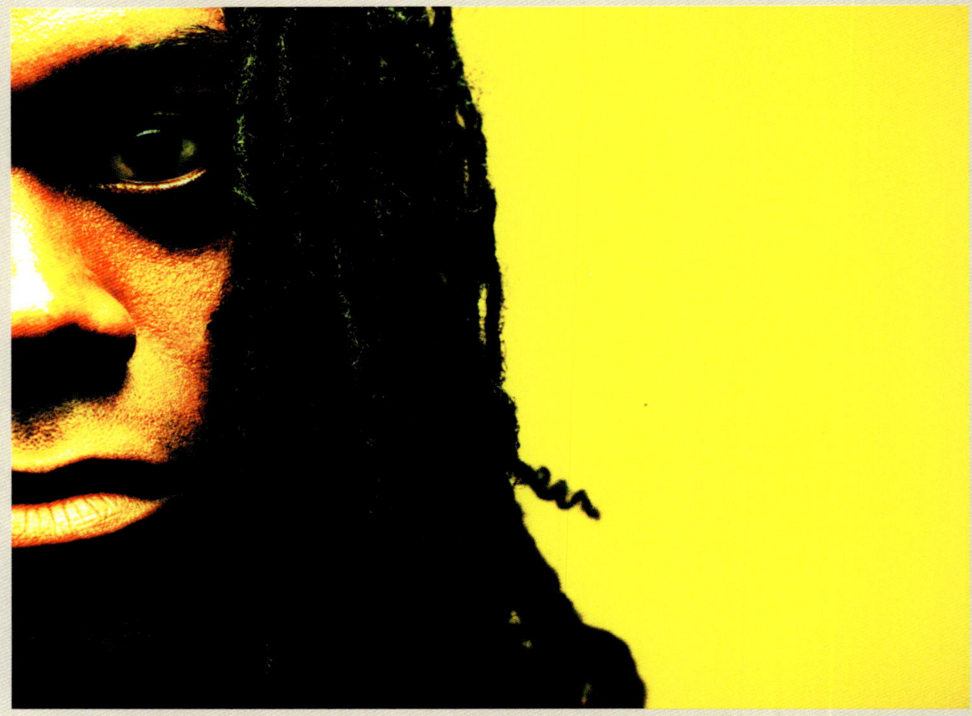

Traditionally stock has always looked to the editorial and advertising markets to keep apace with new stylistic trends. In the future it is possible that some of the trailblazing boutique shops may in turn provide style reference for these industries.

The surge in quality content of some libraries is a determined move to gain an even stronger foothold with high profile advertisers. If this trend continues, the logical extension is towards image buyers commissioning the library to provide bespoke content. This is another reversal of roles, considering that stock has been at best second choice to commissioned work.

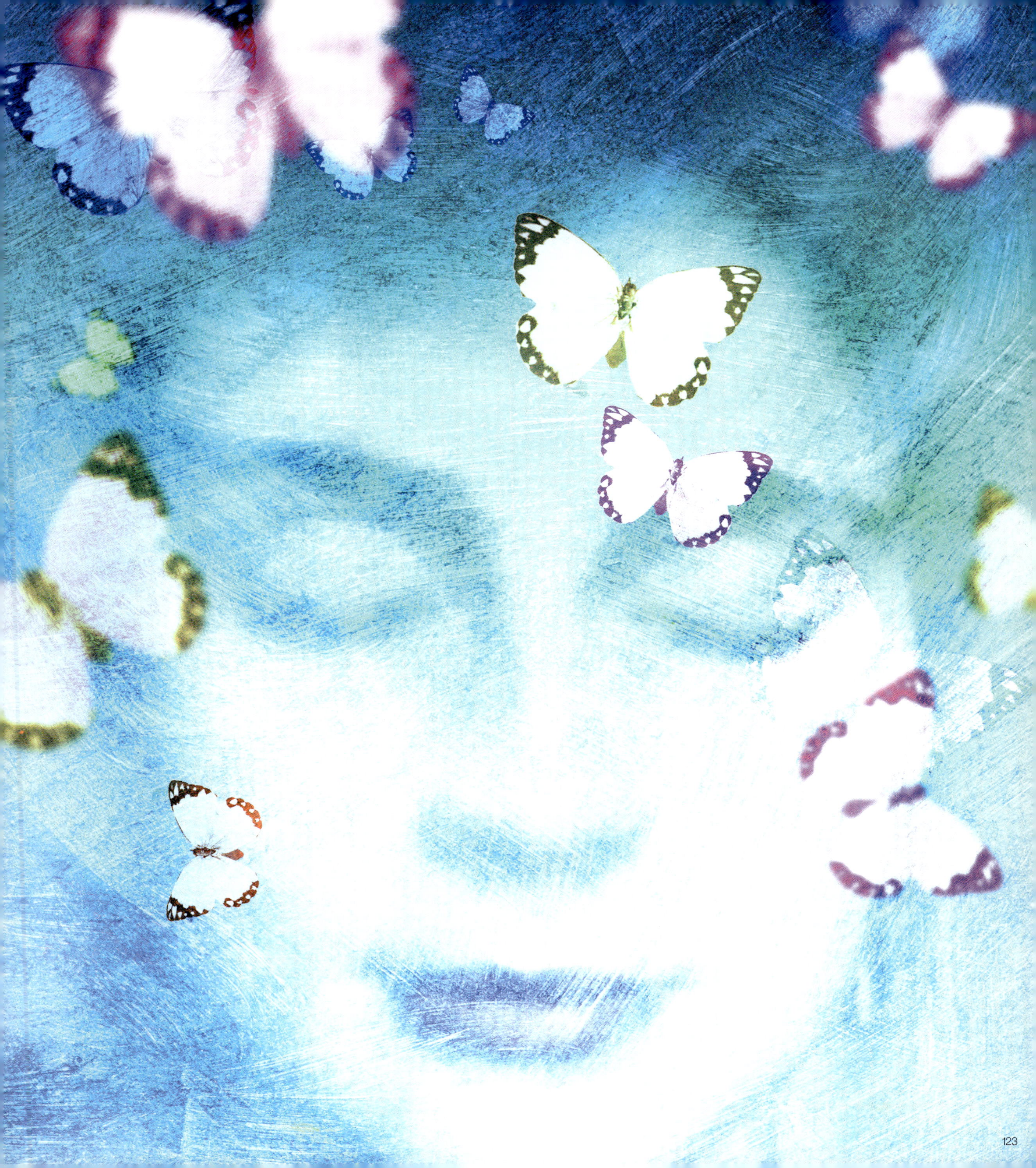

A New Look – A New Angle

Another trend which has found a firm foothold with the quality libraries is the move to use specialist photographers in an unfamiliar or unconnected field. For example, getting a fashion or style photographer to shoot a sports-based disk or business images will give a fresh dimension to the stock stalwarts.

It is likely too that the move to provide more conceptual collections will gather pace over the next few years. Stone once again leads the field with its bright and considered approach to collections where the originality of the concepts pave the way for groundbreaking photography. Recent accomplishments include the image collections 'O2', 'Meet Me' and '623', which mark a departure from the usual business, lifestyle and industry/technology divisions which collections too often fall into.

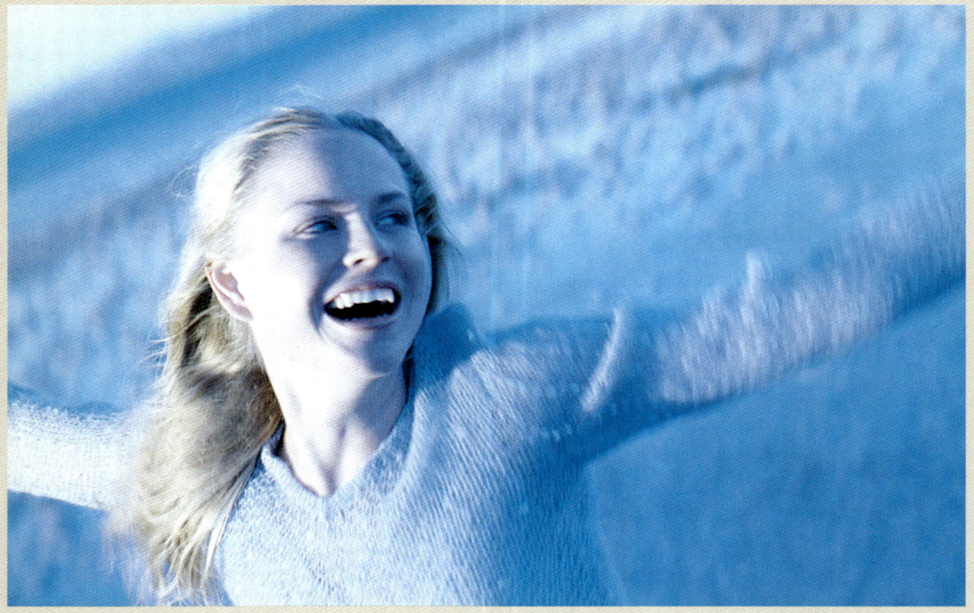

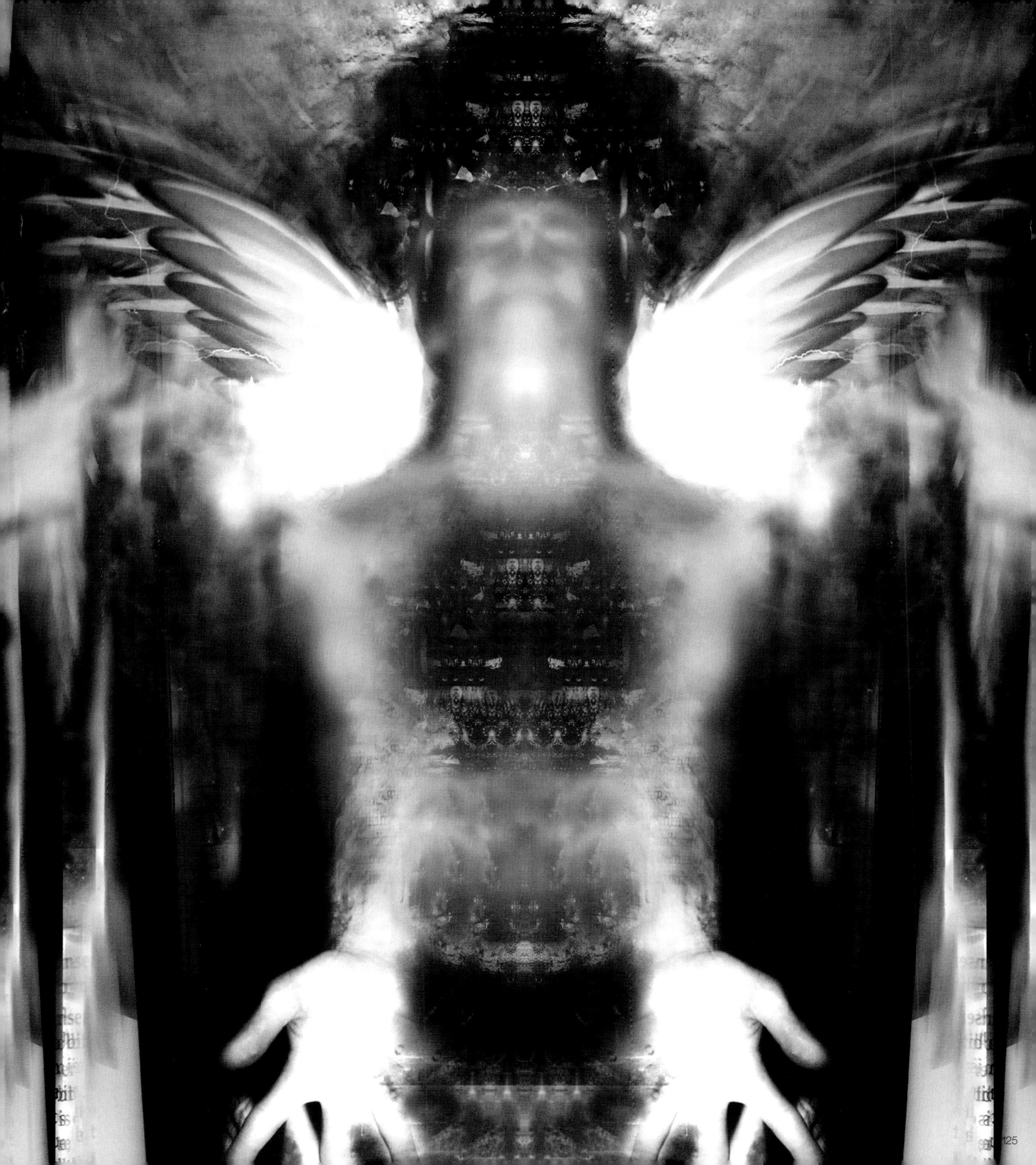

Digital Bias

The way in which content is delivered is also changing, with photographers increasingly taking charge of their own retouching and digital manipulation. With the digital age continuing to gather momentum it is likely in future that libraries will switch forever from providing transparencies to the entirely digital delivery of images. This is not a guess – more of a reality given the pressure of customer demands.

Where once photographers would deliver transparencies for an edit, images might soon be provided solely in digital format which would later be returned to the photographer to not only crop, but to colour correct, retouch and cross-process. This shifting of responsibility is a growing trend benefitting both the photographer and the stock library. The photographer gets his or her images to market much faster and the library doesn't have a backlog of images to process at once. In the future, photographers may even be requested to key-word their own images.

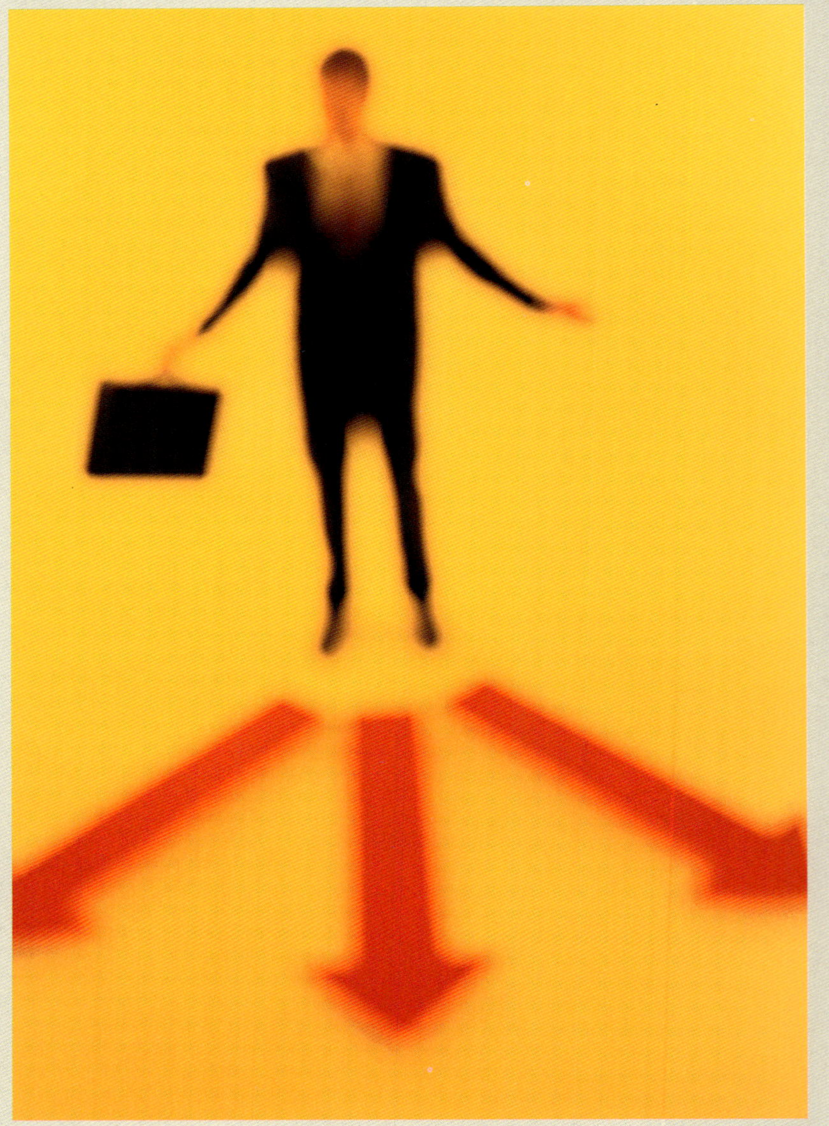

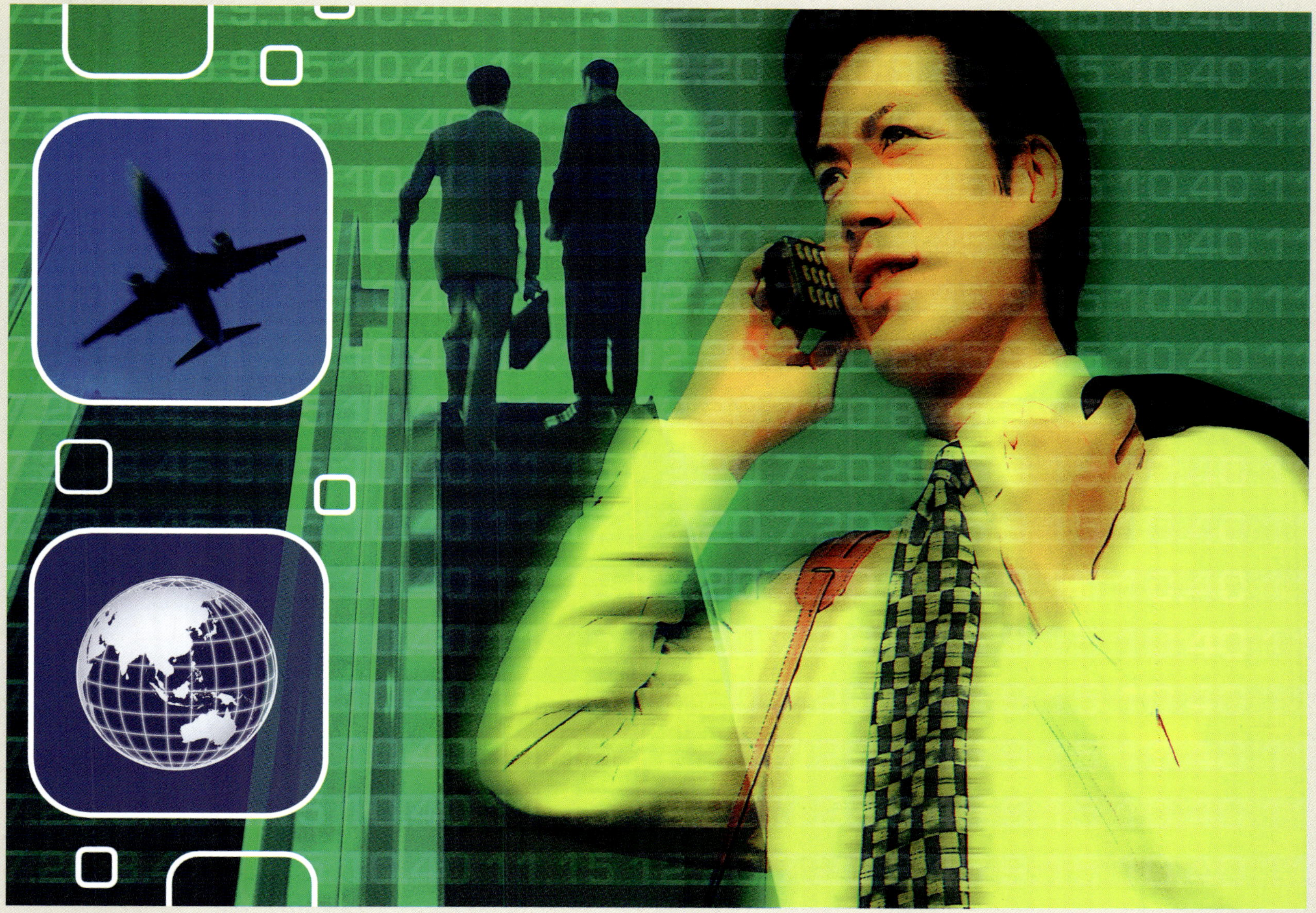

Digital Enhancement

Another trend is to fuse stock photography with digital design. While this concept is not new, the growing requirement for up-to-the-minute photographic treatments may lead compositions to contain elements of high technology or bold graphic forms. When done well, this is an exciting new avenue which can result in an almost true art form. Illustration, once considered a dying art, has been resurrected recently with art directors seeking to combine line drawing with photography. Once again, the results are intriguing and highly original.

Marketing Trends

In the future, there is likely to be a move away from the standard stock catalogue. The present trend is to explore new shapes, sizes and paper texture to feature the images in a more creative way. The web will play a far more prominent role for the simple reason that pictures can be brought to market faster – therefore allowing for a better turn-around in profits. In stock, the time-to-market has always been a frustratingly long wait. Now, with digital imagery and the amazing strides in technology, the web will be king for stock.

E-marketing will also become a much larger part of the process with communications being sent electronically. These could include moving type and flash animation and be very visually-driven. This move has already started – but it will only take off fully when more companies allow for web-based e-mails to go through their firewalls. Given this type of communication, a photographer may want to consider how they can provide content about themselves and their work for even more publicity.

Company Trends

There is another growing trend in the shaping of the actual business model for stock libraries. Currently, the two main economic models are traditional stock (rights controlled) or royalty free. On the horizon – or which may be in operation by the time this book is published – is a hybrid style of pricing and copyright usage. A customer will pay a set rate for one time usage, but the actual cut to the photographer will be larger. This type of hybrid stock library may have funding by a group of photographers or the library may have chosen to be solely dependent on web-based delivery. In other words, there are no CD-Roms, heavy stock catalogues and printed direct-mail pieces to produce, and therefore marketing overheads are able to be cut substantially.

Currently, royalty free libraries, while all of them sell single image, still produce and deliver CD image collections. In the future, it is more than likely that they will cease CD production and just sell single images on-line, negotiating them at a different commission rate than CD collections.

Trends for Photographers

While some photographers lament their lack of commission work, others will see the opportunity that stock provides. For the future, it won't be a question of 'either one or the other'. The expectations will be that smart and lucrative photographers will take advantage of both.

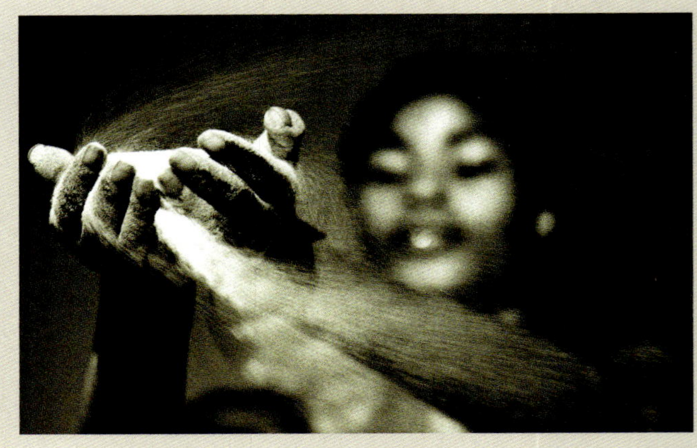

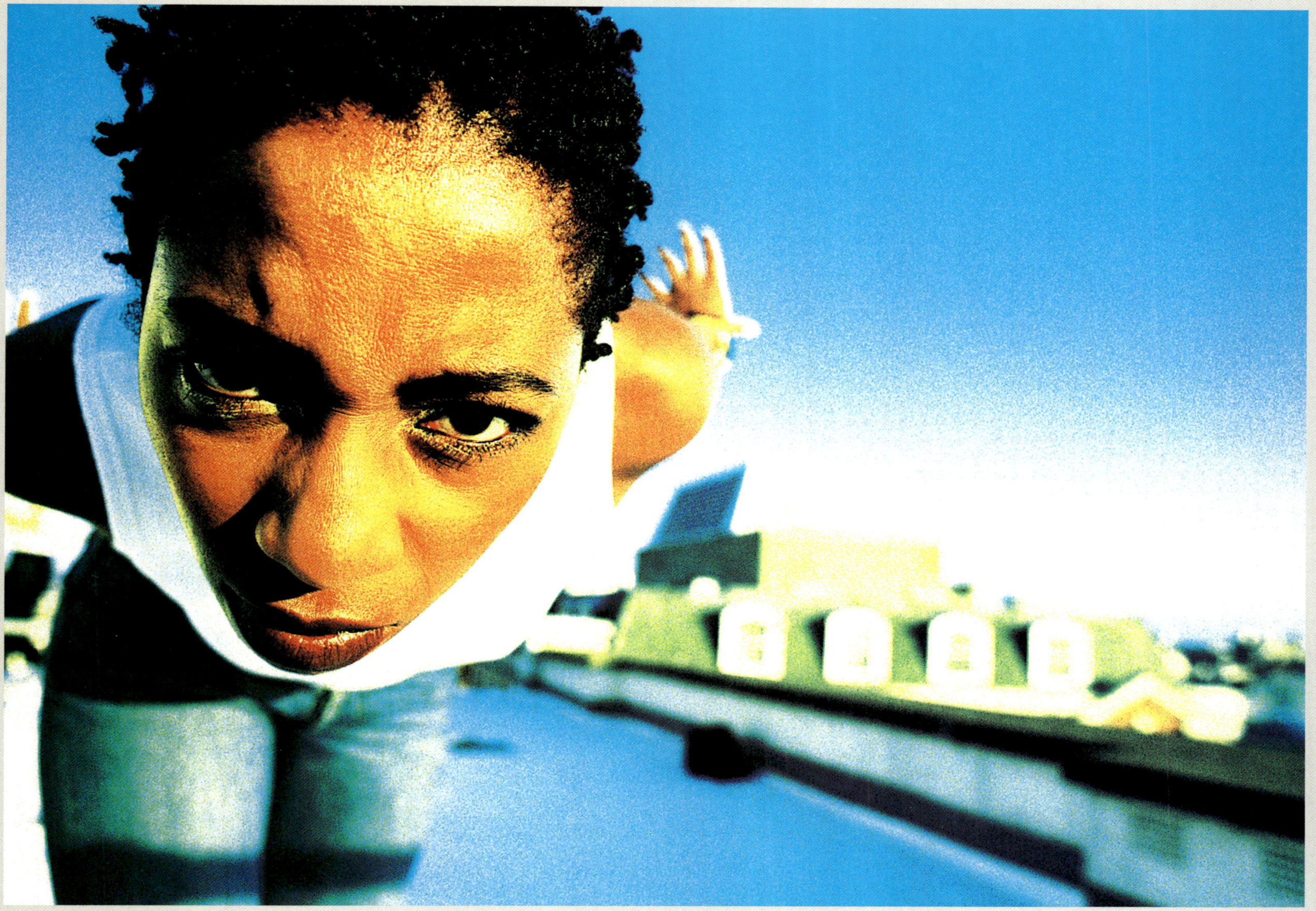

Chapter 7

Most Frequently Asked Questions 130 – 135

We've split this section up so you can see the real insider's view of the industry. The first section focuses on what stock photographers would tell colleagues who want to enter the business. The answers shown are actual responses from professional stock photographers who clearly tell you the real story.

The second section answers questions directed at stock professionals and is entitled 'Industry Section'. Here you'll find out how the decision-makers within the stock library trade choose photographers, what they are looking for and how you can join that 'A' list of photographers who are kept busy year-round.

Photographers Section

Q
What should I look for in a stock agency?
A
On a personal level, many photographers choose agencies that have prestige, a style they feel comfortable with and a good reputation. This good reputation extends to being known in the industry for paying royalties on time and having frontline creative staff who understand how photographers like to work.

Q
How do I approach the company I'm interested in?
A
Many photographers say that they are approached by the stock agencies. The stock industry sources photographers by looking in contact books like **Creative Handbook** and **NY Gold**. They are usually trying to match your style with a current project.
If you have not yet been approached, you may want to first look at a variety of stock industry websites. These companies normally have a section devoted to contributors and here you'll find 'images wanted' and sample shoot lists. Your next step is to call and to ask to speak to the creative acquisitions team. For even better results, you may want to request to speak to the person in charge of whichever sector you feel you are strongest in (lifestyle imagery, business, industry, etc.).

Q
What's the best way of showing my images? Should I include personal work too?
A
One of the ironic things in the stock trade is that photographers are usually chosen for their personal work – yet are asked to shoot something completely different! The best tip is to keep a good balance between your most commercial work and personal – and then ask a friend/colleague whose creativity you admire to help edit the work you'll show. Keep it lean, mean and keen – just like they say in advertising! Lastly, do not show any work you are unsure of or not proud of.

Q
How should I work with the stock agency to interpret the brief/project theme?
A
Having a good working relationship with the stock agency's art director/picture editor is absolutely essential. In essence, they are your client and being clear from the start is important to ensure that the shoot will go well.

Q
I have a drawer full of outtakes from my last shoot – can't I just unload these to the stock company?
A
Yes, some stock companies will purchase these directly and it is called a 'buy-out'. This will mean they will give you a set fee for these images, and no royalties. However, stock companies are moving away from these 'B' quality images. They expect any image added to their collection to be as good a quality as the rest of their entire library.

Q
What about travel images? I took rolls and rolls on my last trip.
A
Travel images are notoriously difficult for the stock industry. Firstly, your images will probably contain shots of the local population. Unless you have model releases from these people, many stock companies will immediately reject them. Also, the travel shots that sell are of recognisable locations, and almost iconic in nature. This may include a new, edgy angle of the Eiffel Tower or a windswept Irish thatched cottage. Keep in mind that travel companies like colour and blue skies, and while retouching with Adobe Photoshop may cure some of the problems, the image that works is something that inspires you to say "Where is that? I want to go."

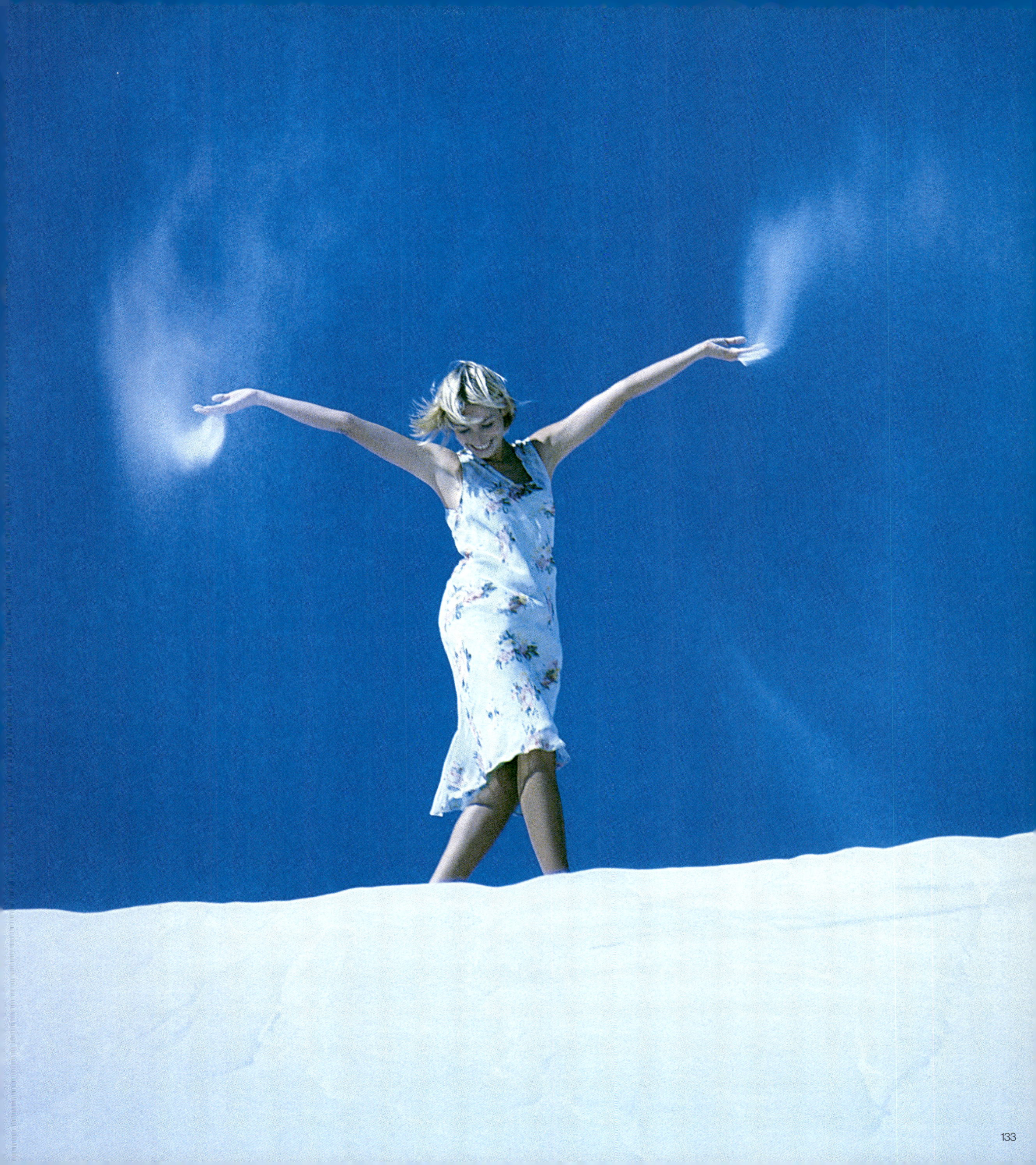

Industry Section

Q

If I invest in stock photography, will I be guaranteed a return?

A

The truth is no. Most companies will not guarantee success no matter how big the outlay on the photographer's part. While we have experience and sales data as to what has sold, trends change. We do work with photographers in partnership – giving advice along the way and recommendations for changes. In the end, however, it is the creative market that makes the final decision.

Q

Can someone make a living by being a stock photographer?

A

Most stock libraries will advise you to use stock photography as supplementary income rather than your full source of cash flow. Stock can be part of the equation, but it is not wise to be solely dependent on royalties. Most stock photographers who have been in the profession for years will tell you about the troughs where one quarter, the royalties are a bonanza and the next quarter they're disappointing. And, unfortunately, there's no simple reason to explain why this happens.

Q

Be honest. Do 'cheesy' images sell better?

A

Interesting question, but in general, the answer is no. If you define 'cheese' as traditional topics combined with well-trodden compositions, there is more of a chance of sales than if, for instance, you do something highly experimental. Take note, however, that the stock industry is looking for photographers who take commercial themes in a new direction. This is where success lies. But as a rule of thumb, with travel images for example – brighter colours, blue skies and happy models are what the majority of people want.

Q

Do you recommend 'buy-outs' or shooting on a 'royalty basis'?

A

This depends on the needs of the stock photographer. If they want immediate funding, for say a personal shoot, most stock agencies will work with the photographer's requests. In general, there are guidelines as to how much an agency will pay for a single image. It is in the photographer's best interests to ask how much photography featuring a similar topic and styling currently draws in royalties. While the stock company won't give you exact figures, most will give you a range. Then, the photographer can make the most informed decision.

Q

What is the absolute worst thing a photographer can do in the initial meeting?

A

Turn up with a plastic bag full of transparencies (slides). This shows a lack of respect for the stock company and a complete lack of understanding of how current companies work. If these transparencies are placed in a portfolio, this is different. Another no-no is to turn up without any knowledge of the stock company. You wouldn't do this on a job interview – don't do it with stock.

Q

Why do some stock photographers get more commission work than others?

A

A couple of reasons. A good track record helps, backed by good chemistry between the stock agency's art director (creative acquisitions person). Someone who has their own team of talented stylists, models and equipment is also viewed as preferable to someone who just has imagination and a good camera. The underlying thing to keep in mind is that it is a partnership between the photographer and the stock company. The more a photographer brings to the table, the more business he will probably get.

Q

If you could describe the ideal stock library company-photographer first meeting and working relationship, what would it be?

A

The photographer would be a referral from a successful photographer we are currently working with. His/her portfolio would have a good balance of personal work and commissioned work, all with captions as to where/how they were taken – plus how the images were used (if they were sold). The photographer would be knowledgeable about the industry, about the actual stock library company, and would have a team of professionals to work with him/her. The photographer would also have done their homework and know about royalties, payment schedules and approximate earnings. There would be chemistry between the stock photography professional and the photographer with both parties willing to work together for optimal results. And, finally, the results of the shoot would show a uniquely creative style and approach all backed by excellent planning and set-up.

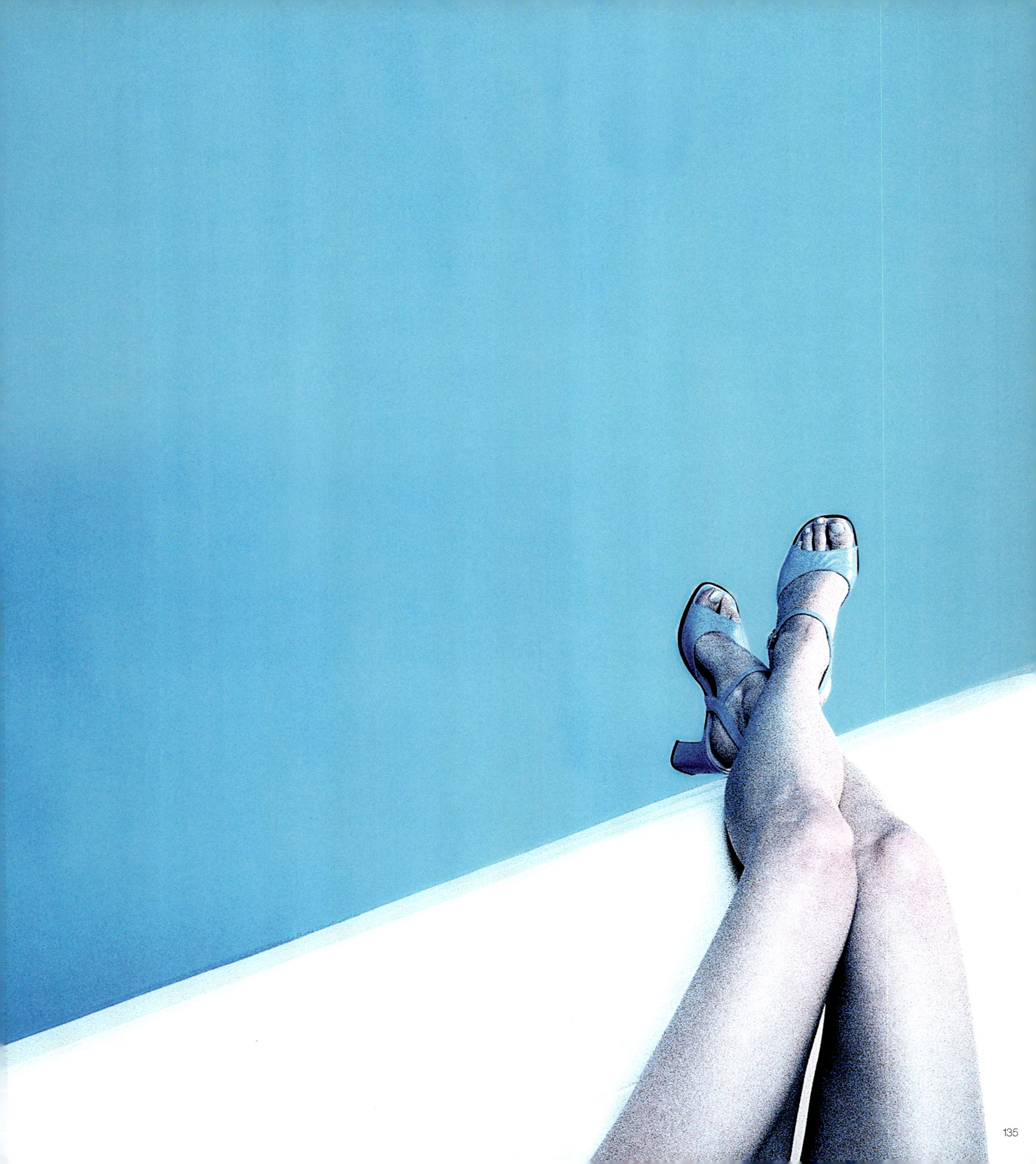

Useful Names and Addresses

Stock Libraries

age fotostock
Buenaventura Muñoz 16
08018 Barcelona
Spain
Telephone
+34 93 300 2552
www.agefotostock.com

alamy.com
6F Milton Park
Abingdon
Oxon OX14 4RR
UK
Telephone
+44 (0)1235 84 46 00
www.alamy.com

Australian Picture Library
2 Northcote Street
St Leonards
NSW 2065
Australia
Telephone
+61 2 9438 3011
www.australianpicturelibrary.com.au

Beneluz B.V.
Zwartelaan 24
2271 BR Voorburg
The Netherlands
Telephone
+31 70 387 1072
www.beneluxpress.com

Comstock Images
244 Sheffield Street
Mountainside
NJ 07092
USA
Telephone
+1 908 518 6200
www.comstock.com

Corbis
(Incorporating Stock Market and Digital Stock plus numerous other historic collections)

15395 SE 30th Place
Suite 300
Bellevue
WA 98007
USA
Telephone
+1 425 641 4505
www.corbis.com/professional

Digital Vision
India House
45 Curlew Street
London SE1 2ND
UK
Telephone
+44 (0)20 7378 5500
www.digitalvisiononline.com

Dynamic Graphics Inc.
6000 N. Forest Park Drive
Peoria
IL 61614-3592
USA
Telephone
+1 309 688 8800
www.dgusa.com

FPG
32 Union Square East
New York
NY 10003-3295
USA
Telephone
+1 212 777 4210
www.fpg.com

Getty Images
2101 Fourth Ave, 5th Floor
Seattle
WA 98121
USA
Telephone
+1 206 622 6262
www.gettyimages.com

Gettyone
(Including: Allsport Concepts, Artville, The Bridgeman Art Library, Energy Film, EyeWire, FoodPix, FPG, HultonArchive, Illustration Works, The Image Bank, The National Geographic Image Collection, PhotoDisc, Stone)

www.gettyone.com

Image 100
3 Soho Street
London W1D 3DG
UK
Telephone
+44 (0)20 7434 1661
www.image100.com

Images Colour Library
Ramilies House
1–2 Ramilies Street
London W1V 1DF
UK
Telephone
+44 (0)20 7734 7344
www.imagescl.co.uk

Image Source
www.imagesource.com

The Image Works
www.theimageworks.com

IPJ
10th Floor DF Building
2-2-8 Minami Aoyama
Minato-ku
Tokyo
Japan
Telephone
+81 3 3479 2865
www.ipjnet.com

Index Stock Imagery
www.indexstock.com

Masterfile Corporation
175 Bloor Street East
South Tower, Second Floor
Toronto
Ontario
Canada M4W 3R8
Telephone
+1 800 387 9010
www.masterfile.com

PhotoAlto
9, rue Pierre Dupont
75010 Paris
France
Telephone
+33 1 44 89 22 22
www.photoalto.com

PhotoEssentials
www.photoessentials.com

Pictor
3307 M Street, NW
Suite 300
DC 20007
USA
Telephone
+1 202 333 0500
www.pictor.com

RubberBall
RubberBall Productions
102 South Mountain Way Dr.
Orem
UT 84058
USA
Telephone
+1 888 224 3472
www.rubberball.com

Stockbyte
www.stockbyte.com

SuperStock Inc.
381 Park Avenue South
Suite 1507
New York
NY 10016
USA
Telephone
+1 212 889 6464
www.superstock.com

Weststock
101 Stewart Street
Suite 800
Seattle
WA 98101
USA
Telephone
+1 206 728 7726
www.weststock.com

Wonderfile
35 East Wacker Drive
Suite 2188
Chicago
IL 60601
Telephone
+1 888 361 9992
www.wonderfile.com

Other Organisations

National Association for Photographic Art
NAPA Membership
31858 Hopedale Avenue
Clearbook
British Columbia
Canada V2T 2G7
Telephone
+1 604 855 4848
Facsimile
+1 604 859 6288

British Journal of Photography
Timothy Benn Publishing Ltd.
39 Earlham Street
Covent Garden
London WC2H 9LD
UK
Telephone
+44 (0)20 7306 7140
Facsimile
+44 (0)20 7306 7000

PDN Online
Photo District News
770 Broadway
New York
NY 10003
USA
Telephone
+1 646 654 5800
Facsimile
+1 646 654 5813
www.pdn-pix.com

Stock Connection
110 Frederick Avenue
Suite A
Rockville
MD 20850
USA
Telephone
+1 301 251 0720
www.pickphoto.com

Glossary of Stock Photography Terms

Adobe Photoshop
A computer software program which allows photographers to digitally retouch images.

Art Director
Usually provided by the stock library, the art director will oversee the shooting to ensure the required look, feel and compositional angles are maintained and achieved.

Buy-outs
A term used to describe a one-time fee offered to the photographer for total rights to an image. Usually, however, the photographer has the right to sell the image themselves but not on an exclusive basis.

Business Model
The economic model used by a library to calculate fees to the photographer, the customer and its distribution chain.

CD-Rom
Literally 'compact disc – read only memory'. Used primarily by royalty free libraries to hold a collection of images based upon a single theme.

Chromes
The American term for transparency or 'tranny'.

Collection
Used to describe a 50–100 set of images based upon a single theme. It can also describe a stock catalogue with individual images also centred on a theme.

Composition
A description of how a photographer literally frames his subjects within an image.

Creative Acquisitions
A term used by the stock industry to describe the team who are the chief liaisons between the photographers and the library. They often act as art directors or have photographic experience themselves.

Cropping
The act of tightening a composition by cutting out unnecessary parts of the image.

Cross-processed
Done at the development stage, this involves the introduction or super-saturation of colours.

Digital Files
Images which are scanned and placed in files which can be placed directly into electronic artwork.

Direct Mail
A description of marketing communications activity that is delivered directly to a customer – can take either paper or electronic form.

Download
The act of electronic transfer between the library's server and a customer's computer.

DPI
Literally meaning 'dots per square inch' – the higher the dpi the better reproduction quality of the picture.

For Placement Only
Describes the act of placing an image into artwork which has not been approved by the client. The image is usually shown in low-resolution format so that the client can understand how the final design will look.

High-res
Short for 'high-resolution', used to describe an image with a large file size which can be printed at up to A4 (US: 8.5 x 11 inches).

Interactive CDs
CD-Roms which allow the user to click on elements to receive additional information or electronic content.

Integrated Campaign
Marketing term meaning the use of more than one media – for example direct mail and advertising.

Jpeg
An image compression scheme that reduces the size of image files, resulting in slightly reduced image quality.

Key-wording
The attachment of words to describe an image. These words are linked to a website's search engine so when the words are requested, the image appears as an option.

Links
A web connection which will take the user to a specific website – used by photographers to showcase their on-line collections or samples.

Low-res
Literally 'low-resolution' images, normally used for placement only.

Marketing Mixture
Differs from integrated campaign in that it describes all available options for marketing on a macro level.

Natural Language Search Engine
An engine on the web which, when he or she is searching for an image, enables the user to type in a full description rather than words connected by commas or plus signs.

Photographic Associations
Groups of photographers linked by their common interests and business goals.

Portfolio Mix
A description of the photographs presented within a photographer's book.

Retouching
The use of digital technology to erase a photograph's flaws.

Royalties
The percentage of sales from his or her image paid to the photographer. Normally distributed quarterly.

Royalty Free
The description of the business model which gives the customer the ability to use an image repeatedly for a fixed price.

Saturation
A description of the colour tones within an image.

Set-ups
Setting for the staging and background for a photographic shoot.

Single Images
Evolving out of the royalty free model of 100-image CD collections, single images refers to the selling of a single image rather than a multiple picture package.

Slides
Also called transparencies, trannies or chromes.

Stock
Generic term describing photography for rent.

Stock Catalogue
Showcase piece for a library's collection of images.

Stock Industry Professional
Generic term for someone who works within a stock library – can be in a variety of positions.

Stylist
Person who dictates clothing, make-up, the look and feel of a shoot and even food preparation.

Traditional Stock Library
Rights-controlled business model which gives the customer limited rights to a photograph's usage.

Acknowledgements

I would like to thank Kate Stevens whose intuitive and practical knowledge of what makes for successful stock was invaluable in the writing of this book; Jo Kennils whose case studies were both fascinating and extremely funny; and-images; John Knill; Carrie Beecroft; Will Woods; Jack Slomovits (name finally spelt right!); Brendan Byrne for participating and a special thank you to Mike Watson at Digital Vision for giving me the opportunity to push the boundaries in marketing stock photography and for his generosity in letting us use these quality images.

On a personal note, I'd like to thank Peter Vines for the use of his trusty old Mac; my parents for their encouragement to write; Gordon Kaye at Graphic Design:usa for his welcome advice and positive views; Markin Abras at MacDirectory for publishing my first article; Angie Patchell and Erica Ffrench, Assistant Editor, at RotoVision for asking me to write this book..., Leanne Botha and Peter Sellberg at SEA Design; and my former colleagues and now friends – Martin Hennessey and Paul Price.

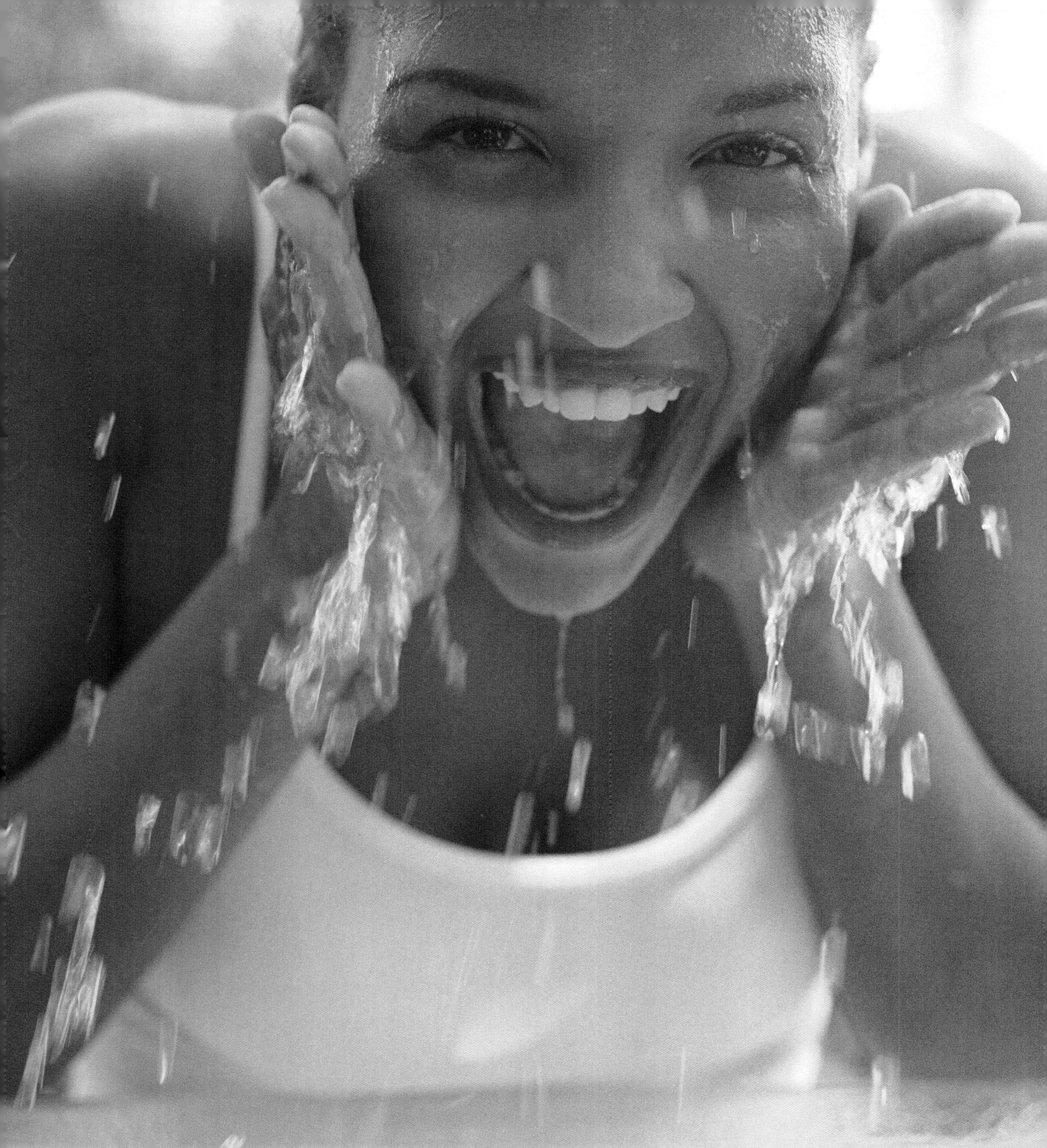

Digital Vision Gallery

Digital Vision is the world's premier publisher and distributor of quality, royalty free imagery. Based in New York and London, the company offers thousands of thematically-related original images which are enjoyed by over 70 countries worldwide.

www.digitalvisiononline.com

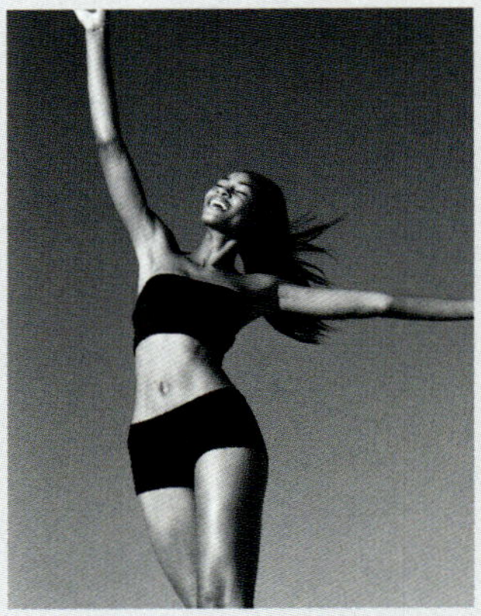

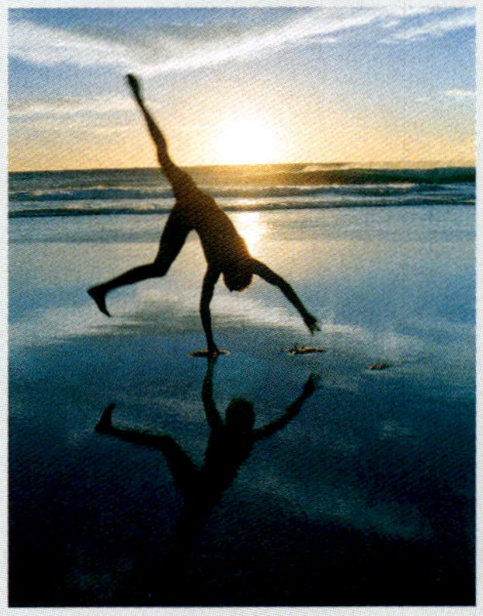

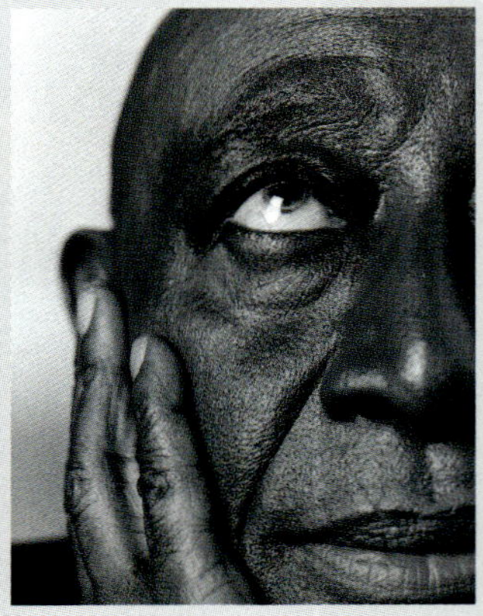

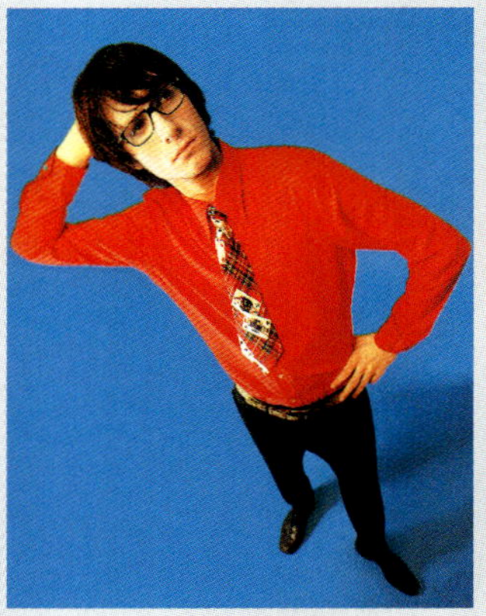

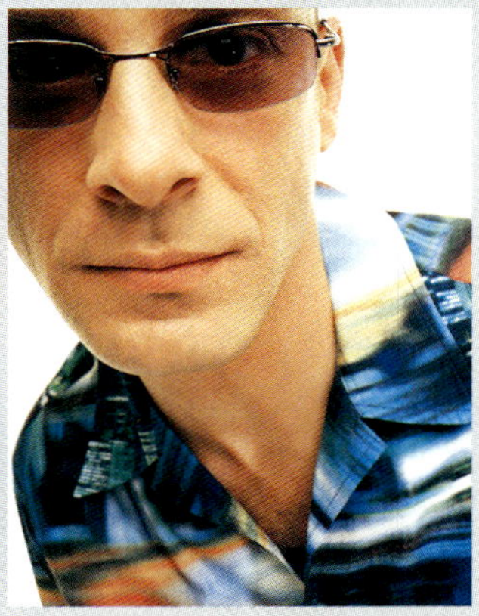

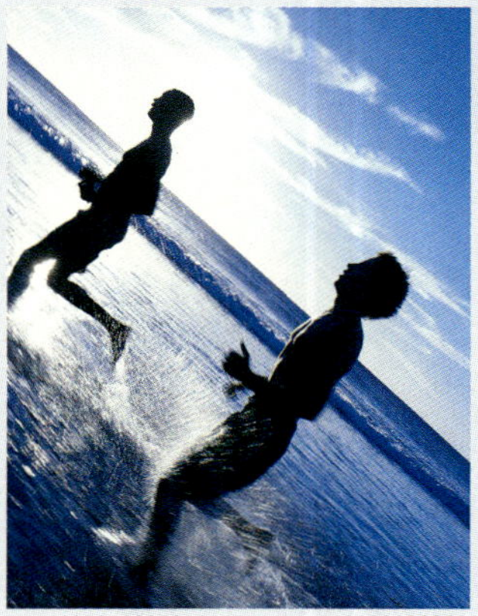

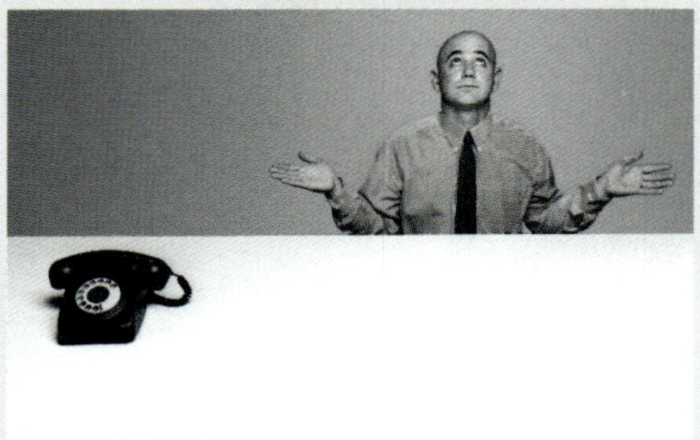

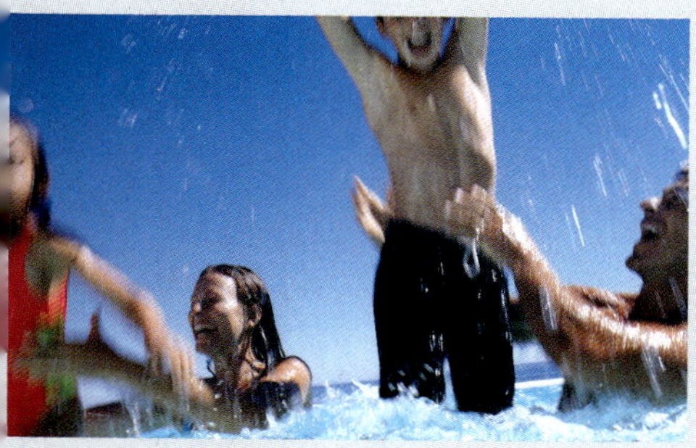
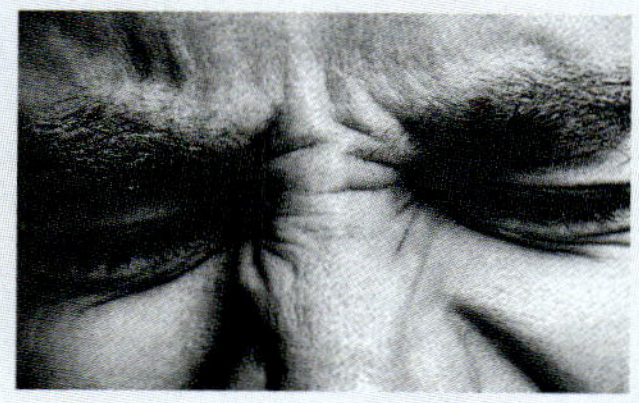
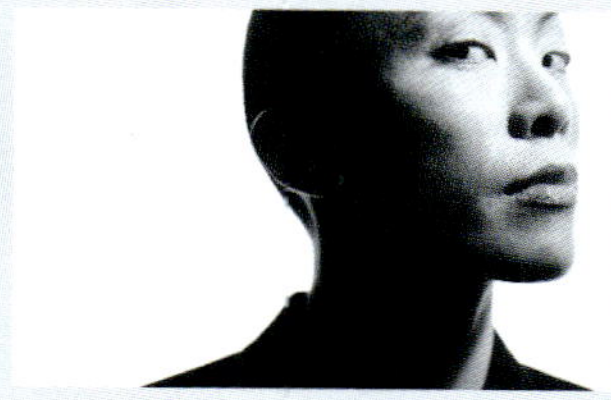
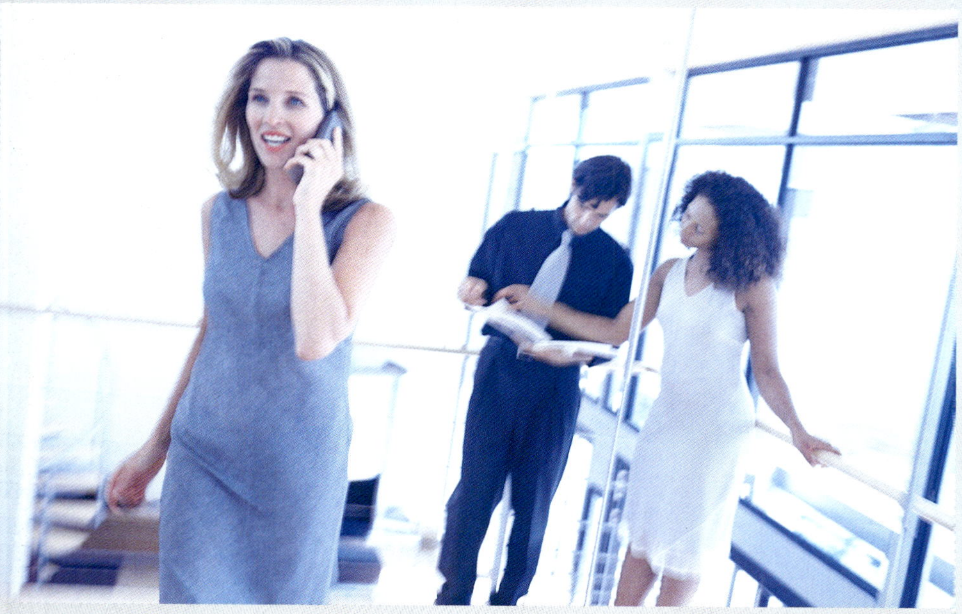
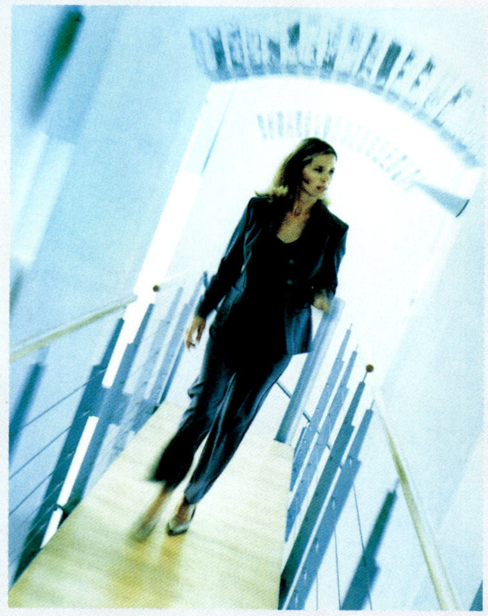
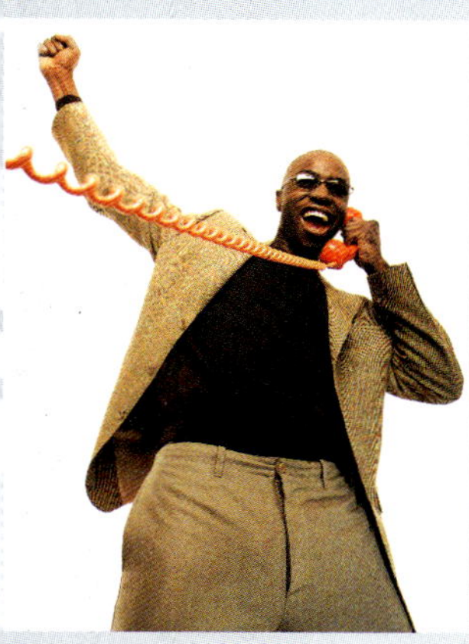
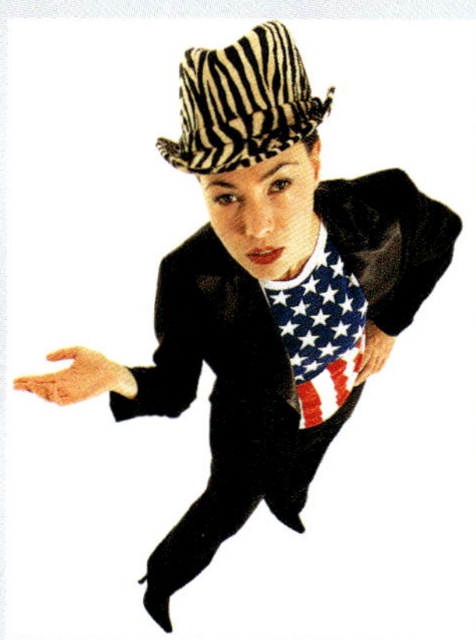
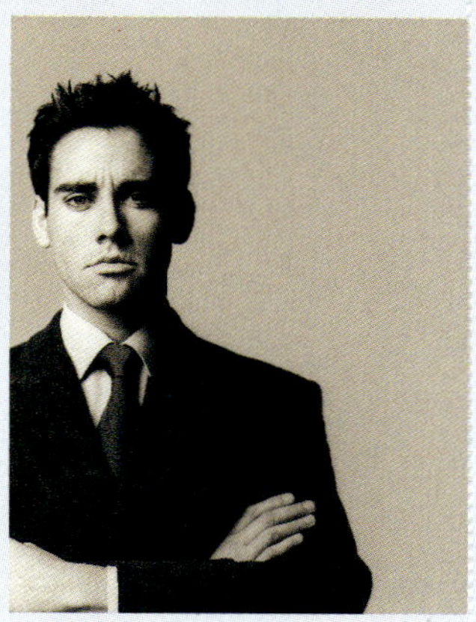